Language Acquisition:
Models and Methods

CENTRE FOR ADVANCED STUDY IN THE DEVELOPMENTAL SCIENCES

Language Acquisition: Models and Methods

Edited by

RENIRA HUXLEY AND
ELISABETH INGRAM

University of Edinburgh

Proceedings of a C.A.S.D.S. Study Group on "Mechanisms of Language Development" held jointly with the Ciba Foundation, London, May 1968, being the third study group in a C.A.S.D.S. programme on "The Origins of Human Behaviour"

ACADEMIC
PRESS

1971

LONDON
NEW YORK

ACADEMIC PRESS INC. (LONDON) LTD.
Berkeley Square House
Berkeley Square
London W1X 6BA

U.S. Edition published by
ACADEMIC PRESS INC.
111 Fifth Avenue
New York, New York 10003

Library of Congress Catalog Card Number: 79-153525
ISBN: 0-12-363450-4

PRINTED IN GREAT BRITAIN BY
Adlard & Son Ltd., Bartholomew Press, Dorking

Contents

Cognition and Language

Clinical

Membership

Study Group on Mechanisms of Language Development held at the Ciba Foundation, London, May 1968.

J. A. AMBROSE
Behaviour Development
Research Unit,
310 Edgware Road, London,
W.2, England

BENEDICTE DE BOYSSON BARDIES
Centre d)étude des processus
cognitifs et du langage,
C.N.R.S., 17 Rue Richer,
Paris, France

URSULA BELLUGI
Salk Institute for Biological
Studies, San Diego, California
92112, U.S.A.

B. BERNSTEIN
Institute of Education,
University of London,
Malet Street, London
WC1 E7HS, England

T. G. BEVER
Department of Psychology,
Columbia University,
New York, New York 10027,
U.S.A.

COURTNEY B. CAZDEN
Harvard University Graduate
School of Education,
Cambridge, Mass. 02138, U.S.A.

J. CHURCH
City University of New York,
Graduate Center, New York,
New York 10036, U.S.A.

SUSAN ERVIN-TRIPP
1636 Leroy Avenue, Berkeley,
California 94704, U.S.A.

B. FOSS
Psychology Department,
Bedford College, London
NW1 4NF, England

H. HECAEN
Centre Neurochirurgical des
Hôpitaux Psychiatriques de la
Seine, 1 Rue Cabaris, Paris
XIVe, France

RENIRA HUXLEY
Department of English
Language, University of
Edinburgh, Edinburgh EH8 9JX,
Scotland

D. HYMES

Department of Anthropology,
University of Pennsylvania,
Philadelphia, Penn. 19104,
U.S.A.

ELISABETH INGRAM

Department of Linguistics,
University of Edinburgh,
Edinburgh EH8 9LN, Scotland

T. T. S. INGRAM

Department of Child Life and
Health, University of
Edinburgh, Edinburgh
EH9 1UW, Scotland

E. S. KLIMA

Department of Linguistics,
University of California,
San Diego 92037, U.S.A.

J. MEHLER

Laboratoire de Psychologie,
C.N.R.S., 54 Boulevard
Raspail, Paris VIe, France

P. ROBINSON

Department of Psychology,
The University, Southampton,
Southampton SO9 5NH,
England

I. M. SCHLESINGER

Israel Institute of Applied
Social Research, Jerusalem,
Israel

HERMINE SINCLAIR

Ecole de Psychologie,
Université de Genève,
Geneva, Switzerland

Developmental Sciences Trust

The study group reported in this volume was organized by the Centre for Advanced Study in the Developmental Sciences in collaboration with the Ciba Foundation, which kindly accommodated the group. The Centre was planned by the Developmental Sciences Trust, which has as its purpose to promote the growth of knowledge about the development of human behaviour and the factors that influence it. More specifically, the Trust aims, first, to stimulate and co-ordinate research in directions where it is most needed and to foster among scientists and teachers in these fields a developmental and multidisciplinary perspective on human nature; second, to encourage the application of knowledge from the developmental sciences by those, in all sectors of society, engaged in coping with or preventing human problems.

At the time of the study group preparations were actively in progress to establish the Centre in its own premises near Oxford. Since then, however, it has unfortunately become necessary to abandon the probject to establish the Centre, owing to failure to obtain sufficient financial support. The description of the proposed Centre included in previous volumes in the present series therefore no longer applies.

However, the demise of the Centre in no way affects the existence of the Developmental Sciences Trust, which will continue to carry out its purposes by other means. The Trust is now in the process of being re-organized; in the meantime it will ensure that the proceedings of each of the five study groups already held as part of its initial programme will be published as planned.

xi

Preface

In May 1968 the Centre for Advanced Study in the Developmental Sciences jointly with the Ciba Foundation held a Study Group on Language Development. This was the third of a programme of five International Study Groups on "The Origins of Human Behaviour".

The Study Group lasted for five days, and was organized so that there should be long periods of time available for discussion of the papers presented and of other related topics which might arise as the result of the meeting of a group like this.

This book presents four types of material: all papers from those participants who were invited beforehand to present formal papers; some of the informal papers from members of the study group who agreed at the time to talk on current research topics; discussion following both types of papers and general discussion of topics which arose independently from the presented papers. The absence of H. Hecaen, who was prevented from attending the conference, has made the clinical section scantier than it might otherwise have been, although his paper is included in this volume.

As editors, we have departed from the actual order in which the papers were presented to the Study Group. The headings, 1. Sociolinguistics, 2. Grammar, 3. Cognition and Language, and 4. Clinical, are necessarily somewhat arbitrary, but this has enabled us to group the discussions into a more coherent presentation than they would otherwise have made. We have shortened the discussion material and these reduced versions have been accepted and in some cases amended by the contributors.

Professor Dell Hymes kindly allowed us to produce an edited form of his contribution adapted from his written paper and opening presentation.

We are most grateful to all contributors for their patient help with all our queries, to Margaret Irving and Brenda Brammar for typing, to Isobel Gawler for her sub-editing work and to M. Atkinson who compiled the index.

Edinburgh University   RENIRA HUXLEY
June 1971   ELISABETH INGRAM

Sociolinguistics

Competence and Performance in Linguistic Theory[1]

D. HYMES

University of Pennsylvania

THE CONTEXT in which this paper developed was one of being invited to address myself to research problems in the study of advantaged and disadvantaged children. Both a linguist and an anthropologist, I am concerned on the one hand with linguistic theory, and on the other with social–cultural aspects of language. From that standpoint, looking at the kinds of research and problems that arise first in an urban community such as New York City, or in education relevant to language, one is struck by the differences in the character, abilities, performance and attitudes of different members of the language community. From that point of view, some of the concepts which are most common, and most salient in linguistics proper, appear not to provide a satisfactory basis for approaching problems where the social–cultural factors are so salient. In particular I am concerned with the notions of competence and performance, as these are approached in modern linguistic theory.

THE NATURE OF THE THEORY

Consider a recent statement, one that makes explicit and precise an assumption that has underlain much of modern linguistics (Chomsky, 1965; p. 3):

> "Linguistic theory is concerned primarily with an ideal speaker–listener, in a completely homogeneous speech-community, who knows its language perfectly and is unaffected by such grammatically irrelevant conditions as memory limitations, distractions,

---

[1] This paper has been adapted by the editors from the written paper and oral presentation of the author, with his approval.

3

shifts of attention and interest, and errors (random or characteristic) in applying his knowledge of the language in actual performance."

The theoretical notion of the ideal speaker–hearer is unilluminating from the standpoint of the children we seek to understand and help. All difficulties confronting the children and ourselves seem swept from view. This means that any attempt to alter and improve children's linguistic ability seems to depend on knowledge we do not yet have.

One way of dealing with the problem of matching application and theory might be to ignore fundamental theory and to pick and choose among its products. One could point to several available models of language, Trager-Smith, tagmemic, stratificational, transformational-generative (in its several variants), and, in England, "system-structure" (Halliday, 1964); one might remark that there are distinguished scholars using each to analyse English; or regret that linguists are unable to agree on the analysis of English; and pick and choose, according to one's problem and local situation, leaving grammarians otherwise to their own devices.

Some linguists, e.g. Labov (1966, 1969), use transformational-generative grammar to study some variant forms of language use, that is, some of the ways in which a speech community is not homogeneous. Perhaps then one ought simply to disregard how linguists define the scope of linguistic theory rather than try to modify their definition to accommodate wider considerations. To do so, however, would be a mistake. A theoretical perspective is essential, and the perspective afforded by transformational generative grammar is particularly valuable because it gives us the concept of an idealized learner, with built-in propensities for language. This does away with the notion of genetic racial inferiority of any particular group, or sub-group.

The linguists' theoretical standpoint then is a necessary one, but not sufficient on its own, because this idealized conception becomes inadequate as soon as it is confronted with real children in a particular environment. When the image of the unfolding, mastering, fluent child is set beside the real children in our schools, the theory begins to seem almost irrelevant because of the difference between the idealized concept and what one sees, and because the theory, so powerful in its own realm, cannot on its own terms cope with the difference between the idealized and the real. To cope with the realities of children as communicating beings requires a theory within which socio–cultural factors have an explicit and constitutive role. We do not possess this theory.

Socio–cultural Factors

The linguist's problem is to explain how a child comes rapidly to be able to produce and understand (in principle) any and all of the grammatical sentences of a language. If we consider a child actually capable of producing all possible sentences he would probably be institutionalized, particularly if not only the sentences but also speech or silence were random or unpredictable. We then have to account for the fact that a normal child acquires knowledge of sentences not only as grammatical but also as appropriate. This is not accounted for in a transformational grammar, which divides linguistic theory into two parts: linguistic competence and linguistic performance.

Competence and Performance in Transformational Grammar

Linguistic competence deals with the knowledge that enables the speaker to produce and understand an infinite set of sentences; this is the meaning of the expression "creative" when applied to language. This competence posits ideal objects, isolated from individual and cultural variables. The theory of performance is the one sector that might have had a specific socio–cultural content; but it is essentially concerned with psychological by-products of the analysis of grammar, not with social interaction. To the linguist, performance is seen as an imperfect manifestation of an underlying system.

The failure to provide an explicit place for socio–cultural factors does not seem to be accidental, nor does the predominant association of performance with imperfection. However, the lack of socio–cultural factors in linguistic theory is more than just a legitimate simplifying device of the sort which any scientific theory demands. It appears to reveal an ideological aspect of the modern theoretical standpoint: that underlying linguistic structure is taken as an endpoint in itself and linguistic use is devalued. This is in contrast to classical antiquity, when structure was a means to use, and grammar subordinate to rhetoric. The advantage of this is that by focusing on readily structurable data, one can enjoy both the prestige of advanced science, as well as retaining the prestige of dealing with something fundamental to human life, in spite of ignoring the social dimension of use.

Roots of the Theory

Chomsky rightly stresses his close relationship with the founders of modern general linguistics. For instance, in de Saussure's linguistics (1959), *la langue* is generally interpreted as the privileged ground of structure and *la parole* as the residual realm of variation (among other things). Chomsky associates his views of *competence* and *performance* with the Saussurian conceptions of *langue* and *parole*, but sees his own conceptions as superior, since they renew the Humboldtian conception of underlying processes. Chomsky's terminology is also superior: "competence" and "performance" change the focus of attention from an object external to man to human abilities; they more readily suggest concrete persons and actions. Indeed, Chomsky's theory can be seen as a culmination and a revitalization of the structural linguistic tradition: no modern linguist has spoken more profoundly of either the internal structure of language, or of its intrinsic human significance. This revitalization flowers, while around it emerges a conception which may replace it before the end of the century. If this occurs, it will be because, just as the transformational theory could absorb its predecessors and handle structural relationships beyond their grasp, so new relationships, relationships with an ineradicable social component, will become salient, requiring a broader theory to absorb and handle them.

Thus Chomsky does not take an isolationist view of linguistics. He wants to re-unite it with psychology and philosophy. If we accept the need to make linguistics part of a larger field of concern, it would be arbitrary to consider only that part of linguistics which is part of psychology and philosophy of mind, and not to consider with Sapir (1949) that aspect of linguistics which is part of a science of social man.

THE THEORY IN THE LIGHT OF CULTURAL DATA

Individual Differences

As a contrast to the ideal speaker–hearer, consider Bloomfield's description of two Menomini speakers:

> ". . . White-Thunder, a man round forty, speaks less English than Menomini, and that is a strong indictment, for his Menomini is atrocious. His vocabulary is small: his inflections are often barbarous; he constructs sentences of a few thread-bare models. He may be said to speak no language tolerably. His case is not uncommon among younger men, even when they speak but little English." On the other hand, there are others like Red Cloud Woman who ". . . speaks a beautiful and highly idiomatic Menomini . . . (and) speaks Ojibwa and Potawatomi fluently . . . Linguistically, she would correspond to a highly educated American woman who spoke, say, French and Italian in addition to the very best type of cultivated, idiomatic English" (Bloomfield, 1927, 1964, p. 395).

We are dealing with a differential competence within a *heterogeneous speech community* which as Bloomfield suggests, is due in some indirect way to the impact of the conquering language. Red Cloud Woman illustrates the competence of a multilingual speaker, but in fact even a fluent monolingual speaker is probably master of several functional varieties within one language.

Cazden (1966) has reported on the relevance of social class in the development of mastery of the full range of functional language varieties. In general, upper social status children are more advanced linguistically than lower social class children; but these children may be better at some aspects of communicative competence, e.g. ritual verbal games (see Ervin-Tripp, this volume).

Within the present view of linguistic competence, there is no way to distinguish between abilities of pure speakers and of poor speakers. Sentences from either type would be referred to a common grammar. Perhaps it can be said that both types share competence with regard to recognition and comprehension of speech. While that would be an important (and probably true) fact, it has not been the intention of the theory to distinguish between models of competence for reception and models of competence for production. Since the theory intends to deal with the "creative" use of language, that is, with the ability of a speaker to devise novel sentences appropriate to new situations, it would seem to be a retrenchment, if not more, to account only for a shared ability to *understand* novel sentences produced by others. In some fundamental sense the competence of the two types of speakers may be very different. The more versatile users of a language have lexical and syntactic knowledge which the others do not.

Status of Language Varieties

Certain languages, or functional varieties of one language, are regarded as having different values and different appropriate uses within a speech community. Across speech communities such judgements may differ. Amongst the Kurds for instance, Arabic is thought superior for expressing religious truths and Kurdish best for everything else, while Berbers may find Arabic superior to Berber for all purposes except intimate domestic conversation (Ferguson, 1966). This sort of differential competence has nothing to do with individual "disadvantage" or "deficiency". In view of the combination of community diversity and differential competence, one should not accept the presence in a community of a widespread language, say, Spanish or English, at face value; it is necessary first to determine its true status in terms of competence, and until this is done one should put the name of language in quotation marks. (Clearly there is need for a theoretically motivated and empirically tested set of terms by which to characterize the different kinds of competence that may be found.) In an extreme case what counts as "English" in the repertoire of a community may be only a few phonologically marked forms (Iwam of New Guinea). Types of English in general constitute a continuum, perhaps a scale, from reduced to more expanded varieties, somewhat cross-cut by the different uses and adaptation of the same original material. A linguist analysing data from a community on the assumption "once English, always English" might miss and sadly misrepresent the actual competence supposedly expressed by his grammar.

Acceptability

Social factors not only influence the competence of individual speakers and the status of functional language varieties; there is also a social component at the heart of grammar. Newman reports (1940) that the words he recorded from Yokuts speakers were mostly short, composed of stem and one or two suffixes. He noticed that the underlying rules of suffixation allowed him to construct words having four or five suffixes; and though his informant found them perfectly meaningful, he also found them comical. To the Yokuts' feeling for simplicity the words were grammatical monstrosities. Communities may draw a line of acceptability within expression; where the line is drawn may change over time within the community, and may differ between communities with identical grammars. Indeed, the drawing of the line of acceptability may be a function of personal culture. (This concept of personal culture derives from Sapir (1938), and has been developed in various ways by Wallace (1961a), Goodenough (1962), Hymes (1964) and others.)

Group Usages

The constitutive role of socio-cultural factors has been stressed by Labov. Phonological features might be expected to be a case of perception and cognition determined by purely linguistic factors. Yet, Labov (1965) writes:

> "The contention that native speakers can hear phonemic distinctions much better than nonphonemic distinctions was not borne out by the evidence. Indeed, one might say that the ability to perceive distinctions is determined largely by the social significance of the distinction to the listener."

Without taking sociological features into account, it may be impossible to account for, for example, the phonological characteristics within a speech community. Labov (1965) investigated the presence and absence of post-vocalic /r/ in the speech of New Yorkers. In terms of notions of a homogeneous speech community, the result is chaos. On the other hand, one can predict the probability of /r/ knowing the speaker's social class, age, the speech situation and what Labov calls his "linguistic insecurity index", a measurable feature which allows for hypercorrection in nervous people (see Ervin-Tripp, this volume). Here again phenomena that belong to the domain of linguistic competence show diversity and pattern that have a social basis.

Further, Labov has documented cases of dual competence in reception, and single competence in production for lower class Negro children. They comprehend sentences in either standard or non-standard phonology, but produce only substandard phonology when they speak themselves. Conversely, the peasants of the Burundi in East Africa (Albert, 1964) present an interesting case of dual productive competence. These peasants may command the verbal abilities which are valued in the culture, but they cannot display them in the presence of a herder or other superior. In such situations appropriate behaviour is that in which "their words are haltingly delivered, or run on uncontrolled, their voices are loud, their gestures wild, their figures of speech ungainly, their emotions freely displayed, their words and sentences clumsy". Clearly the behaviour here is general to all aspects of communication, including the grammatical; it is a "competence for incompetence", as it were.

Work with children and with the place of language in education, therefore, requires a theory that can deal with a heterogeneous speech community, differential competence and the constitutive role of socio–cultural features. Those whose work requires such a theory know best how little of it can be specified; but two things can be said. First, linguistics needs such a theory too; i.e. concepts that are unquestioningly postulated as basic to linguistics (speaker–listener speech community, speech act, acceptability, etc.) are, in fact, socio–cultural variables, and only when one has moved from their postulation to their analysis can one secure the foundations of linguistic theory itself. Secondly, the notion of competence may itself provide the key. We turn now to an examination of these central linguistic notions, in the light of the phenomena discussed.

EXTENSION OF NOTION OF COMPETENCE/PERFORMANCE

Competence for Use

We have to account for the fact that a normal child acquires knowledge of sentences, not only as grammatical but also as appropriate. A child acquires a repertoire of speech acts, is able to take part in speech acts and to evaluate the speech acts of others. This is a competence which is integral with attitudes and values concerning language and integral with competence for the interrelation of language with other codes of communication. Attention to the social dimension is thus not restricted to the subtractive effect of social factors. The engagement of language in social life has a positive, productive aspect. There are rules of use without which the rules of grammar would be useless. Rules of use are not a late grafting. Data from the first years of acquisition of English grammar show that children do develop rules for the use of different forms in different situations (Ervin-Tripp, this volume).

The existence of competence for use may seem obvious, but if its study is to be established and conducted in relation to current linguistics, then the notion of competence and performance must themselves be critically analysed and their formulations revised. The chief difficulty with present linguistic theory would seem to be that it requires that the study of the phenomena of concern to us here should be identified with the category of performance; language use is equated with performance.

Confusion Over Competence and Performance

This confusion is seen in Chomsky's defence against the charge that generative grammar slights the study of performance:

> ". . . the only studies of performance, outside of phonetics . . . are those carried out as a by-product of work in generative grammar. In particular the study of memory limitations . . . and the study of deviations from rules, as a stylistic device . . . have developed in this way" (Chomsky, 1965; p. 15).

However, if (outside phonetics) only by-products of generative grammar qualify as studies of performance, what is to be said of more than two thousand years of rhetoric and poetics, and of investigations of the use of language in social interaction and cultural behaviour? If these investigations are not performance, then the equation of performance with use of language has reduced the notion of "use" so much as to exclude most aspects of speaking. If these investigations *do* deal with performance subject-matter, then the term "study" is oddly restricted to just those investigations that arise as generative grammar by-products. In either case, the notion of the study of performance and the equated notions of theory of performance: theory of language use have been fatally constricted from the standpoint of the communicative development of children. Only implementations of a model of grammar, viewed from the standpoint of the model, are admitted. But to take a model of grammar as the sole starting point is to prejudice any arrival at an adequate and revealing understanding of speech.

In these respects, I think one sees the distorting effect of using the one term "performance" for two distinct things, of the correlative withholding of "competence" from the second of them, and of the recurrent dichotomy between underlying knowledge and actual performance, so that the sense in which performance entails its own underlying knowledge is obscured. If the only underlying competence expressly recognized as such is grammatical, then of course only grammatical competence can fulfil the role of providing the indispensable basis for the study of the use of language. Then studies of the use of language conducted prior to or independently of the development of explicit generative grammar may with some justification seem irrelevant, although one might argue for them, just as Chomsky argues for traditional grammars, that much of what they say is sound. But once one makes clear the difference, within the realm of the non-grammatical itself, between that which is actual behaviour and that which underlies it, the whole situation changes. The objection to merely external studies of speech still holds: competence must be the central concern. But arbitrary restriction of the domain of underlying knowledge can be ended; the methodological spirit of generative grammar can be extended to the whole sphere of the abilities manifest in speech. The identification of underlying competence with grammatical competence was, if not a grammarian's *hubris*, the product of a particular theoretical period. There *was* a need to establish the view that a grammatical system had a deep structure radically distinct from observed data (cf. Chomsky, 1965; p. 16), and that abilities manifest in speech could not be explained without reference to it. This need may have motivated the primary insistence on the contrast between rules of grammar and actual behaviour. Now that the battle is won, one can attend to the relation between rules of grammar and rules of use.

To develop the concept of underlying competence for use requires a socio-cultural standpoint. To develop that standpoint adequately, one must transcend the present formulation of the dichotomy of "com-

petence/performance", and the associated formulation of the judgements and abilities of the users of a language as well. The grammatical
factor is one among several which affect communicative competence.
Underlying communicative behaviour, there are several systems of
rules reflected in the abilities and judgements of the users. In the linguistic theory under discussion, judgements are said to be of two kinds: of
grammaticality, with respect to competence; and more generally of
acceptability, with respect to performance. The critical analysis just
given of the second of each pair requires analysis of the first as well.
Moreover, it requires that explicit distinctions be made within
the notion of "acceptability" to match the distinctions of kinds of
"performance", and at the same time, the entire set of terms
must be examined and recast with respect to communication as a
whole.

If an adequate theory of language-users and language use is to be
developed, it seems that judgements must be recognized to be not of
two kinds but of four:

(i) whether (and to what extent) something is formally *possible*;
(ii) whether (and to what extent) something is *feasible* in virtue of
the means of implementation available;
(iii) whether (and to what extent) something is *appropriate* in relation
to a context in which it is used and evaluated;
(iv) whether (and to what extent) something is in fact done, actually
performed, and what its doing entails.

(i) *Whether (and to what extent) Something is Formally Possible*

This formulation expresses an essential concern of present linguistic
theory for the openness, the potentiality of language and generalizes it
for cultural systems. When systemic possibility is a matter of language,
the corresponding term is *grammaticality*. Indeed, language is so much
the paradigmatic example that one uses "grammar" and "grammaticality" by extension for other systems of formal possibility (see Burke,
1945). For particular systems, such extension may well be the easiest
course; it is much easier to say that something is "grammatical" with
respect to the underlying structure of a body of myth, than to say in a
sense that it is "mythical". As a general term, one does readily enough
speak of "cultural" in a way analogous to "grammatical". We may say,
then, that something possible within a formal system is grammatical,
cultural, or, on occasion, communicative (cf. Hymes, 1967) as distinct
from ungrammatical, uncultural or non-communicative.

(ii) *Whether (and to what extent) Something is Feasible*

The predominant linguistic concern here has been with psycholinguistic factors such as memory limitation, perceptual devices, awkwardness or ease of structural properties, such as nesting, embedding or branching. Such considerations are also relevant to cultural anthropology: Wallace (1961b) says that the brain is such that "culturally institutionalized folk taxonomies will not contain more than 26 entities and consequently will not require more than six orthogonally related binary dimensions for the definitions of all terms". With regard to the cultural, one would take into account other features of the body and features of the material environment as well. With regard to the communicative, the importance of the notion of available means of implementation is obvious.

As we have seen, question (ii) defines one portion of all that has been included under the heading of performance, so a more specific term is needed here. *Feasible* would seem to be suitable both for linguistics and for the cultural as a whole. (No general term for this property in cultural behaviour has been proposed, so far as I know; Chomsky (1965; p. 63) has used "feasibility" in a distinct, but not wholly unrelated sense.) Moreover, the implementational constraints affecting grammar may be largely the same as those that affect all of cultural behaviour. Certainly, with regard to the brain, substantial identity would seem likely.

(iii) *Whether (and to what extent) Something is Appropriate*

The term "appropriate" is introduced by Chomsky with regard to the possibility, provided by language, of "reacting appropriately in an indefinite range of new situations" (1965). The relation of sentences to speech events and to context of situation is certainly at issue here; but verbal, as well as extra-verbal, context must be taken into account. The interdependence of the two kinds of context in their relation to grammar has long been noted (see Waterhouse, 1963; Gunter, 1966).

Verbal context has been lumped together with psycholinguistic constraints under the general heading of performance and, correspondingly, acceptability: "The unacceptable grammatical sentences often cannot be used, for reasons having to do, not with grammar, but rather with memory limitation, intonational and stylistic factors, 'iconic' elements of discourse (for example, a tendency to place logical subject and object early rather than late . . .), and so on" (Chomsky, 1965; p. 11). As the preceding analysis has stressed, questions of implementation should not be confused with questions of additional kinds of rules (such as those of style): the former are distinguished here as matters of feasibility, the latter as matters of appropriateness. Within cultural anthropology the term "appropriate" has been used in the ethnographic work of Conklin, Frake, and others, and has been extended to discussion of linguistic theory (Hymes, 1964). "Appropriateness" readily suggests the required sense of relation to contextual features. Since any judgement is made in some defining context, it may always involve a factor of appropriateness, so that this dimension must be controlled even in a study of purely grammatical competence. From a communicative standpoint, judgements of appropriateness may not be assignable, either to the linguistic, or to the cultural sphere; rather, the two will intersect, if not largely coincide. (One might think of appropriateness in grammar as the context-sensitive rules of sub-categorization and selection to which the base component is subject; there would still be intersection with the cultural—cf. Newman and the Yokuts above, and the implications of Tyler (1966), De Camp (1971) and Labov (1969), for inclusion of cultural features in the contexts of rules.)

Chomsky's concern with appropriateness would seem to be with its *possibility* with regard to *new* situations, as evidence of the unboundedness of language, not with its rule-governed nature. Grammar itself, however, provides only for the possibility of appropriateness, not for the fact. In virtue of grammar new sentences are possible; which of the infinite number of possible new sentences will be appropriate in a given new situation depends on other sectors of cultural behaviour. Chomsky himself discusses the need to specify situations in mentalistic terms, and refers to proper notions of "what might be expected from anthropological research" (1965, p. 195). Here would seem to be recognition that an adequate approach to the relation between situations and sentences must be "mentalistic", entailing a tacit knowledge and hence competence. But so far as explicit statement of theory is concerned, the notion of competence (knowledge) remains restricted to the grammatical. There is no suggestion as to what might contribute to judgement of sentences in relation to situations, nor how such judgements might be characterized. The lack of explication here might be defended on the grounds that the grammatical theory is not concerned with such matters; but the need to place linguistic theory within a more general socio–cultural theory is shown by its inconsistency on just this score. The footnote quoted above rejects treatment of situations in non-mentalistic terms, as betraying "a complete misunderstanding of what might be expected from anthropological research", yet its own terms leave no place for the subject except "performance", whose description as "the actual use of language in concrete situations" (1965, p. 4) sounds suspiciously like the very approach to which one is opposed.

From the standpoint of grammar, appropriateness is the notion under which rules of use, rules of speaking, enter (cf. Hymes, 1971). Sentences will be seen as judged for acceptability in terms of their appropriateness under rules governing relations between scenes, participants, genres, channel, and the like—who can say what, in what way, where and when, by what means and to whom? From the standpoint of a single underlying structure, one will be concerned with explaining a choice of alternative realizations—"To end the Vietnam war is easy", "It is easy to end the Vietnam war", "Ending the Vietnam war is easy", "The Vietnam war is easy to end"—which may be suitable within a particular style of speech or writing.

(iv) *Whether* (*and to what extent*) *Something is Done*

Study of communicative competence cannot restrict itself to occurrences, but it cannot ignore them. Structure cannot be reduced to probabilities of occurrence, but structural change and rules of speaking are not independent of them. The capabilities of language-users do include some (perhaps unconscious) knowledge of probabilities, and shifts in proportions of occurrence, as indicators of style, appropriate response, and the like. One problem is that a quantitative predominance may be treated as a qualitative absolute, exceptions being ignored or not even noticed. Another is that the number and proportion of features required to mark a style or variety of language vary greatly. In some cases only one or two features will stamp discourse as "archaic", "vulgar", or the like. The relationship of occurrence to social valuation is a necessary part of sociolinguistics.

Statistical properties are not in themselves revealing, but one must consider them when speakers find them so. Kučera (1955) reports that Prague speakers begin conversation in one linguistic variety, and move gradually to another, less formal variety, through a process of introduction and gradual change in the frequency of less formal features. Status-implicated features of Japanese are said to be manipulated in a similar manner. Again, in usual linguistic theory no distinction is made between competence of speaker and hearer. Even within a monolingual community, however, one must provide for "the distinction between the merely and marginally possible and the actually normal: between what one will accept as a hearer and what one will produce as a speaker" (Quirk, 1968).

It is a criterion of a structural analysis that it provides for the *absence*, the non-occurrence, of a feature as well as for its occurrence: something may be possible, feasible, appropriate, and not occur. Rules of speaking must account for silence, both as the appropriate act and as marked by the absence of the appropriate act (e.g. absence of a response to a summons, or of a further remark by the maker of a summons, once answer has been given). As a general term, *occurrence* here covers diverse phenomena. It serves only to make a point, especially important for work that seeks to change what is done.

Finally, this fourth category allows for what Garfinkel (1971) explains as the application of a medieval principle, *factum valet*: "an action otherwise prohibited by rule is to be treated as correct if it happens nevertheless". And, of special importance, this dimension is needed to allow a place for work by Labov, which incorporates quantitative relations and conditions into transformational generative rules, as well as to allow for the problem of the assimilation of quantitative properties to qualitative, normative status, posed by Labov with regard to rules of grammar and verbal interaction (rare phenomena often being treated as non-occurring, very frequent phenomena as absolute).

The four questions which I have raised may be asked from the standpoint of a system, or from the standpoint of persons. Interest in competence, however, dictates the second standpoint here. So far the argument has been to extend the notion of competence as tacit knowledge from grammar to speaking as a whole. If, however, the factors of differential competence, heterogeneous speech community, and constitutive role of sociocultural features, are to be adequately studied, the most general term for human capability in regard to speech must be extended yet further. I should therefore take *competence* as the most general term for the speaking and hearing capabilities of a person. This choice is in the spirit of present linguistic theory, if at present against the letter. Competence is understood to be dependent upon two things: (tacit) *knowledge* and (ability for) *use*.

Knowledge, then, is distinct from competence and from systemic possibility, to which it is related empirically by being a sub-part of it. This distinction allows one to deal with differential competence due to differential knowledge. Cazden (1967), by utilizing what is in effect systemic possibility as a definition of competence, was forced to separate it from what persons know and do: the "competence" underlying a person's behaviour was labelled a kind of "performance". Her procedure may be inevitable once one tries to adapt the original notion of competence to facts of personal knowledge. As mentioned above, it seems preferable to interpret knowledge as relevant to all four parameters of communication.

Ability for use is introduced to allow for the role of non-cognitive factors, such as motivation. Like *knowledge* it may relate to all four parameters, i.e. individuals may differ in ability to use knowledge of each. In speaking of competence it is important to ignore affective and volitional factors which are relevant to the theory of education and to research design and explanation (as the work of Labov indicates). Socio-linguistic work recurrently finds that *self-identity* is crucial to differential competence and to heterogeneity of speech communities (e.g. as a source of linguistic change). Failure to consider this goes together with the simplistic assumption that sheer quantity of exposure should shape children's speech. This view is commonly held by teachers and the public. Linguists may recognize it as a version of the fallacy espoused by Bloomfield, that quantity of interaction explained linguistic change (1933). Non-standard speaking children in fact hear as much television and radio as other children, and of course, hear their teachers all day. These facts puzzle some teachers; the point is that identification and motivation are what count, not exposure. At Columbia Point school in Boston in July 1968, after a discussion sparked off by these questions concerning exposure, the one black mother present later volunteered: "You know, I've noticed that when the children play 'school' outside, they talk like they're supposed to in school; and when they stop playing school, they stop".

Turning now to actual use and actual events, the term *performance* is now free for this meaning, but with several important reminders and provisos. The "performance models" studied in psycholinguistics are to be taken as models of aspects of ability for use, relative to means of implementation in the brain, although they could now be seen as a distinct, contributory factor in general competence. In sum, the goal of a broad theory of competence can be said to be to show the ways in which the systematically possible, the feasible, and the appropriate are linked to produce and interpret actually occurring cultural behaviour.

It is too early to propose a precise model of the interrelations of the linguistic portion of competence and the rest. At least 3 abstract possibilities would seem to exist (Fig. 1).

Perhaps one should contrast a long and a short range view of competence, the short view being interested primarily in understanding innate capacities as unfolded during the first years of life, and the long-range view in understanding the continuing socialization and change of competence through life. In any case, here is one major respect in which a theory of competence must go beyond the notion of ideal

(a)	Linguistic Competence	+	(other) Communicative Competence
	Linguistic Performance	+	(other) Communicative Performance

(b)	Communicative Competence
	Linguistic Competence
	Communicative Competence
	Linguistic Performance

(c)	Communicative Competence
	Linguistic Competence
	Communicative Performance
	Linguistic Performance

FIG. 1.

fluency in a homogeneous community, if it is to be applicable to work with disadvantaged children and with children whose primary language or language variety is different from that of their school. Belief in the possibility of change presupposes the possibility that competence which has unfolded in the natural way can be altered, perhaps drastically so, by new social factors. One is assuming from the outset a confrontation of different systems of competence within the school and community, and focusing on the way in which one system affects or can be made to affect the other. Problems of the interpretation of manifestations of one system in terms of another arise: what Weinreich calls *interference* (1953). Since interference involves features of language and features of use together, one might adopt the phrase suggested by Alfred Hayes,[1] and speak of *sociolinguistic interference*. (More generally, one would speak of *communicative interference* to allow for the role of modes of communication other than language; I shall focus, however, on phenomena of language and language *per se*.)

When a child from one background enters a situation in which the communicative expectations are defined in terms of another, misperception and misanalysis may occur at every level. As is well known, words may be misunderstood because of differences in phonological systems; sentences may be misunderstood because of differences in grammatical systems; intents and innate abilities may be misjudged because of difference of systems for the use of language. The notion of socio-

[1] At a conference held in 1965 at West Point Farms, sponsored by Yeshiva University, Department of Educational Psychology and Guidance.

linguistic interference is of the greatest importance for the relationship between theory and practice. First, a theory of sociolinguistic interference must begin with heterogeneous situations, whose dimensions are social as well as linguistic. (See, for example, Labov and Cohen (1967) on relations between standard and non-standard phonological and syntactic rules in Harlem, and between receptive and productive competence of uses of the non-standard vernacular.) Secondly, the notion of sociolinguistic interference presupposes the notion of sociolinguistic systems between which interference occurs. This points to a variety of researches that might otherwise be overlooked or set aside. (For instance some people object to utilizing research on "second-language learning" in programmes for Negro students because of the offensive implications of the term.) The notions of sociolinguistic interference and system require a conception of an *integrated theory of sociolinguistic description*. Contributions towards such a theory have found it necessary to start, not from the notion of language, but from the notion of a *variety* or *code*; and they have been forced to recognize *that the question of whether languages and dialects are historically related or not* is entirely secondary to their status in actual social relationships. First, there is the need to put language names in quotes (pp. 7–8). Secondly, the degree of linguistic similarity and distance cannot predict mutual intelligibility, let alone use (cf. Hymes, 1968). Thirdly, from the functional standpoint of a socio-linguistic description, means quite different in scope can be employed in equivalent roles.

In short, we have to break with the tradition of thought which simply equates one language, one culture, and takes a set of functions for granted. In order to deal with the problems faced by disadvantaged children, and with the problems of education in much of the world, we have to begin with the conception of the speech habits, or competences, of a community or population, and regard the place among them of resources of historically derived languages as an empirical question. What must be known is the attitude towards the objective linguistic differences, the use made of them. Only on the basis of such a functionally motivated description can comparable cases be established and valid theory developed.

With regard to sociolinguistic interference among school children, much relevant information and theoretical insight can come from the sorts of cases variously labelled "bilingualism", "linguistic acculturation", "dialectology" or "creolization". The value of an integrated theory of sociolinguistic description to the practical work would be that (i) it would attempt to place studies, diversely labelled, within a

B

common analytical framework, where one can talk about relations among codes, and types of code-switching, and types of interference between codes; and that (ii) by so doing one could make use of the theory while perhaps avoiding connotations that attach to such labels as "second-language learning". I say perhaps, because it is very difficult to avoid unpleasant connotations for any terms used to designate situations that are themselves intrinsically sensitive and objectionable.

William Stewart's suggestion (1965) that some code relationships in the United States might be better understood if seen as part of a continuum of cases ranging to the Caribbean and Africa, for example, seems to me from a theoretical standpoint very promising. Most code relationships in the United States do not involve different languages, but they do involve relationships among different codes, and the full series illuminates the part. Stewart has assigned them different labels of dialect, creole, pidgin language, bilingualism, along a common sociolinguistic dimension. Overcoming different labels for underlying sociolinguistic dimensions is a task in which theory and practice meet.

Let me now consider briefly, in the context of interference, a principle that makes the broader perspective of communication essential. We only need to mention for them to be recognized, phenomena of intonation, tone of voice, expressive phonetic features, and other parts of paralinguistics; phenomena of the body idiom, gesture, and other parts of kinesics (Goffman, 1963); and all that Edward Hall (1961) designates as the "silent language" and the "hidden dimension". Yet it is remarkable how easily we forget them. In Cazden's review article, she makes an important critical point, namely that a common finding may easily be given two quite different interpretations, and her example may be evidence of the point I wish to make now. Bernstein has interpreted a greater use of "I think" among higher-status subjects in terms of egocentricity-sociocentricity contrasting with "ain't it", whereas Loban (1966) has taken a like result as evidence of cognitive flexibility (grouping it with "I'm not exactly sure"). The question arises: did Bernstein's English subjects say "I think"in an egocentric way, and did Loban's California school children say "I think" with cognitive flexibility? Clearly, the import of data cannot be assessed apart from the co-occurring set of intonational and expressive signals.

The question of communicative interference poses itself here in two ways. There is first the problem of interference between differing sets of expressive signals; of this there are many examples in education and the transmission of information. Steven Polgar (1960) reported some years ago that Mesquaki Fox children near Tama, Iowa, interpreted the normal loudness of voice and directness of teachers as "meanness" and getting mad. The Lakota word for "white man" is etymologized as "fast-talking, argumentative", literally, "bad-mouth". The normal patterns of friendly interaction, verbal and non-verbal, among Negroes in Oakland may be seen by Lakota there as frightening. (I am indebted to Luis Kemnitzer for these observations.) Second, there is the problem of interference with regard to the relations between co-occurring codes within a single message. The principle of concern here can be put as an instruction: *"Find out where the information is."* A child is making use of a set of modalities, as he or she communicates, and interprets communication, and in discursive communication language is only one modality. With non-vocal communication, there is not only the fact that "body idiom . . . is a conventionalized discourse" (Goffman, 1963), but also the possible interdependence of kinesic behaviour and linguistic structure. Birdwhistell (1971) finds among Americans both a set of particular movements (markers) that occur regularly with or in substitution for syntactic features (pronominal, pluralization, verbal, tense, expression of area and of manner), and a kinesic stress system which expresses certain syntactic combinations. One of the essential features of Bernstein's model for restricted and elaborated codes is that the grammatical and lexical restrictiveness of the restricted code is accompanied by intensified perceptual paralinguistic activity. I have found Bernstein's model very useful cross-culturally when taken as defining ideal types, although one finds that the dimensions joined in the two types prove empirically distinct. In such a case the two parties to a communicative exchange may be putting information in different places, and looking for it in different places. The situation is further complicated by what the late Dutch linguist de Groot called "the law of the two strata", namely that when the discursive and the expressive import of a message conflict, the latter signals the real intent. Quite possibly some teachers are not understanding their students at all, and some children are understanding their teachers all too well! In any case, a theory of competence that is to be of help must provide for tacit knowledge of an array of signals and a battery of functions; what is signalled lexically in one case may be signalled by expressive intonation in another. The theory of competence cannot be limited to the referential use of language alone.

More generally, one must reckon with the fact that any act that is subject to a rule of conduct is a communication, and that seemingly trivial details of situational propriety can have major consequences. Such properties are subsidiary to verbal discourse in our usual thinking about education, and yet their maintenance or infringement may overrule discourse content. Consciously or not, from an individual's use of the verbal and non-verbal idiom of social gatherings, others make inference to his regard for others and himself, involvement, motives, and indeed basic character and mental health (see Goffman, 1963; esp. pp. 216–48). Lack of attention due to lack of sleep may be read as rejection and hostility (and even come to be accepted by the sleepless one as a correct interpretation).

In these respects the continuity or discontinuity of communicative patterning from family to school is of crucial importance. As an example, in Hawaiian first grade an Anglo teacher may act on the assumption that the children should stop, become quiet, and give simultaneous attention to her, so that she need give information only once. That the children do not comply may be attributed to many things about them, perhaps, but not to lack of communicative competence on her part. In fact patterns of communication in the families from which the children come make the methods unsuccessful. A teacher who knows these patterns turns to one child with the information, and so quickly attracts the successive attention of the others, accomplishing her purpose in a period of time in which another teacher would perhaps still be attempting to obtain the situation she thinks necessary for information to be given (Stephen Boggs, personal communication). Clearly the motives and character of the two teachers will be differently interpreted by the children. This most general level of the notion of communicative competence implies a concern with a corresponding theory of description; much more needs to be said and learned about both.

With regard to education and children, the goal of an integrated theory of communicative description should be to guide accounts of the range of communicative settings, functions and means and their interrelationships, acquired by children. The school setting would be one, but not the only one; and a major purpose should be to place the school setting in the context of other settings, so as to delineate the true communicative abilities of the children and to show the extent to which the performance in school settings was not a direct disclosure of their abilities, but a product of interference between the system they possess and the system that confronts them. In part the problem is one of conflict of values and perceived interests (cf. Labov, 1965). Indeed, since the beginnings of stratified society and the use of writing, it has been characteristic of the greater part of mankind that a desired or required communicative competence has confronted man as an alien thing, imposed by a power not within his control. In the complex circumstances of our own society it is hard to see how children can be expected to master a second system, complementing or replacing their own, if the process is not perceived as intrinsically relevant or enjoyable, preferably both.

What sorts of interference may occur; what sorts of learning and change may be required, cannot of course be postulated in advance. Sometimes the question will be simply of dialect markers, of the social, rather than the referential, or expressive, information called for in the situation. Sometimes the question will be one of added skills in the use of syntax or routines; sometimes a total style of communicative conduct; but it should be repeated that one major problem concerns the communicative patterns, attitudes, and consciousness of those whom the children encounter, e.g. teachers of reading (cf. Labov, 1967; Labov, Cohen and Robins, 1965). One major need for change is in the schools and surrounding communities.

CONCLUSION

I began with limitations of a linguistic theory, and introduced considerations to broaden it. With discussion of each of a number of topics, the starting point of thought has momentarily shifted from language to social life. Such shift of starting point and orientation reflects a basic property of a broad theory of competence and description whether sociolinguistic or more generally communicative: it is essentially sociocultural. A linguistic theory in the narrow sense, in so far as it deals with use, starts with language and looks out from there; structure precedes, functions follow. Discussion that starts with such a theory tends to follow the same course. A theory of the sort needed here starts with social life and looks in at language; thus functions guide, structures follow. Communicative means generally are viewed in terms of the patterning of communicative acts and purposes. The essentially sociocultural character of an adequate theory can be brought out by three assumptions that such a theory makes:

(i) each social relationship entails the selection and/or creation of communicative means considered specific and appropriate to it by its participants;

(ii) the organization of communicative means, in terms of social relationships, confers a structure that is not disclosed in the analysis of the means separately;

(iii) the communicative means available in a relationship condition its nature and outcome.

These three assumptions are rather simple and obvious; to take them seriously, however, is to define a kind of investigation almost wholly unsystematized and theoretically little understood. To take the first assumption, a social relationship gives rise to a use of communicative means that distinguishes it. It is probably a sociolinguistic universal that the speech of men and women can be distinguished in every society, yet articles on men's and women's speech only refer to cases when markers of the distinction intrude themselves into the ordinary analysis of the language. For the vast majority of societies the markers have not so intruded, so we are largely ignorant. This very fact is evidence of the second assumption: the way communicative means are organized in terms of a social relationship is unlikely to appear unless one begins with the social relationship, and then looks for the means. The third assumption is perhaps the simplest, the most obvious, and for some reason, the most resisted by some linguists. It says, with reference to language, that what skills people have available affects what they can do. In it lies the heart of the element of truth in what is often called the Whorfian hypothesis.

It is of course not mandatory that the term "linguistic theory" be used in one particular way. If one wishes to reserve "linguistic theory" for the narrower sort of competence, then "sociolinguistic theory" (and communicative theory) will do for a broader sort of competence. What is essential is that concepts of the nature of language and its use be not pre-empted in the name of "linguistic theory" by a narrow view. The understanding of the language use involves attention not only to participants, settings, and other extra-linguistic factors, but also attention to purely linguistic phenomena, and the discovery and statement of new features, organization and relationships in the data of language itself, when viewed from the more general perspective of social relationships. What is essential is that conceptions of speakers, listeners and competence take into account, as quite normal in the world, the situations of diversity of codes. One must see the child as acquiring and achieving narrowly linguistic and broadly sociolinguistic (and communicative) competence together.

Discussion

BEVER: The trouble with the way in which the notions of competence and performance were originally described was that it looked as though linguistic grammars succeeded in being the descriptions of the internal structure of the language. There was always a flaw in that right from the start: the basic data, which the grammar of competence depended on, were themselves pieces of performance, the behaviour of having intuitions about sentences. So at its very inception, grammar was not the crystal-pure nugget of ideal form that we would have liked to have. However, it is a profitable scientific heuristic to have a simplified body of data, and this was obtained by saying that we would only treat so-called grammatical sentences. Your plea, that we must treat language with respect to more problems than just the problem of grammaticality, was already inherent in the theory, since grammaticality was seen as a psychological notion. But your suggestion that we can resolve our difficulties through study of the interaction of language and its social function is incorrect. This study is important in its own right, but it will not resolve the problem of the relationship between a linguistic grammar and speech performance.

KLIMA: We have to remember the difference between sentences and utterances. A sentence is a linguistic construct, and it is this which competence describes; an utterance is a matter of performance and as such involves not only English grammar, but also intention.

MEHLER: I believe there is a problem in defining competence in the classical way. All along there has been confusion between defining competence as the machine that can produce clean simple outputs, and defining it as describing underlying processes, that is mechanisms. We have linguistic intuitions about what competence should be about, but in order to look at the minimal machine, one has to study it at the outset, not at the adult stage, because then the problems become too complicated. However, if you look at a child, and try to determine what the minimum machine should be in order to generate everything, you come to another problem: and that is, that performance limitations are supposed to concern memory, among other things. Now, it is generally presupposed that the memory changes; but I believe on the contrary that memory changes are changes in the way in which people encode things, that is to say that they are qualitative changes. It may be then, that competence has to be defined as a dynamic process, and what you have to postulate are a set of minimal rules, so that you get a system that can learn things later. This makes competence very much more impoverished than Katz, for instance, would have us believe. It also means that from the beginning, competence would have to be something that is not purely linguistic. The rules we need are probably some very general rules, which allow us to learn, among other things, the linguistic rules.

HYMES: I don't regard my position as incompatible with the original position. One of the points I want to make here is simply that there are people who use this dichotomy to distinguish between some things which are worthy of study and others which are perhaps not—"mere performance data". I am also trying to make clear some distinctions that I think are not always made explicit. First of all there is the notion of the potentiality of the system, the extent to which something is possible, given a formal system. This is relevant both to the study of language and to the study of culture, apart from language. Secondly, there are those phenomena which have been associated with performance, that is, the study of the extent to which something is practical or feasible, given the means available at the time. Thirdly, I want to include under "acceptability" of an utterance, not only the judgement of an individual in the abstract, but also acceptability as it is evaluated by members of the speech community with regard to the situation, or with regard to their opinions and views. These three things seem to me to be rather distinct and to need to be sorted out.

CAZDEN: Do I understand you right? You are still talking about the rules, the knowledge that underlies behaviour; but you are saying that in order to explain language usage you have to consider more than the knowledge of grammar. You are saying that you must include, in the notion of competence, knowledge of rules of style and rules of social interaction, and so on.

HYMES: Yes, and this may lead to different kinds of competence in people who grow up in different cultural contexts. For instance, there may be things that are general about Indonesian speakers who are raised in a multi-lingual context, which might not necessarily be true of children who are brought up to speak one language only. The situations they are in may have effects on their use of language and their ability to use language and the meaning of language to them.

BERNSTEIN: The social class contexts are very relevant here. I am thinking for instance of young boys in school, who have great difficulty in producing either speech or writing which is acceptable to the people within the educational system. On the other hand, if you listen to the same boys in the street discussing a ball game, or something else that has excited them, they can produce very rich and complex linguistic structures with complete communicative control.

CAZDEN: I think we should be very careful here not to confuse differences with deficiencies. One can speak of a deficiency if, given a universal developmental pattern of some type, certain children go through it more slowly, or later, than other children. Social class differences are often thought of as deficiencies, but you can only talk about these as deficiencies against certain criteria. Labov (1966) describes non-standard speakers of English, who cannot repeat standard English sentences without errors; but the reverse could also be true, standard English speakers may have more errors speaking non-standard English sentences. These are differences in linguistic rules and, it seems to me, cannot be considered as deficiencies on any criterion.

HYMES: But when Labov actually pressed his kids very hard, saying "this is what I said, and this is what you said; *now* repeat what *I* said", the kids replied with the same non-standard form. I actually asked him what happened when he asked middle class kids to repeat non-standard forms, and he told me that they could produce the non-standard form.

BERNSTEIN: Again, this could be due to the fact that middle class kids understand the game you are playing with them, whereas working class kids don't necessarily.

HYMES: Well it seems to me that we have come near to what you might call the problems of ethnographic description of the kinds of communicative activity in which these children take part. Let me give you some examples, from the anthropological field, concerning the interaction between sociological factors and linguistic factors. Peter Gardener (1966) did some fieldwork recently in southern India, among a tribal people called the Puliya, describing their socialization patterns. There is no agriculture and no industry, and the society is neither particularly co-operative nor particularly competitive; so children are led neither to be particularly inter-dependent nor to be aggressively competitive with each other, but simply to busy themselves with their own concerns in reasonable spatial proximity. He observed that, by the time a man was forty, he practically stopped speaking altogether. He had no reason to speak. People there, in fact, just didn't talk much and seldom seemed to find anything much to talk about, and he saw this as a consequence of the particular kind of socialization pattern.

Another thing which is quite striking in some societies, especially in agricultural societies, is a differential role for men and women. In a number of different places around the world there is a restrictive role for women in communication. Public speech, for instance, is almost exclusively a male prerogative, but as a sort of compensation, women are allowed to express personal feelings. Often this is accompanied by special marking of the situation, particular use of the voice, or by special intonation patterns. One finds this among the Aurecanians in Chile (Hymes, 1970), where women are excluded from public speech; they talk among themselves but not in the presence of men; when an interchange is necessary, they address men through an intonational process. Among the Ashanti of Ghana (*ibid.*), speech is reported to be looked upon as intrinsically dangerous; for instance, children and babies are believed to share a special code with each other and with certain spirits. If a mother is giving birth, another infant is not allowed in the same room. They believe that if children were allowed they would tell the baby in the womb how tough life is, and then it would be a difficult delivery because the baby would not want to come out.

Another relevant thing here may not only be how a child makes its first utterances, but how the society interprets these utterances. In our society, and in many other societies, the first utterances are often thought of as being labels, pointing out and naming objects. Among the Alor in Indonesia, a child's first utterances are regarded as a demand for food. Among the Chaga in Africa (*ibid.*), a child's first utterances are taken as attempts to manipulate persons around it. It is almost as if the child's first utterance is a projective test for the cultural value system. There are certainly differences among societies as to the motives they give to the child's utterances and this may have quite important consequences for what role speech plays in the learning of the language.

Social Backgrounds and Verbal Skills

SUSAN ERVIN-TRIPP

Berkeley, California

THERE HAS BEEN a great deal of public discussion in the United States recently about research on differences in verbal skills in children according to social background. This discussion arises from the crisis in our schools, but is typically ill-informed about the varieties of meaning which "social differences in verbal skills" may have, and their theoretical implications (e.g. Olim *et al.*, 1967; Lawton, 1968). My purpose here is to clarify a set of categories in order to distinguish sharply between skills which ought to be measured differently, have different pedagogical implications, and possibly different origins.

My attention to this matter has been sharpened by the cross-cultural research programme of our group in Berkeley, California. The first statement of this programme is the *Field manual for cross-cultural study of the acquisition of communicative competence* (Slobin, 1967). From this imposing title you can see that we owe a great deal to Dell Hymes, both in frame of reference and specifically in ranges of issues to consider.

The *Manual* summarizes past work, proposes problems to be studied and suggests methods pertaining to three aspects of child language development. One section deals with the traditional domains of phonology, syntax and semantics, but with the intent of enabling comparisons to be made between data collected from a variety of different languages. Another section is concerned with the influence of environment on the child's language through beliefs about language, formal and informal instruction, and exposure to different kinds of input. Courtney Cazden will deal with most of these matters. A third section is concerned with the development of social features of language, with competence in its use, not merely in its structure. This topic will be my main concern in this present paper. My question is very simple: what are the ways in which children's language behaviour may differ in different social groups?

LINGUISTIC RULES

Children who live in the same larger community may belong to sub-communities using different underlying linguistic rules. In the case of dialects, the differences may be relatively superficial but have import-ance socially and in the encounter of two dialects in the teaching of reading by a speaker of one to a speaker of another. For example, Roger Shuy (Shuy *et al.*, 1967) found in a study of black and white informants in Detroit that there was a high correlation between social class indices and negative concord rules:

(i) I don't want any apples;
(ii) I don't want no apples;
(iii) Nobody wants any apples;
(iv) Nobody don't want no apples.

In addition, blacks had higher frequencies of multiple negation in sentences containing indefinites than whites.

The strength of these differences in sentence-processing rules can be seen from the work of William Labov with Harlem teenage boys (Labov, 1966, 1970). Under optimal testing conditions with a group he knew well he developed an imitation game which included both standard and non-standard sentences. He found that the boys had a marked tendency to extend negation to all indefinites, and yet might believe they had imitated accurately.

(v) Nobody ever took an airplane;
(vi) Nobody never took a airplane.

In cases other than negation, it became clear that the boys could correctly interpret standard English utterances but could not produce them:

(vii) I asked Alvin whether he knows how to play basketball.
(viii) I asked Alvin did he know how to play basketball.

Just as (v) and (vi) are translations, (vii) and (viii) are translations showing comprehension of the tense feature but a different rule of auxiliary inversion, in output.

One difference between Standard English and NNE (Non-standard

Negro English) of black adolescents which is of interest because it carries meaning in the use of invariant *be* as a main verb.

    (ix) It don't be that way;
     (x) She be in the office;
    (xi) She in the office.

While the semantic interpretation of this verb remains uncertain, studies of contextual variation suggest that it usually carries an implication of habitual, iterative, or general occurrence. Thus (x) implies a regular rule that 'she be in the office' at this time, but (xi) (which has NNE copula deletion) that she is only momentarily in the office on this occasion.

The examples one finds in texts of NNE suggest a contrast quite like that in Standard English between

   (xii) He walks to work (every day);
  (xiii) He is walking to work (right now).

The difference between the habitual or general and the short term event is often difficult for foreigners to learn and they make errors indicative of failure to make the semantic distinction appropriately between sentences (xii) and (xiii). Thus NNE appears to carry out in the copula a distinction present in the rest of the verb system, whereas it is neutralized in standard English copulas. Black children in the United States find it difficult if they use *be* in this sense to translate and "correct" these utterances into "proper" English (as their parents and teachers pressure them to do), and the presence of the semantic distinction is not usually understood by white teachers who hear it. I would assume that many West Indian children in England who heard versions of Creoles at home are like our speakers of NNE in comprehending the standard English they have heard without always being able to produce it consistently, and in being misinterpreted by their teachers.

DEVELOPMENTAL RATE

The evidence that we have suggests that the vast majority of linguistic rules are alike in the different varieties of English. But children might differ in the *rate* of mastery of shared rules. For such comparisons, test structures must use the dialect of the child's milieu, and fundamental rules in the child's capacity, not his frequency of output which is subject to stylistic preference. Cazden (1970) mentions that the black children in the day-care centre where she did her study of training language development were similar in morphemes per utterance to middle class white children of the same age. Shriner and Miner (1968) found no class differences in morphological development of 4-year-olds, in the Berko (1958) kind of test situation. The widespread belief that there are class and ethnic group differences in developmental rates, leading to "verbal deprivation" requiring compensatory linguistic training, seems extremely ill-founded. We simply do not know whether there are reliable differences in the rate of development of basic linguistic skills, in the emergence of fundamental milestones such as the ability to understand or imitate multi-word sentences, subject versus object, and imbedded sentences. The little evidence we have suggests no differences.

SOCIO-LINGUISTIC RULES

This unfamiliar category will require elaboration. Socio-linguistic rules differ from linguistic rules in that the prediction of the linguistic form to be generated, or the interpretation of one in the corpus, entails the use of social categories. These rules, as I see them, are of 3 general types.

The first are *alternation rules*, in which the selection between linguistic alternatives depends on some social feature or a series of features (in terms of ordered alternative possibilities). The second person pronoun in French, or first-naming an addressee, provides a vivid example. A person who calls everyone indiscriminately by his first name seems to be violating some kind of rule of address. The violation is usually, however, not interpreted as a linguistic slip but as a breach of etiquette. If the form used is part of the set of possible alternatives in the system, we may view the speaker as too forward, too shy, and so on.

The rules for address in English, which I have analysed systematically elsewhere, give examples of the kind of social categories I mean; they include relative age, rank, child *vs.* adult, sex. Some situational categories are relevant, for example courtroom; if a son were a lawyer and his father the judge, he would not call his father "Dad" in court. The address system of the courtroom supersedes, and in ordered choices is prior to all other determinants except for child versus adult.

These social categories require ethnological analysis. Age difference in the Korean rules means one day; in my rule, about fifteen years. Even an apparently simple category like "child" requires that one identify the age and social conditions making one an adult in a community.

Children begin to reveal alternations based on social features at a very early age. One can find whisper versus shout, and baby talk intonation to infants by the time a speaker is 2. Any child who contrasts "hi" and "good morning" to different addressees, who contrasts "please" with "gimme" or who has learned, if he is multilingual, which language to use according to addressee or situation, has an alternation rule *if* there is evidence of productivity of the pattern.

William Labov made the important discovery that much linguistic variation is not just "free variation"; the proportions of each alternative can be predicted given the linguistic context and certain social features. In these cases there is a socio-linguistic alternation rule which determines, not the particular alternative used, but its probability. Violation of the rule consists in using a feature too much or too little, with consequences for the social categorization of the speaker (e.g. social class) or of his intent (e.g. deference, formality, nervousness). In Labov's study of New York City speech (1966), he found that post-vocalic /r/ has a frequency dependent on the speaker's age, social class, formality of eliciting situation, and score on a "Linguistic Insecurity Index" developed by Labov. The frequency can be predicted by a linear equation, and hence is certainly not a random variable. Contractions such as "he's tired" or deletions in NNE such as "he tired" depend also on linguistic and semantic context. For child learning, this systematic inherent variation demands a new complex type of learning, since it demands a probability matching which cannot be readily accomplished by classroom exercises or formal rule-learning.

A second type of socio-linguistic rule concerns the constraints on alternations arising from surrounding or co-occurrent choices, so they are called *co-occurrence constraints*. In the most extreme form they exist in language-switching, but we all have some constraints in style-switching which join formal lexicon, formal grammar and more carefully monitored articulation. When Mme. Sinclair said *répertoire* yesterday (with a uvular /r/) instead of English *repertoire* in the midst of an English sentence, she was realizing French lexicon with French phonemes regardless of the larger English context. This I call a vertical constraint, since the phonological features are determined by the lexical selection rather than neighbouring phonological choices. On the other hand, Richard Diebold (1963) described Greek–English bilinguals who have a horizontal phonological constraint, so that phonological continuity exists from an English context into borrowed Greek lexicon, or vice-versa. In the latter case, which is probably more common in garden-variety bilingual communities, one might say that a phonological set carries across a whole utterance, just as the grammatical morphemes of an utterance may all be from one set regardless of the lexical or content words. Fischer's (1958) study of New England children noted that formal words like *write* took *-ing* as a suffix, whereas words used in play accepted *-in* as a suffix, so we have *writing*, but *fishin, hittin, shovin*. Regular co-occurrence rules imply a fairly consistent differentiation of styles. Our impression from the material we have so far both on multilingual and dialectal styles suggests that children are rather inconsistent at first, especially if audiences are capable of understanding both varieties. Selections may "mark" the speech socially (for instance in role-playing games) initially, but drift readily back to "normal" style, or there may be fairly free alternation.

The third category of socio-linguistic rules is the *sequential rule for speech events*. The Anglican or Episcopal *Book of Common Prayer*, for example, identifies speech events such as marriage ceremonies and baptisms, specifies a sequence of units within each event and defines within each frame what the paradigmatic alternatives are and even some factors that condition the selection, such as whether it is Advent or Easter. Informal events may also have structure, as Schegloff (1968) has shown for telephone calls. There are relatively fixed segments in telephone calls, governed by rules, e.g. the called person speaks first. What he says may be predictable, or at least fall within a small range, such as "hello" here, "moshi-moshi" in Japan. If I approached a stranger in the street, and said "How do you do. My name is Susan Ervin-Tripp. Where is the Post Office?" he would probably be surprised. There is something wrong; the pattern for such requests for public information normally would not include greetings or self-identification, either being suitable to a different type of conversation but not this one.

How early do children have rules of this sort? Children do, of course, memorize rote strings quite early; by school age, Navajo children may know the whole Blessing Way Ceremony by heart. My 18-month-old child picks up the telephone and says "Hello, fine". She never reverses the order, nor uses this sequence except for the telephone. She lacks any conditionality of response; at the other end may be a recycling recording but it makes no difference to what she says. The simple boundaries of greetings, thanks, farewells are a beginning. By the time children have games they have obviously some knowledge of generalized rules of sequence with alternative contingencies; this is the test for having a rule rather than a specific rote sequence: an example is the complex structure of the "dozens", a form of black adolescent mutual insult.

FREQUENCIES OF OPTIONAL STRUCTURES

The great bulk of studies of differences between speech of children in different social groups concerns not linguistic, or socio-linguistic competence or rules at all, but the frequency of structures present in all speakers to varying degrees of use. The purpose is not to find out whether children are competent to understand and produce relative clauses, but how often they use them. Differential use could of course reflect the kind of socio-linguistic rule difference mentioned above, if it should be found that one group employed as a regular means to signal social meanings a style alternation involving this feature, and the other did not. We know too little now to know if this is the case for any features studied. Bernstein and his colleagues have developed the richest studies of this sort, well motivated by theory. They have found that there are many differences in frequencies according to social features of the family, in texts of the same type, for linguistic features such as preference for pronouns versus nouns with modifiers, preference for active versus passive verbs, use of rank-shifting.[1] Hess (1965) and his colleagues have similar findings for black families in Chicago. In both cases the differences appear to be related to the uses to which language is put within the family. Williams (1969) interprets these differences as a kind of playing safe, sticking close to context, since the differences disappear when tasks are interpretive and require elaborated speech.

DEVELOPMENTAL RATE FOR STRUCTURAL OPTIONS

The differences found in the London research between cross-sectional samples of children in different social classes are in many cases strikingly like the developmental differences within one class in American research. For example, the number of noun modifiers and the frequency of rank-shifting both increase with age and with social rank. It is this correspondence that leads writers to speak of retardation when talking of differences. If there were a difference in developmental rate, it would be relatively impermeable to situational manipulations or slight and short-term instructional programmes which in some studies have marked effects as if differences are rather due to performance customs.

FUNCTIONS OF SPEECH

Social groups differ in both the *uses* to which they put speech, and the *value* they place on skill in these different uses. The beginnings of

[1] See Editor's note, p. 63 for grammatical terms.

speech usually include at least 5 uses that can be seen in young children around one: pointing out and naming, requesting, predicating, playing with speech, and influencing the social reactions of others. Later on we find other uses: very grossly these may include coding and storage of information for oneself, and communication with others about objects, relations, emotions, abstractions, and beliefs unknown to the hearer.

I think it could be said of both the early and the later uses that social groups differ very markedly in their elaboration. Predicating (talking about things that the hearer is also aware of) is very elaborated in middle-class families; in experiments these children frequently do better in making explicit descriptions as though their parents had played "known-answer" descriptive games with them. Here the Bernstein group has some good data on parental encouragement, and Hess and Shipman (1965) found that the mother's ability to elicit appropriate descriptive speech from children was related to other important variables. In many social groups play uses may be elaborated considerably even in later childhood in such things as secret languages and rhyming games. We have some evidence of high development of uses of this kind in the black groups we have studied. The use of language for coding and storing new information is more highly elaborated in some groups than others. Several studies have shown differences in intra-social class communicative success when the task was talking about objects or arranging them spatially. It is possible that these differences arise from what Bernstein has called the emphasis on *explicitness* in middle class descriptive behaviour, from greater experience in speaking with strangers in general terms; some evidence suggests these class differences can readily disappear with a little experience.

How a social group evaluates skills in these uses of language is quite different from the frequency of a particular use of language. In a café, a great deal of requesting goes on verbally but no value attaches to it as a skill. In some children's groups we have found that a rote-memorized repertoire of oral tradition, of songs, poems, and stories, is highly valued. In the Harlem adolescent community that Labov studied, a ritualized insult known as "signifying" or "the dozens" involves a formal structure in which there are obscene statements about relatives. The originality of the statement in conformity with the structural rules is recognized and appreciated, and everyone knows who is good at these combats. On the other hand, the 13-year-old boys did not know who in the group was illiterate. It was not that reading was disvalued; it was totally irrelevant.

Why should we take these categories into account when studying child language? First, because if we are concerned with the development of competence in its most narrow sense, the kind of difference referred to on p. 30 above, then the other differences constitute noise. At the very least it is necessary to know enough about them to remove or counteract their consequences in assessing that competence.

For many of us, the characterization of social differences and how they arise is a foreground problem. As we have widened our awareness of the rule-governed range of options in language, we have raised new issues for study in the development of children's capacities. But more than this, our cross-cultural studies have impressed us with the major role of social features in the generation of performance. As more models of processing are developed, we believe that models which treat children as grammatical automata will seriously founder in accounting for behaviour outside the narrow constraints of the laboratory. Children's language development involves far more than grammar and phonology. We talk about generative theories which account for producing and interpreting novel but appropriate speech; in contrasting children from different social milieux we become aware that children's developing skills include coming to say the right thing in the right way at the right time and place as defined by their social group. So our task is far greater than we used to suppose. And of course if we understand better the range of competence of school children in terms of the features entering into their use of language, we hope to be in a far better position to understand and mitigate the failure of our schools.

Discussion

SCHLESINGER: You treat socio-linguistic rules as being entirely parallel to linguistic rules.

ERVIN-TRIPP: I certainly think that everything that can be said about linguistic rules can also be said about socio-linguistic rules. For example, the problem of a distinction between inferred competence and observed performance exists in both cases. The distinction between logical rules following criteria of simplicity and formal constraints *versus* processing strategies representing psychological events in real time exists in both cases. I don't see any difference, at least in these respects.

SCHLESINGER: I agree with you. This means that we have to enlarge the concept of competence. The concept of the competence of the idealized speaker-hearer doesn't seem to be sufficient.

ERVIN-TRIPP: But I do want to distinguish clearly between two meanings of the word "competence". One concerns basic rules which everyone masters who is a member of a community: if you fail, you are ignorant, an outsider, a social bore, or a bit strange. The other type of competence involves ranked skills where the criteria of success can be formally defined but where success is beyond the capacity of some individuals. As I said, Labov (1966) has described the formal structure of the game of "dozens" which anyone can play who is in the Harlem teenage male street-gang community. But the boys can rank each other on skill, on competence in doing well, just as we know good raconteurs and joke-tellers. It may be, of course, that some of these differences in competence in the second sense can be formally characterized, as Labov has proposed in the case of narrative structures, and raconteur skill. I have found these two uses confused in some discussions.

HYMES: Perhaps I could amplify a little on what Labov found. In a community like New York City, you get a great deal of difference among persons with regard to their speech, whether they say "thing" or "ting", whether they refer to the "garr" or the "guard", and so on. Many of these indicators go with different social class or different ages. Speakers use some of them to place each other on the social scale but they don't necessarily use all available indicators, they only use some; Labov calls these markers. For instance, the use of *r* is a recent prestige pronunciation in New York, but New Yorkers over 40 of all social classes do not notice whether an *r* is present in anybody's speech; therefore for them it is not a marker. Finally, there are stereotypes; these are consciously remarked on, being indicative of class status, whether or not they have any reality in actual speech. Again, *r* is an example, New Yorkers under 40 think they use it; they rate it as a class marker, but only a few upper middle class individuals use it at all regularly in casual speech. This could well become a new stereotype. An example of a variable rule is the presence or absence of the copula, a New Yorker may say *he crazy* or he may say *he's crazy*; but this is not a matter of free variation, it is a matter of probability, which is conditioned by various linguistic factors. The copula is more likely to be left out if the predicate word is an adjective and it is more likely to be left out if the subject is a pronoun. Now, if you take variable rules (phenomena that sometimes occur in the production of speech and sometimes not) together with the evaluation which is given to these phenomena by the members of the speech community, this is a place where social change and linguistic change could come together. Indeed, Labov suggests that this may be an explanation of linguistic change over time.

BEVER: What is being said here is that every rule has a certain probability assigned to it and there are certain consistent situations in which the probability for each individual rule may vary. For instance, there are some circumstances where you are more likely to use the passive construction and some where you are less likely to use it. But that doesn't seem to me to change the nature of competence or of linguistic theory; in fact I don't think it is a contribution to linguistic theory in itself. I think it is a contribution to the problem of the interaction of linguistic theory and social variables.

HYMES: I don't think it is enough to call this statistical and leave it at that. I would have thought that Labov's view, and mine also, is that these factors are somehow intimately or intrinsically part of the linguistic competence of the speaker. Even if we take a formal linguistic point of view, Labov accounts for various phenomena that grammarians have so far thought of as being in free variation, that is, a matter of chance. Until Labov started looking for factors that might account for the presence or absence of the copula, this had simply been thought to be a matter of free variation; and he has shown both that the phenomenon is conditional linguistically and that it is a matter of probability.

The Hunt for the Independent Variables

COURTNEY B. CAZDEN

Harvard University

DR. ERVIN-TRIPP (this volume) has outlined the ways in which children's language can differ across individuals or social groups. If you think in terms of research design, she has provided a taxonomy of the dependent variables in research on the social factors affecting language development, that is, the ways in which children's language can be said to differ. I cannot do the same for the social factors themselves—the independent variables—because the problem is to find out what it is that seems to make the kinds of differences she characterizes.

Research on social factors has so far dealt largely with only two of the differences she outlined: differences in the rate of acquisition of linguistic rules and differences in the frequency of use of optional linguistic structures. There is increasing interest in the social factors which affect the acquisition and maintenance of different grammatical rules systems, and different language functions. In education, for example, they are probably more important than features of children's language to which traditionally more attention has been paid, but until the differences in children's language in these latter categories are more fully specified, there is little to relate social factors to.

I will not try here to outline what we have found out about aspects of a child's world that seem to make a difference. One characteristic of all the evidence to date is that it is only presumptive evidence. It is almost all based on correlational data; and no matter how high or well replicated the correlations, we are still left with only a presumption of any causal relationship. Reviews of this research are readily available (e.g. Cazden, 1966; Ervin-Tripp, 1966). Instead, I will simply discuss briefly some recent findings.

Eventually, we will probably find two kinds of social variables: one which has a *pervasive* impact on the development of language and cognition in general, and another which has a *differential* impact on language in contrast to its impact on other aspects of cognitive development. The terms "pervasive" and "differential" are taken from Lesser's study of ethnic and social class differences in primary mental abilities (Lesser *et al.*, 1965). He had four tests of "primary mental ability", reasoning, spatial ability, arithmetic and "verbal ability" which in fact is vocabulary; four ethnic groups, Jewish, Chinese, Negro and Puerto Rican; and two social classes. The scores for each test were turned into Z scores, to make comparison meaningful, and profiles were drawn over all tests for each ethnic group and both social classes. He found that ethnic origin had a differential impact on the test results: the Jewish group scored highest on vocabulary, the Chinese scored highest on spatial ability, and so on; whereas the social class variable had a pervasive impact, the two social classes in each ethnic group having similarly shaped parallel test profiles, with the lower class group scoring consistently below the higher social class group. (Lesser has since obtained a very close replication in Boston of the original New York data; Stodolsky and Lesser, 1967.) On a less global scale, nutrition deficits in pregnancy are probably one example of a pervasive factor, while relative opportunities for conversation with adults may be a differential factor.

Though Lesser restricted himself to vocabulary, one could go further and talk about differential impact on the various aspects of language development itself. There has been some discussion about universal versus language-specific features of any given language. I find it easier to consider these as ends of a continuum rather than as a simple dichotomy:

$$\text{language universals} \longleftrightarrow \text{language specifics}$$

We can then place the components of linguistic competence along this continuum. On one level of discussion, grammatical structure as a whole can be considered more universal, while vocabulary is more specific; on another level, within grammatical structure, subject-verb-object word order may be more universal, while noun and verb morphology is more specific. I predict we will find that variation in a child's experience will affect acquisition along this continuum in different ways or to different degrees. The acquisition of components of competence towards the left, or more universal, end should require less exposure to samples of speech, show less variability across children, and be reflected in a shorter learning period and fewer errors on the part of any one child. Conversely, acquisition of the more language-specific components of competence towards the right end of the continuum should require more exposure, show greater variability across children, and be reflected in a longer learning period and more fluctuations and errors by each child. A language intervention programme has been designed for preschool children on the "specificity hypothesis" that the development of different levels and functions of language (cognitive, emotive, communicative) requires different experience and will benefit from different training (John and Moskovitz, 1968).

Social factors to which some attention has been paid can be grouped into three categories: (1) characteristics of the language which the child hears; (2) characteristics of the patterns of interaction which he is engaged in; and (3) characteristics of the non-linguistic environment or context. Our knowledge of social factors can also be categorized according to its certainty, from the weakest to the strongest: (a) evidence of an interesting and theoretically plausible feature of the child's environment; (b) correlations between such features and some aspect of the child's language; and (c) causal relationships tested in a manipulative experiment. Combining the 3 categories of social factors and 3 degrees of certainty, we get a 3-by-3 table with 9 cells into which we can place all the research in this area.

TABLE I. NATURE OF THE EVIDENCE

		Discovery of feature in environment	Correlational data	Manipulative experiment
Aspects of the environment	Language child hears	1A	1B	1C
	Interaction	2A	2B	2C
	Non-linguistic environment	3A	3B	3C

I will give brief examples of substantive findings and/or methodological problems of research in each cell, drawing largely on the research which Dr. Bellugi and I have done with Roger Brown on the language acquisition of 3 children—Adam, Eve and Sarah (Brown, Cazden and Bellugi, 1969; Cazden, 1968; Brown and Hanlon, 1970). It is the research I am most familiar with, and it is one of the few projects which has information on mother-child interaction rather than just recordings of child speech.

1A. Bever's call for an ecological survey of the child's linguistic environment fits here. We know virtually nothing about the total input to any child's "language acquisition device"—either utterances addressed to the child or spoken in his presence. How does it vary in quantity, intelligibility, grammaticality and complexity?

2A. One example here comes from an interesting feature of an otherwise uninteresting form of parent–child interaction we call "the naming game". Sarah is the working-class child in the Brown sample, and Sarah's mother plays this game often, at least when Harvard people appear with a tape recorder. To keep Sarah talking, she goes around the room or takes out a picture book and asks "What's this?" and "What's that?" During one visit, when Sarah was less than $2\frac{1}{2}$, "What's that?" was asked about inanimate objects 37 times in a row followed by a switch to "Who's that?" for a picture of a lady. It seems plausible that this pattern of interaction may signal to the child a division of the non-linguistic world into non-human and human. Admittedly, the mother may have confused things because she asked "Who's that?" about the moon and called it Mr. Moon.

1B. Here we do have correlational data on the relationship between frequency of certain linguistic structures in the child's environment and order of acquisition of those structures by the child. Consider one example from Adam and one from Eve (Brown *et al.*, 1969). For a while Adam sprinkled *s*'s on third person singular impersonal pronouns, producing utterances like *Its fell* and *Its works*. When we looked for features of his mother's speech which might be responsible, we found a simple matter of frequency: she was more apt to follow *it* with a form of the verb *to be* (usually *is* in contracted form) and more apt to follow pronouns with a main verb—*It's blue* but *She went home*. Perhaps this explains why for a time Adam thought that *its* was simply a variant pronunciation of the pronoun itself.

We have similar evidence of a correspondence between frequency in parent speech and order of acquisition of prepositions by Eve. When Eve was 18–21 months old, her mother used *in* and *on* approximately three times as often as she used *with*, *of*, *for* or *to*. Later, when Eve was 22–24 months old, she supplied *in* and *on* correctly 90 per cent of the time while the correct percentage for each of the other prepositions was between 67–77 per cent. Note that it is not sufficient to demonstrate that *in* and *on* appear first in the child's speech. Because they are more common in English in general, they would be likely to appear first in our transcriptions even if in fact all the prepositions had been learned at the same time. That is why we computed the percentage of instances supplied to instances required.

As an interesting addition to this finding, it turns out not to matter in what particular prepositional phrase the child has heard *in* or *on*. Once he starts using a particular preposition, it pops into all the phrases requiring it—*in the waste basket, in the book*, etc. It is not the case that the child has learned by imitation particular phrases as whole chunks. If the frequency in the child's environment is operating at all, it is operating in providing him with material for learning rules, it is not providing him just with models for imitation.

So far I have been talking of a research design where you look at a feature of one child's language and relate it to some feature of the language to which he is exposed. Such a relationship can then be compared across a set of mother-child pairs. In an alternative design, one looks at differences among children and relates those data to differences among the mothers. Here one needs a metric for comparing the children: chronological age is the usual basis of comparison. Alternatively, one can use the child's mean length of utterance (MLU). Holding chronological age or MLU constant in comparisons of language development is comparable to holding chronological age or mental age constant in comparisons of intellectual development. Like mental age, MLU is a global measure, and equating children on such a measure may yield additional information on the relative development of more specific abilities. When we tried both bases of comparison for the acquisition of noun and verb inflections, we found that Eve was by far the most advanced in terms of age; but if MLU was held constant instead, Sarah was relatively more advanced in the provision of inflections and function words generally than in the amount of information she conveyed by content words (Cazden, 1968).

2B. Here we have important evidence on the lack of importance of some aspects of parent-child interaction which many people outside this conference group insist must make a difference. We have data, at least for Adam, Eve and Sarah, which suggest that reinforcement in the form of approval or disapproval cannot be operating. There is no indication in our records that approval or disapproval is at all contingent on the degree of well-formedness of the child's utterance; and if approval isn't contingent, it can't have any effect (Brown *et al.*, 1969). Brown has also shown that reinforcement does not operate on the more subtle level of differential communication effectiveness. He looked at the child's "yes-no" questions, "wh-" questions and negations for a period of time when they were sometimes well formed and sometimes not. There is no evidence that the child communicates more successfully—in the sense of getting more appropriate actions or answers—with well-formed utterances than with less mature ones (Brown and Hanlon, 1970).

3A-B. The non-linguistic environment can affect the child's development in two ways: it can affect the nature of the language the child hears and the patterns of interaction he engages in. That is, part of the effect of row C will be through its influence on rows A and B. If the people in the child's environment are adults or children, rows 1 and 2 will not be the same. Adults have different beliefs about language and children, about how to talk to children and how to induct them into appropriate speech behaviour. The Berkeley cross-cultural study of which Dr. Ervin-Tripp is a co-director (Slobin, 1967) hopes to obtain information on these questions.

The non-linguistic environment can also have an effect by influencing the way in which the child attends to and processes whatever language he hears. For example, Kagan (1968) has found that when mothers talk to their 4-month-old infants, college-educated ones provide more of what he calls "distinctive vocalization"; when talking to their infants, these mothers less often provide simultaneous tactile or kinaesthetic stimulation by touching, tickling or picking the infant up. Because college-educated mothers by and large have children whose language develops faster, one could claim correlation data for cell 3B, but whether distinctive vocalization really makes any difference we don't know. Kagan hopes to conduct a manipulative experiment (3C) to find out.

The question is of some practical significance, for instance in planning television programmes for young children. Language heard on television comes in a highly non-distinctive form, simultaneously with attention-grabbing visual stimuli; but on the other hand television makes it possible to manipulate the relationship between word and picture. A large-scale project in the United States is now starting to plan a television programme for pre-school children to go on the air in 1969–70.[1] I hope we can try out various forms of distinctive and non-distinctive language on that programme.

1C. Column C contains manipulative experiments and, as I suggested earlier, very few such studies exist. Bellugi (1967) has put forth one suggestion: since children seem to learn the complex system of English auxiliaries from very fragmentary data, perhaps the acquisition of that

[1] The programme referred to is the now famous Sesame Street.

system could be aided by more systematic presentation, in natural conversation, of all the forms that auxiliaries can take.

2C. One feature of parent-child interaction, which does correlate (2B) with the child's rate of language development when age is held constant, is the extent to which parents provide grammatical "expansions" for their child's telegraphic utterances. I attempted to test the causal connection in this relationship by deliberately providing intensive expansions for some children and intensive non-expansion (or "extensions") for other children. I was unable to demonstrate that expansions are helpful, but the sample was small and other explanations are possible (Brown *et al.*, 1969). The important point is that many more manipulative experiments will have to be done before we can make strong statements about social factors affecting language development.

Social Factors and Language Development in Primary School Children

W. P. ROBINSON

University of Southampton

INTRODUCTION

AT A PSYCHOLOGICAL level we may agree that the language we command affects our capacity for communication both with ourselves and with other people. When material to be comprehended or learned is presented verbally, or when verbal answers are required, the language we have available constrains our verbal and non-verbal behaviour. Experimental results support the view that language influences our habitual manner of perceiving and thinking. Such results do not imply that we are unable to make discriminations beyond our normal use of language; that our experience cannot transcend our language; but they do illustrate how our present and future abilities to acquire and use many types of knowledge and understanding depend upon our ability to understand and produce appropriate speech and writing.

That this might have significance in sociology was made explicit by Bernstein's transposition and elaboration of the Sapir-Whorf hypothesis to the sociological level of analysis (Bernstein, 1961a, b). He has argued that, within what is often treated as a single speech community, there may exist broadly based social differences in language usage. In its simplest form his argument is that, while the middle class has access to both "elaborated" and "restricted" codes, the working class, especially its lower stratum, is generally confined to a particular "restricted" code. These two "codes" have different linguistic structures and behavioural functions.

According to Bernstein, the working class "restricted" code has a predominantly social function serving to maintain or change the nature of an immediate role relationship: it defines the type of bond existing between persons in a face to face situation. The "elaborated" code is a vehicle for the communication of all manner of information about the physical and social world. Linguistically the "elaborated" code lends itself to an exploitation of the full range of grammatical, lexical and semantic possibilities of the language, whereas the postulated "restricted" code exhibits among other features a simpler grammar, with fewer completed structures; less use of subordination; less complex verbal and adverbial structures. The restricted code has a narrower lexical range, and a higher incidence of clichés and tags to check up on the listener's agreement.

A full description of the two codes can only be made in the light of data as yet uncollected or unprocessed, but one point that has emerged concerns a contextual feature of the codes, viz. the relationship between what is said or written and the non-verbal events being discussed. The "elaborated" code is firmly anchored to the external world: its essence requires that it change and grow as a function of new understanding of this world. For the "restricted" code such correspondence is unnecessary: when you ask "How are you?" you do not require an accurate diagnosis; the latent social functions of the code make the verbal content relatively unimportant. Not only are the grammar and lexis relatively unsuited to generally accepted educational objectives, but its semantics are also directed towards other ends.

We could demand more information about these codes and we could embark upon a critical evaluation; to date we have preferred to use the ideas as guides to research. The socially-orientated "restricted" code and the everything-orientated "elaborated" code are conceived as ideal types rather than discrete entities; it would be rash to demand too precise a specification too soon.

RESEARCH

Empirical evidence showing social class differences in the speech and writing of adolescents has given general support to the fruitfulness of Bernstein's distinction, but these studies were confined to a description of general linguistic differences between the codes (for a bibliography, see Robinson and Rackstraw, 1967). The present investigations of primary school children cover, not only the code differences, but also the correlates, the antecedents and consequences of such differences. The initial goals of the research were to describe variations in school performance and link these to variations in verbal behaviour. This presupposes the existence of a taxonomy of the grammatical, lexical and contextual features of the language. For our linguistic analysis,

Halliday's Scale and Category Grammar has been the major system used (Halliday *et al.*, 1964; see Editors' note, p. 63).

In the second stage the goals of our investigations were to link the variations in verbal behaviour to differences in parent–child interaction. In order to discover the sociological constraints on the child–parent interaction, it was necessary to describe the constellation of attitudes and capacities which lead parents to adopt the child-rearing practices they do, and to relate these attitudes and capacities to the social structure. A similar chain of influences can be traced through the educational system, and this was taken into consideration in the design of the inquiry.

Because all the data are not yet processed, I shall concentrate on a description of the sources of data and on the four main areas in which results are already beginning to emerge, these are:

(1) social class differences in mothers' attitudes;
(2) social class differences in the mothers' reported behaviour in two situations, and the replies of their children for similar problems;
(3) the speech of primary school children and its differential association with social class;
(4) an attempt to change the expected life chances of a group of working class children by employing a special "Use of Language" programme intended to switch the children from a "restricted" to an "elaborated" code.

The original sample of children was chosen from the 39 Local Education Authority primary schools in a predominantly working class London borough. About 350 children in 13 schools were involved. A year later six schools in a middle class area added a further 150 subjects. For both groups we collected data from children, mothers and teachers, but so far only data concerning children and mothers have been analysed.

Data from Mothers

Maternal interview (i). Almost all mothers of the children in the sample were willing to be interviewed, but of these not all mothers were approached. The 351 interviews made were conducted about two months *before* the children started at primary school. Both closed and open-ended questions were asked. Roughly, the data can be broken into five sections:

(1) basic demographic data, age, size of family, type of housing, jobs and education of both parents, etc.;

c

(2) knowledge of the educational system in general and primary schools in particular;

(3) attitudes to features of the educational system, including reports of behaviour relevant to the preparation of the child for school;

(4) attitudes to and reported behaviour concerning play, toys, reading, and children's questions;

(5) reported behaviour in discipline situations: what is done, what is said and explained to the child, and the reasons for the action taken.

Maternal interview (ii). This interview was conducted 2 years after the first and comprised more detailed extensions of the areas already examined. Among additional problems investigated were:

(1) the perceived role of language as a vehicle for instruction in social and non-social skills;

(2) attitudes and behaviour concerning speech faults;

(3) the structure of decision-making in the family, particularly decisions affecting the child;

(4) definitions of anti-social behaviour and strategies for handling it.

Data from Children

So far data of three types have been collected:

(1) *Standardized tests of intelligence and achievement*. The English Picture Vocabulary Test (Brimer and Dunn, 1962), the Crichton Vocabulary Scale (Raven, 1951), and the Coloured Progressive Matrices (Raven, 1963) were each given within a month of the child's entry to infant school. The Wechsler Intelligence Scale for Children (Wechsler, 1965) was given one year later. The children from the mainly working class borough were also given a standardized English attainment test after a further year.

(2) *Teachers' ratings*. At the end of the first year, and half way through the second year, the teachers rated children in their class on a number of scales including co-operativeness, attentiveness, answering and questioning, brightness and the likelihood of success in school.

(3) *Speech samples*. Within the first three weeks of entering primary school, each child performed a series of tasks in a structured but informal interview usually lasting half an hour. The interview started with the child bringing a painting or model to the interview room and talking about it. Then the children constructed a model room with furniture and family figures and answered several questions about these.

They told three stories about three sets of pictures, described objects and events in three postcard reproductions of paintings by Trotin, told a story about what a child did on a free day, explained how to play one of three games, and described and explained the behaviour of a toy elephant. It is difficult to see how one could select a representative sample of a child's speech, but it was hoped that the variety of the requirements of these tasks would give a useful sample. The speech was recorded on tape and a similar sample was collected 20 months later.

Other situations were used for the collection of particular data from specially selected sub-samples of children, e.g. answers to "why" questions, perceptual and verbal discrimination tasks and paired associate learning.

RESULTS

The results obtained so far can be reported under the four headings given above, although it may be useful to specify the general tactical approach to the data derived from the maternal interviews by way of introduction.

Data from Maternal Interviews

The sociological and social psychological data have so far been analysed in three main ways:

(1) the development of indices based upon the results of factor analyses, and combining only scores which have known relationships with each other;

(2) initial contrasts of the knowledge, attitudes and reported behaviour of middle and working class mothers;

(3) preliminary examinations of associations between relevant maternal characteristics and the intelligence test scores of children.

The ultimate intention is to specify the antecedents of variations in the children's speech, intelligence test scores and other behaviours in terms of the social psychological situation of the family and to relate these variations in turn to sociological measures. Another way of expressing this would be to state that we intend to explain social class differences in terms of social psychological variables, at least as far as the learning of the children is concerned.

The development of indices presupposes a mastery and completion of the coding of responses and the availability of suitable computational programmes and machinery. Neither was ready to hand, but initial processing is nearly complete. A Communication index and an Attitude to Toy index have already been shown to have strong relationships both backwards to social class and forwards to the intelligence test scores of the children. (Differences in "toy ideology" are associated more strongly with non-verbal than verbal intelligence test scores, suggesting some types of learning experience which may be relevant to non-verbal test performance; Bernstein and Young, 1967.)

Attitudes of Mothers

First runs have been made of social class differences on a variety of questions directed at knowledge, attitudes and reported behaviour. Among significant comparative differences (Jones, 1966) are the following:

(1) The middle class mother prepares herself and her child for school. He is told about active and passive aspects of his role at school and about similarities between home and school.

(2) Middle class mothers are unlikely to fix a firm boundary between home and school, are satisfied with present possibilities for interaction with school, and think they should support the teacher. If the child doesn't learn, they think that something can be done, that the teacher or child is likely to be at fault. They believe the teacher is the most likely person to diagnose the trouble.

(3) They have a favourable attitude both to basic educational skills (reading, writing and arithmetic) and to play, and believe that play is educationally important.

(4) They see toys as having exploratory and developmental functions. When they buy toys for a child, they report that the child's age and sex are taken into account as well as the explorative and physical properties of the toy.

(5) They are likely to read frequently and regularly to the child and to give various reasons for reading. They see reading both as a sign of the bond between mother and child and also as a means of providing information. Both middle class mothers and their children are much more likely to be members of a library.

The preliminary data suggest a host of further differences awaiting discovery. The problem is not to find significant differences, but to locate distinct clusters of variables that may serve as major indices for descriptive and explanatory purposes. Modern techniques of factor analysis are proving informative in the areas of communication and discipline so far examined. It is hoped that factor analysis will eventually reduce the data to manageable proportions and help to suggest a pattern of possible links to explain the variability of the children's behaviour. The problem is made easier and harder by the high positive correlations among the scores. These high associations yield impressive general factors, but make it difficult to isolate other factors.

Reported Behaviour of Mothers and Children

Reported behaviour in disciplinary situations. The mother's control procedures are providing interpretive problems partly because there are variations in the amount as well as type of control, but a summary statement, which does not do great injustice to the data, would posit that at one behavioural extreme is physical punishment and, at the other lie "complex verbal appeals" to the child about the effects his behaviour has on both the behaviour and feelings of specified persons, such as himself and the mother. The implication is clear. At one extreme the child receives a minimal amount of information, mainly confined to a connection between the stimulus complex of the discipline situation and the punishment. At the other extreme the child is offered facts about the physical and social world and how these affect people; he is given information about points of view other than his own and he is encouraged to consider his actions from a long term point of view. The data have been subjected to preliminary cross-breaks only, but it is apparent that simple physical punishment is more frequent in the working class and the more informative appeals in the middle class. It should be noted that the concern has been confined initially to restrictive controls, how the mother copes with problems. Techniques and reasons for rewarding have not been examined.

From our investigations we found that the middle class child seems to be learning that wrongness is not a total concept in and of itself; the wrongness of an action can be inferred from higher order principles relating to consequences and other people. This suggests the beginning of some hierarchical system with a deductive potential. The working class child largely meets appeal to authority, often backed up with force, and has little chance of developing any differentiating attitude. If we ask whether there is any evidence of differential learning by the children, we can examine the answers they gave at 7 to questions about morality. The working class children were more likely to give answers like "Because I'll get thumped" in reply to "Why shouldn't you steal?" There is a correspondence to what has been made available for them to learn. Two features of middle class answers may be noted: middle class children were more likely to specify any authority they cited and were more likely to mention the consequences of their actions for *other people*, both what others would have to do and how they would feel. These answers have similarities with the personal appeals used by their mothers.

Child's questions and mother's responses. Brandis and Henderson (1970) report that middle class mothers are more likely to answer difficult questions and are prepared to chatter with the child in a greater variety of situations. Robinson and Rackstraw (1967) examined replies made by mothers to 2 "where from" and 4 "why" questions supposedly posed by their child. Answers were classified in terms of the amount, accuracy, context and type of information made available. The children were grouped by sex, verbal IQ, social class and the communication index. Although intelligence test scores and sex had some relevance to the variety of answers, social class was the major differentiating variable; there were striking similarities in the behaviour of adults and children from the same social class. At the age of 7 the children were asked to give answers to identical and similar questions, but only the analysis for girls can as yet be reported.

(a) Probability of response. Middle class mothers, more often than working class mothers, said they answered the questions. Middle class 7-year-old girls answered more of the questions put to them by the investigator than their working class peers.

(b) Amount of information. When mothers gave answers to the question where the water in the tap comes from, middle class women gave more units of information in their replies. The question "How do you ride a bicycle?" elicited more units of information from middle class girls than from working class ones.

(c) Accuracy of information. The preliminary findings on this are not clear, though there seems to be more irrelevant answers to "why" questions in working class girls.

(d) Classification of "why" questions. When working class mothers are asked questions like "Why do leaves fall off trees?" they are likely to give appeal to regularity—"They always do"; or, more crudely, they take the fact referred to in the question and repeat it as an explanation, "Because they do". Middle class mothers usually attempt some sort of explanation in terms of cause or purpose, often in terms of class inclusion or category; a syllogism is displayed to the child: leaves are living things, living things die, leaves die. When their 7-year-old daughters were asked the same question, the middle class girls were more likely to answer in terms of categorization, the working class in terms of regularity.

Speech of the Children

Grammatical analysis. The social class comparisons made on the total of approximately 350 grammatical categories, counted over the total speech sample of each child gave no pattern of significant differences.

Form class analysis. Two types of analysis were made of speech from a sub-set of the speech tasks. Both a token and a type count were made of speech from the Picture story, the Trotin cards, and the Elephant. From this it became apparent that middle class children used a wider range of nouns, adjectives, and verbs than working class children matched on intelligence test scores, sex and communication index (Brandis and Henderson, 1970). A second analysis, on the narrative picture story and the descriptive Trotin cards, showed that middle class children varied the proportions of form class tokens and types across tasks more than working class children (*ibid.*).

Nominal group structure (Hawkins, unpublished). Without controls for any other possible sources of variation, analyses were made of the nominal groups used in the picture stories and Trotin tasks. Middle class children used slightly fewer pronouns than working class children, but the working class used significantly more pronouns whose referents were not made verbally explicit (exophoric!). This was true of pronouns at head and modifier on both tasks (see Editors' note, p. 63).

Other differences included the use of both epithets and rank-shifted clauses at head, epithets other than "big" or "little" as modifier, two or more ordinatives, and intensifiers before epithets.

Form and content of answers. An analysis was made of answers to three questions, the main one was "How do you play Hide and Seek?" Middle class children gave more precise and general answers, making fewer inappropriate assumptions about their listener's knowledge of the game than working class children. They used more abstract linguistic structures and made clearer linguistic differentiations (Rackstraw and Robinson, 1967).

In answer to 29 "why" questions, middle class girls, aged 7, differed from working class girls on several counts (analysis for boys not yet completed). For "when" questions they were more likely to use an absolute rather than a relative time reference (e.g. on June 26th) and for "why" questions they used fewer appeals to regularity and authority and more to categorization, cause and purpose. They gave answers which were more appropriate and complete, both grammatically and contextually (a closer correspondence with events). These differences are similar to those found for mothers (Robinson and Rackstraw, 1967).

Two extra analyses are worth a brief mention because they go beyond social class as a differentiating variable (Robinson and Creed, 1968; Coulthard and Robinson, 1968). In these, sub-samples of lower working class girls were divided into "elaborated" and "restricted"[1] code users on the basis of the language they used in the speech sample. The linguistic criteria used to contrast the children were (1) number of sub-ordinate clauses, (2) number of rank-shifted clauses, (3) number of adverbial groups, (4) number of different modifiers, (5) number of different verb tenses. These indices were generally consistent in their ordering of subjects ($w = 0.75$, $p < 0.001$), suggesting that it would be permissible to sum ranks across each index. In a "Spot the Difference" experiment conducted 18 months later, girls who used an "elaborated" code made fewer perceptual errors than those who used the "restricted" code and gave more accurate verbal descriptions of differences seen, with perceptual discrimination scores partialled out. A similar linguistic differentiation was made in the investigations into answers to 29 "wh-" questions when the children were 7. Elaborated code girls differed from restricted code girls in the same direction as significant middle/ working class differentiations on 13 out of 19 such differences (Sign test, $p = 0.048$).

Evaluation. An interesting methodological point is illustrated by the failure to find social class differences in grammar over the total speech sample, in contrast to the success in finding differences for more detailed analyses in specific contexts. The suggestion is that it is more fruitful to perform particular analyses for discovering the pattern of social class differences than to try to solve the problem with a sledgehammer. The differences found bear a remarkably good correspondence to those specified by Bernstein (1961b) as being markers of "restricted" and "elaborated" codes, while the two last-mentioned investigations imply the possibility of moving on from social class to a specification of more direct relationships between language and behaviour.

"USE OF LANGUAGE" PROGRAMME

Aims and Description of Programme

The Language Programme was designed by the Unit psychologists, D. M. and Georgina A. Gahagan (1968), to make speech and language more important in the children's lives than it would otherwise have

---

[1] These labels may well be wrong in this instance. It would have been better to write in terms of "complexity".

been. It aimed to improve and expand the range and type of grammatical and lexical categories available to the children, to relate this usage to the external physical and social world and so to equip the children with an increased awareness of new ways of describing and discussing the world. In terms of Bernstein's theory, the aim could be summarized by saying that the objective was to provide an opportunity for children to develop an elaborated code.

Four factors limited the scope of the programme: it had to be inexpensive to run; when necessary it had to be adapted to over-crowded and materially inadequate classrooms; because it was carried out during school hours, the time it could occupy had not to interfere with normal work in basic skills; and it had to be carried out by teachers who had received no special training.

The programme was limited to 20 minutes a day, during which two or three tasks were used by the teachers. Most tasks had graduated degrees of complexity and difficulty to add interest and vary the demands upon the children. At first, the children played a passive role but eventually they were responsible for thinking up, evaluating, and discussing the problems posed within the tasks.

I will give a few examples to illustrate the tasks. The O'Grady game was expanded and elaborated. It was intended to develop the children's awareness of physical and social differences and to train them to act appropriately in a given context. To succeed, children had to analyse their own attributes and those of relatives, friends and objects. At a later stage the children had to devise their own categories and discuss results. New vocabulary was introduced in an "I spy game". In a game called "The Surprise Box" the children had to describe to another child the nature of unseen objects. "The Five Minute Story" (listened to on tape recorders) also offered new vocabulary, exposed the child to increasingly complex syntax and contained sentences with deliberate errors, which the children were encouraged to spot. Telephones were used for children to describe familiar objects to each other without mentioning the usual name. "Question Time" and "News Time" were made use of to develop vocabulary and the syntax of questions and statements. "Picture stories" were frequently used: in these children were given sets of pictures and had to discuss all possible features of the social and physical situation. Pictures were omitted and the order of presentation was altered, so that the children could develop an inferential and hypothetical approach to the stories.

The teachers who worked with the Language Programme children met fortnightly with the Unit psychologists to discuss the techniques and materials for the programme and the psychologists visited the class-room weekly to check that agreed procedures were being used.

The schools in the Language Programme study were a sub-set of the original 30 per cent sample of those in the borough. There were three groups each consisting of three classes, matched on the IQ distribution of children leaving their attached junior schools during the preceding 3 years. The experimental group (E1) were given the programme just described. The two control groups were not given the programme; but in the first control group (C1) the teachers took part in fortnightly seminars, conducted by Professor Bernstein, during which they discussed infant school teaching, planned various projects, carried them out and evaluated them. This was designed to off-set the Hawthorne effect. The second control group (C2) had no treatment.

Three means of evaluation of the Language Programme are to be pursued: (1) comparisons in specific experiments intended to tap limited aspects of performance under controlled conditions, (2) comparisons on standardized tests, and (3) comparisons of the grammar and lexis of the children's speech. No results from this third source can as yet be given.

Four experiments can be reported with the emphasis upon E1/C1 comparisons, although experiments normally contained additional variables such as IQ, sex, or code differences. The experiments were run when the programme had been in progress for at least four terms.

Evaluation with Experiments

G. A. and D. M. Gahagan have completed two investigations, both giving encouraging results. The first was a paired-associate learning task in which the child had to respond with an appropriate stimulus word; the list comprised 8 pairs. Boys and girls ($N = 54$) aged between 6 years 9 months and 7 years 3 months were required to produce sentences linking the stimulus and response words of 8 pairs of items presented pictorially, prior to learning the pairs by the method of anticipation. Children who had participated in the Language Programme (E1) produced more different verbs linking the stimulus and response items and took fewer trials to criterion than either of two groups of control children (C1 and C2). Verbal intelligence test scores (E.P.V.T.), obtained at the onset of the Language Programme, were not related to the number of different verbs produced, but were related to the learning measure. A significant negative correlation was found between trials to criterion and the number of different verbs produced (Gahagan and Gahagan, 1968).

In a second experiment children were shown sets of four pictures arranged in a sequence. A fifth picture to complete or include in a specified gap in the story had to be chosen from four other pictures. E1 children of medium IQ (E.P.V.T., 95–106) made more correct responses than comparable C1 children.

The third experiment "Spot the difference" (Robinson and Creed, 1968) also showed the relative superiority of E1 girls. Compared with C1, E1 girls made fewer errors of perceptual discrimination. They pointed to more differences and were more adept at describing the nature of differences they did notice.

A secondary analysis of their total output of speech in this situation (Coulthard and Robinson, 1968) revealed several grammatical and lexical differences between the groups. In grammar, E1 girls included more nominal groups in clauses and more often used clauses to qualify a head (often a noun). Although they did not use more single modifiers, they were more likely to use two or more modifiers in a nominal group. C1 girls used simple rankshift more frequently, but the reverse held for complex rankshift. Lexical differences included a greater number of adjective types by E1 and a higher incidence of rare adjectives of colour. These results imply an increased facility for handling complex nominal groups and a greater variety of lexical units to insert in the grammatical structure.

In each case significant differences were obtained in directions consistent with the objective of orienting the experimental children towards the use of an elaborated code. In a fourth investigation which required the subjects to give answers to 28 "wh-" questions, of 19 significant differences found between middle and working class girls, 14 showed differences between E1 and C1 girls in the same direction, two showed no difference and three were in the reverse direction. On a Sign test this shows that the behaviour of the E1 girls was more similar than that of C1 girls to the middle class ($p = 0.006$).

Standardized Tests

Creed and Robinson attempted to analyse the special abilities and knowledge demanded by sub-tests on the W.I.S.C. and were able to set up an expected pattern of differences between E1 and C1 children. The analysis was confounded by the nested factor of different schools, but it is noteworthy that pairs of girls (but not boys) matched for E.P.V.T. scores taken a year earlier did show significant differences in favour of E1 girls on the vocabulary ($p < 0.001$), similarities ($p < 0.001$) and comprehension ($p < 0.002$) sub-tests. Information, arithmetic and the performance tests showed no differences. This test was given after the programme had been running for two full terms.

Gahagan and Gahagan administered a standardized English attainment test after 2 years of the programme and found that E1 girls were making substantially higher scores than either of the control groups (C1 and C2).

Evaluation

The assessment of the efficiency of the Language Programme is still in bits and pieces, but several conclusions can be drawn. It does appear that such intervention can have significant effects upon the performance of children, and hence that such programmes might be a desirable addition to the curriculum of primary schools catering for linguistically disadvantaged children.

One unexpected result was the apparent success with girls, but failure with boys. No solution of this mystery has yet been found; the materials and tasks do not seem to have been biased in favour of girls; the teachers do not report any bias in their behaviour; there is no evidence that boys differed from girls in intellectual capacity in such a way that the programme was beyond their abilities or beneath their needs. A single hint is given by the fact that on average the girls are rated by the teachers as more co-operative and attentive than the boys. One untested suggestion is that normative sex roles may be relevant such that while it is respectable and perhaps admirable for working class girls to be "good at language", such skills might be considered unmanly in boys, being seen as incompatible with other positively valued attributes such as toughness, mechanical abilities, and physical prowess. If this is so, and it should not be difficult to test, primary school teachers have an awkward hurdle to jump before they can begin teaching. This result does raise with some force the point that any special intervention programmes must be geared to the particular values and capacities of the children towards whom they are directed.

SUMMARY AND CONCLUSIONS

Although we are not yet in a position to integrate the assorted facts discovered, it does appear that Bernstein's theoretical framework is strongly supported by the evidence. Both mothers and children exhibit varieties of orientation to the world at large and language in particular which are a function of social class.

For the working class mother language is one weapon in an armoury of control strategies: in discipline situations there is a preference for non-verbal strategies and abrupt commands, while questions from their children to obtain information are responded to with attempts to control, contain or ignore them. This contrasts with the middle class mothers who convey more information in answer to questions and appear to encourage such curiosity, and who apparently treat discipline situations as opportunities for giving information. The one mother ignores and controls in both situations, the other emphasizes learning through language. It is not surprising that these differences are reflected in the speech of their children. Relative to 5-year-old working class children, their middle class peers have developed an elaborated linguistic structure for talking about objects and their attributes (nominal group) and they use a greater variety of lexical items to expound categories. Their language usage differs from situation to situation and bears a closer correspondence to the features of the non-linguistic world. They make their meanings verbally precise and unambiguous, and make fewer assumptions about the listeners' familiarity with their own world.

The educational advantages of the middle class child have not been discussed, but they are clearly considerable. That schools could mount cheap, easily administered programmes to help offset this differential is implied by the positive results with the "Use of Language" programme.

EDITOR'S NOTE

The Grammatical Apparatus Used in the Survey

The Survey uses an early version of the grammar of Halliday and his associates. A *nominal group* consists of a *head*, usually a noun or a pronoun; optional *qualifiers* which may follow the head, and *modifiers* which may precede the head. Modifiers are ordered in places; *epithets* (adjectives) occur nearer the head than *ordinatives* (cardinal and ordinal numbers, comparative and superlative adjectives), and ordinatives occur nearer the head than *deictics* (articles, demonstratives etc.), as in the following diagram.

modifier			head	qualifier
deictic	ordinative	epithet		
the	first	red	rose	of summer

When a clause is used inside another clause, or a phrase inside another phrase, the embedded clause or phrase is said to be *rankshifted*, e.g. *What I'm thinking* is none of your business.

Discussion

BEVER: Both moral development and the development of causality concepts are very interesting problems, but not linguistic problems proper. It may be that the child goes through a period of dependence on contiguity as a principle for causality; or a notion of immanent causality, which apparently your working class mothers and children have. Similarly, in moral development you may be able to show the notion of explicit punishment or immanent justice to be the basis for moral judgments, as strategies which the child goes through before developing a full moral system. The same developmental principles may apply; the child starts with a certain basic set of capacities and then attempts to modify these, both in the case of moral development, and in the case of the development of perceptual causality.

However, what we were talking about was something specifically related to the perception of language and its bearing on language development which is a little different. What *you* are talking about is other aspects of the child's cognitive development. I was raising the question really of how far one could treat these two problems in a similar way, and no more. What we are trying to do is to point out that specific perceptual strategies exist, and that children have the capacity for developing them. To try to make an exhaustive list would be silly; the point is to demonstrate that they exist and to explore their interaction with general perceptual capacities, in the case of language perception.

SINCLAIR: There seems to be an important supposition beneath everything that has been said; a supposition which I don't agree with, and for which I think we have negative evidence. This is that concepts like logical classification, or causality relationships could possibly be acquired, or at least helped along by verbal information from the mother. Now, in the experiments we have done on causality in the child or on logical concepts, we have never been able to find any relationship whatsoever between *class*, or whatever you like to call it, and the development of these concepts. It seems to me that if there is influence, it is the other way round. Certain linguistic structures can be acquired by children who have developed a certain concept of causality and classification. In that case, the influence of what they hear around them is important. But to assume that a mother saying something about leaves falling off a tree develops a concept of causality is, as far as our evidence goes, completely out of the question.

ROBINSON: Our problem is to account for the differences which we eventually find.

SINCLAIR: And you suppose these to be the result of different ways of talking in childhood?

ROBINSON: We assume this to be one relevant factor.

CAZDEN: This seems to me to be an example of this business of correlation and cause. You have a correlation between some linguistic things and some cognitive things and you assume that the directionality is one way.

ROBINSON: Are you saying that the environment in which the child develops is virtually irrelevant?

SINCLAIR: Irrelevant, as far as the basic concepts and their formation is concerned.

BEVER: But it is surely a source of information.

SINCLAIR: Yes indeed.

ROBINSON: Yes, and this is a source of information which you then cannot use to help you process further information? Why do leaves fall off trees? You mean to say the person who is told that they always fall off every year has no different life chances from the person who is given some other sort of explanation?

HYMES: It is certainly an observed fact that various populations differ to some extent in the way in which they interpret things causally. These differences must have some explanation.

ROBINSON: Our problem is that we find this *within* a society, that a social class seems to be a relatively pervasive variable in the sense in which Dr. Cazden uses the term. Whether this is a cultural difference or not, I don't know. I think one might have to distinguish here between what Bernstein calls object relations, and person relations. In one sense, person relations can be self-fulfilling prophecies, in a way in which relations in the physical world are not.

BEVER: But object heuristics in our opinion are not based on instruction from parents. They are based on discoveries by the child. I would like to encourage you to continue research into the same sort of phenomenon in moral development. I think it is very possible that the child extracts moral principles and moral inductions, not from what the person says about specific questions, but from what the person does.

SINCLAIR: If we work on the child, feeding him verbal information, we get what Luria and his collaborators always found—a better fixation of attention to relevant features of the problem. We never get an inner structuration of the problem, leading to what Bever and Mehler call the new strategy. These are two quite different things.

E. INGRAM: Could you give an example of what you mean by attention to features?

SINCLAIR: There is the well known conservation experiment of pouring liquid from one glass to another. You can quite easily teach children who do not have terms for *long* and *thin* and *fat* etc. to use such words; then they will be able to describe any type of object in these terms. However, if you put the conservation problem again, they will still say there is more in the higher, thinner glass. If you ask "why?", they say "Well, the water goes up higher, because the glass is thinner". They have all the elements they need to deduce that because the glass is thinner, then the water goes up higher, so it is the same quantity; but they will not take the last step. Whereas children who have none of the linguistic terms available, who do not speak French for instance, will get the concept across if they have achieved the cognitive structure, even though they may not have the vocabulary.

MEHLER: They do have terms in other languages.

SINCLAIR: Even some children from very disadvantaged backgrounds, as we have seen, who do not know the terms in their own mother tongue, once they have got the strategies, will be able to get it across. Sometimes with gestures: "it's big like this (height), but not big like this" (width). Teaching children verbal information leads to the better fixation of the relevant features, nothing else.

HYMES: It doesn't change the rate of structuration?

SINCLAIR: This may be a help to them, I do not know.

Language and Roles

B. BERNSTEIN

University of London

WHAT I AM essentially interested in is not language by itself, but the process of transmission, the internal structure of the communication processes. What I really want to know is how the order, which is external to the individual, becomes a psychological reality; and I am interested in language in communication because this is one of the means by which the culture is made psychologically active within the individual, through the several socializing agencies. These agencies allocate roles to the child; within the kinship system, within the age group system, within the school system and within the work system. All of these interact in some way with the language that the child learns. So, if we are going to consider questions of language and language use, then we are necessarily forced into the wider question of the relationship between roles and codes, and we must also take into account the context in which the roles are played when the communication takes place.

Let us first consider context. Take a group of men, who are being marched up and down by a man who is shouting at them, and he is saying "Go left!", "Go right!" or "Go to hell!". Now this is a very limited context and the individuals who are operating within that context have a very small range of alternatives available to them, and the behavioural expression to these alternatives is also limited. The soldiers march, or turn about, or stand still, and the man who shouts has only a very limited number of verbal choices open to him, in fact every word that is said can be predicted and is predicted. The sergeant could be shouting nonsense words, the correct movements would still be executed; there is no new piece of information being transmitted, the information is common to all members of the group. The verbal message can have no semantic content. Now, if within this role system any person wants to transmit a piece of individual information, then he cannot do it by variations of linguistic usage, because of the

contraints of the context. The only way he can do it is in some extra-
verbal way. For instance, a soldier can signal private meaning by how
he wears his cap, or how he ties up his boot laces. The controls on the
channels through which new information is going to pass is sociological.

Not all contexts are quite so restricted as this one. Take another
example, a man and a wife, at night, talking to each other and the
woman says to the husband: "Darling, isn't it time?" and the husband
says "No", and the wife says "Oh darling, it is time, isn't it?" and the
husband says "If you want it, darling"; and the wife says "You do it
tonight, please", and he says: "I always do it, don't I?" and she says
"Oh well, I'll do it"; and then she goes out into the kitchen to make a
cup of tea. An observer might not be able to interpret this conversation
unless he knew the history of the relationship, the roles and how the
roles are verbally realized—he might come to a very wrong conclusion
about the content of such a communication. From the language in this
situation, we could not predict very well. We certainly cannot predict
the lexical choices; but there may be a certain rigidity in the use of
syntax, so it may be possible to predict at the syntactic level. Where the
individuals share a common culture, a common set of identifications, a
common set of expectations, the code that is being used may operate
under certain restrictions, probably of a syntactic nature; it would be a
restricted code. My point is that certain constraints in lexical and syntactic selections are of social origin; that there is a relationship between
the roles which individuals have acquired and the verbal realization of
these roles and interactions.

Finally, there are contexts in which prediction is much less possible
even at the syntactic level. These are situations in which new or individual
meanings have to be communicated. When a speaker cannot assume
that the listener knows in advance what he is going to say, when his
intention cannot be taken for granted, then the speaker is forced to
become much more explicit. Neither his syntax nor his lexis can be
predicted. I am suggesting that a particular social role has to be learnt,
which has to do with the production of novel meanings. This is a role in
which you have to cope with the separation from others, the weakening
of shared assumption; you have to tolerate your difference from others.
In order to produce the elaborated code which is necessary for the
transmission of new information at the verbal level, it is conceivable
that there must be some kind of role history which enables you to cope
with the isolation involved in the creation of novel meaning. I would
also like to suggest that where you have elaborated codes there is a
selective attention paid to language; the language use itself becomes an

object of special perceptual activity. Where codes are restricted, the attention is not to the language, but to the message, whether through the verbal channel or through the extra-verbal channels. When codes are restricted, the meanings will tend to be communalized rather than individualized or specific.

Let me restate this from the point of roles. Roles can be distinguished in terms of the range of alternatives and of the kinds of substitutions that can be made in that performance. We can refer to the range of alternatives in terms of discretion: if a role has a wide discretion, a vast range of alternatives is available to the player; if a role has low discretion, there are fewer alternatives available to the individual. Where there is low discretion the alternatives that are taken up are likely to be more communalized. The roles which have wide discretion are likely to give rise to less communalized choices; there is more scope for the individual. A child is accorded a role, in line with the cultural expectations of the group he belongs to, and then he only gradually learns the alternatives within that role. This is easily seen if we compare different cultures. For instance, a mother in our culture will not pick a little boy up and carry him all day. Japanese children are not expected to learn table manners until they are 6 or 7, whereas south-western Pueblo children are supposed to know how to eat correctly by about two and a half. The roles that are accorded to children vary also with social class and with the sex of the child. It is, for instance, conceivable that a girl's role in the working class is much more complex than a boy's role, because a girl is much more likely to act as a mediator between parents and siblings, more likely to take control over her younger sisters and brothers and less likely to play any part in the activity-dominated peer group of the boys. On the other hand, we find that middle class mothers explain less to the girl child than to the boy and are more coercive over the girl than over the boy, so the girl here is socialized into a submissive role, which the boy is not.

Before I go on to talk about the correlations between roles and codes, I should like to take up two other points. In the first place, I want to distinguish between two basic kinds of meaning. One kind of meaning refers to inter-personal and intra-personal relationships, which I could call person meanings, and the other refers to relationships between objects, which I want to call object meanings. I assume that if we did linguistic descriptions of object meanings, we might find that the syntax and lexis are rather different from the syntax and lexis of person meanings. I relate this to the finding that girls appear to be linguistically more mature than boys. This could be an artifact due to the eliciting techniques which we use for children. These techniques are often highly person-oriented, rather than object-oriented. If we took care to present object-related meanings as well as the person-oriented meanings we might find that boys did better on the object-related meanings.

Next I would like to introduce the concept of closed-type role systems and open-type role systems. A closed role system reduces the range of alternatives for the realization of verbal meanings. Where there is such a reduction in the range of alternatives, the more communal or collective the verbal meanings are, the more rigid the syntactic and lexical selection, and so the more restricted the code. The more closed the role system, the more it will tend to evoke the code which I have called restricted. On the other hand, an open role system permits a range of alternatives; and the greater the range of alternatives, the more individualized the verbal meanings, therefore the more flexible the syntactic and vocabulary selection and therefore the more elaborated the code gets. The open/closed dimension interacts with the object-meaning/person-meaning dimension.

We might find, for instance, that a role system may be open in relation to object-meanings, but closed in relation to person-meanings, or vice versa. This may in fact be different for the children from the same family: the role system may be open in relation to the girl in terms of person-meaning, but closed in terms of object-meaning; and this may be reversed for the boy. Open and closed role systems must also be related to types of family control, and types of social control. Peter Robinson has talked about control so I will not go into that here. In the area where the role system is open, there is an induced motivation to explore, to seek out meanings; where the role system is closed, there is little induced motivation to explore a great number of meanings. Where the role system is open, the individual child may learn to cope with ambiguity and isolation in the creation of verbal meanings, because he may have much more complex choices; where the role system is closed the child may have to forgo such learning, because in such situations the drive is to create verbal meanings in social contexts which are unambiguous and communalized. If an open role is forced on a child, where he has previously accepted a closed role system, it may create considerable tension in him. Conversely if a closed role system is pushed on a child, who has hitherto experienced an open role system, then he may also be in difficulties. A child who is expected to communicate in elaborated codes, when he has previously only had to communicate in the restricted codes, may be under considerable strain.

When I try to relate restricted and elaborated codes to role, to closed and open role sets, to personal meanings, I do not pretend to furnish any explanations which invalidate any other kind of explanation, I am simply trying to relate what, to me, are sociologically relevant factors. I am suggesting, for instance, that unless a child has the opportunity to learn to act a certain role he may not be able to learn to use the appropriate code which that role involves; and that the range of roles, which a child learns, may have effects on his ability to use language. For instance, there is no doubt that there is considerable difference between the use of language of girls and boys in the working class, and that this may be related to the greater complexity of the girls' role-set, as against the more simple roles which boys are expected to play. Interestingly enough, this shows up particularly in the complexity of the noun phrase, as used by working-class girls at 5 years of age.

Limitation of the Term "Language"

GENERAL DISCUSSION

HYMES: It seems to me that we tend to use the term "language" for everything we are interested in. I would like to propose that we use *language* in as narrow a sense as possible. I think it would help if we restrict *language* to mean that with which linguists deal in terms of underlying structures; for the other subjects which we have also called "language", we could talk about "verbal behaviour". There might be a set of rules in between to link the two, which could be distinguished as rules for speaking, or rules governing speech as a form of conduct. This might clarify some points along a possible continuum of reference, which are all being described as "language" at the present moment. This is a terminological proposal, and I don't want to be prescriptive about how we deal with it. If you prefer, we could have language$_1$ and language$_2$.

Another possible approach would be to use another term for the kind of structure linguists refer to: we could call it "code" or something. But if we persist in using a single term for all these different aspects of a situation, we will go on being hopelessly confused.

ROBINSON: Yes. I must admit, in terms of the linguist's narrow use of the word, my own use of "language" was inappropriate. I should perhaps have called it "verbal behaviour".

HYMES: The structure of language; the use of language; the acquisition of language; these things may all affect one another, and interact with one another. If we use one term "language" for all of them we will really be confused and obscure all the interactions.

CHURCH: I think you and I are in agreement. What I dislike is the use of empty abstractions. We spend too much time talking about the structural properties of language and make much too little reference to the people who speak the language. I want to drag these abstractions back into the context of children growing up and learning to speak. The contrast that I see is between studying the formal aspects of language

73

and studying the total corpus of what the child says; the putting of the world into words. We should aim to arrive at a different kind of analysis, in terms of the psychological functions of different kinds of communicative acts.

HUXLEY: May I make a defence of pure linguists? I agree with Dr. Hymes that language is used to cover a great number of different activities, and that these should certainly be differentiated; but the examples in Dr. Church's paper (this volume) would be described in a linguist's terms as use of antonyms, predications, and ordering relations. I must assure you that, in semantics, linguists are certainly concerned with these problems, particularly in regard to children.

CHURCH: Yes I agree. But partly, you see, what I am saying is that we need more semantics and less grammar.

HUXLEY: But linguistics involves both.

CHURCH: Yes; but, at least in the United States, developmental psycholinguistics has been preoccupied with grammatical analysis, and has almost forgotten about semantic analysis.

HUXLEY: I think there is a good case for putting grammar first in one's approach to the problem. Until you have examined the structures and have found some syntactic invariants in terms of distribution, you are not in a very good position to go further and differentiate the semantic invariants that children express with a particular syntactic apparatus which may be available to them.

HYMES: We must register too that the second generation of transformational linguists have cast their approach much more in semantic terms.

CHURCH: I think it is perfectly possible that you can start the other way round—start working with the semantic functions of language in reference to the real world and then examine the grammatical, syntactic and compositional properties of language as subordinate to these. In general, children don't talk language without some kind of meaning, function, goal, or whatever. We do have the Ruth Weir kind of thing which seems to be a purely abstract exercise in language, but this is highly atypical of the ordinary everyday linguistic behaviour of children. In fact, they are usually talking about *things* and they are talking to somebody. For instance, I was very pleased to see the Bellugi study of question-asking (see Bellugi, this volume); but again I found it much too grammatical and too little semantic. What is the variety of question? What is the child asking about?

KLIMA: There are two things here. There is the questioning and there is the interrogative form of English; now both have a reality, and I

think a linguist finds the interrogative form, in itself, rather interesting.
CHURCH: Yes, but it is perfectly clear, for instance, that you cannot rely on the interrogative form alone in deciding what the child means. He can ask "why" in a great many different senses.
KLIMA: Of course; furthermore, no one says the intention of the interrogative form is necessarily to get an answer.
CHURCH: The child finds a great many different linguistic mechanisms for saying essentially the same thing; his intention can be constant while his linguistic forms vary.
KLIMA: There is a whole continuum of the intent of a particular utterance. There is also, I insist, a certain reality to form.
HYMES: Even more seriously, it would seem to me, in relating these two things, there is the question, at each stage of the child's development, of what linguistic mechanisms are in fact available. This development is to some extent separate from the functional use of them.
CHURCH: I am the most thorough-going environmentalist you could find around, and this is basic to my argument. Unless one looks at the linguistic environment and the forms contained there, then one is very likely to misunderstand the linguistic, cognitive, intellectual development of the child. It is for this reason that it makes very little sense to me to talk about the properties of English in general, rather than *this* situation of spoken English or *that* situation of spoken English.
BEVER: Every linguist agrees with that. In fact, often they say that all a given grammar can really describe, if it is a detailed grammar, is one person's idiolect; but then, by comparing with different people, you can begin to see what they do in fact have in common.
CHURCH: Yes, and this is perfectly appropriate for linguistics. What I am questioning is its appropriateness for developmental psychology.
CAZDEN: Roger Brown made a suggestion about the interaction of grammar and semantics, which was that the first verbs that seemed to receive a past tense were verbs like *smashed*; *banged*; *dropped*—where the instantaneous quality of the action and the fact that it was inherently over by the time it was discussed might be the beginning of the triggering of the use of the past tense. I am sorry that when I was testing the inflections, I never really followed that up. The whole question of this interaction between the grammar and the semantics seems to me not only a very intriguing one but also a step in the direction of the even more complex kinds of interactions which Professor Hymes was asking us to think about.
SINCLAIR: At a much later age, when we ask children to describe actions which we have just performed in front of them, the question is

always put in the same way: "Tell me what happened"; that is to say, it is put in the past tense. We find that the children introduce some kind of distinction between duratives and non-duratives. All the actions that take some time, like *laver*, are put in the present. I will say: "Tell me what happened" and the child will say: "The boy washes the car" or rather, in English, "is washing the car". Whereas when the action is *breaking* something, he will say: "the boy broke the stick"; and the distinction is quite clear. 5 to 6-year-old children always answer in the past tense when the action is momentary or non-durative and in the present when it is durative action, even though the question was always put in the past.

Grammar

Learning Grammar: From Pivot to Realization Rule

I. M. SCHLESINGER

*The Hebrew University, Jerusalem; and the
Israel Institute of Applied Social Research*

As the title of the paper suggests, I am one of the psychologists who still cling to the old-fashioned view that grammar can be learnt. For some time now, a nativist view of language acquisition has had some vigorous spokesmen. Their claim is essentially that the language acquisition device cannot be assumed to operate merely on the basis of known principles of learning theory, because the linguistic input to the device is not sufficiently rich to yield a grammar by applying these principles. Therefore, it is argued, the device (*alias* the child acquiring a grammar) must be equipped with powerful innate constraints which determine the form of the grammar that is acquired.

What is objectionable about such an explanation is that it is no explanation at all. Even if the nativist were right that the learning-theory approach is untenable—and I shall argue further on that he is not— this would not constitute any support whatsoever for his own approach. To see that this is so, imagine a learning theorist using the same type of argumentation. He first enlarges on the difficulties attendant on any attempt to provide a genetically based explanation for language acquisi- tion. After having proved to his satisfaction that genetics is "in prin- ciple" incapable of explaining how deep structures are handed down from generation to generation, our learning theorist smugly concludes that, therefore, deep structures must be inferred by the child from the corpus of speech he encounters. Such an argument would of course not be accepted. It would be correctly pointed out that the task of learning theory does not end here; rather, it begins here and the learning theorist must show *how* deep structures are inferred from the corpus. I submit that the nativist is in the same position as this imaginary learning theorist: his claim is not strengthened by merely pointing out the weaknesses of an empiricist position.

Further, the arguments advanced so far by the proponents of nativism do not seem to me to disparage the view that grammar is learnt. Their arguments are based on generalities and amount to little more than saying: "I dare you to show me how a child can learn deep structures which are hidden so well that it takes a linguist to find them!" Of course there could hardly have been anything but such general pronouncements, because there is no well-developed learning account of the acquisition of grammar (except for the initial phases of learning). In the absence of a theory which can be criticized, nothing is left but to forestall attempts to construct such a theory by declaring these to be out of the question "in principle". This way of argumentation has been refuted convincingly by Crothers and Suppes (1967), and I shall not enlarge on it here.

What we need, then, are not war-cries but theories. There is no sense in ruling out on *a priori* grounds either a nativist or a learning theory. If someone suggests a theory based on innate constructs and rules, we should ask *which* constructs, or rules, or ways of inference are innate, and *how* they are inherited; just as the onus is on the learning theorist to state what is learnt and how it is learnt. The convenient formula, "This could not have been learnt, therefore it must be innate", cannot be accepted in lieu of theorizing. Let us then not look for ways of succeeding in theorizing without trying; instead, let us try.

In the following, I intend to sketch the bare outlines of an explanation of how grammar is learnt. The details remain to be filled in, and this can be done only after much further study.

Let us start by examining the alleged difficulties of a learning theory approach to acquisition of grammar. These have to do with the concept of deep structure as developed by Chomsky (1965). According to this view, the surface structures which the child is exposed to are derived from deep structures by means of transformations. The child cannot understand an utterance unless he recovers the deep structure which underlies it. Now, it is hard to see how some of the information contained in the deep structure could have been obtained by the child from the utterances he is exposed to. Specifically, the problem arises in regard to the following aspects of deep structure:

(1) the branches of the P-marker which represents the deep structure are ordered, and this order may differ from that in the surface structure;

(2) in the deep structures there appear major categories—like NP, VP, etc.—which are highly abstract entities, and are nowhere apparent in the surface structure.

So far, no explanation has been forthcoming of how the child arrives at such deep structures, which does not assume that something or other is due to his innate capacity. But, unless it is substantiated by positive evidence, the claim that something is innate does not amount to an explanation; it amounts to throwing your hands up before the complexity of the phenomenon to be explained. The following proposal is based on the assumption that the deep structures which the speaker and listener operate with are not exactly those which currently figure in generative grammar. In particular, I suggest that they contain neither information about grammatical categories nor about order. This information is introduced through transformations which convert the deep structure into the surface.

This changed conception of deep structures makes it possible, as I shall try to show, to give a learning account of language acquisition. But this is not the only motivation for introducing such a change. The necessity for hypothesizing a somewhat modified form of deep structures became apparent in considering a model for the production of utterances. Elsewhere (Schlesinger, in press) I have argued that the linguistically relevant aspect of the speaker's *intentions* must serve as input to such a model. These may be formalized as input-markers or *I-markers*. The I-marker contains concepts, and the relations holding between these concepts; the speaker realizes the concepts in the form of words and the relations holding between them by grammatical means, such as word order and inflection.

Now, the notion of relations between words is not novel. Chomsky (1965, pp. 68 ff.) has shown that functional relations can be defined in terms of category symbols appearing in the P-marker of deep structure. Thus, the object of a VP is the relation holding between the NP of this VP and the whole VP, and so on. But note that the reverse is also true: information regarding grammatical categories (NP, VP, etc.) can be extracted from the relational notions. I suggest therefore that it is these relations which appear in the I-marker. Since relations and categories can be retrieved from each other, I-markers and P-markers are similar to each other. The main difference is not in the information they contain but in the form in which this information appears. The reason why I have proposed I-markers rather than P-markers for the performance model is that in I-markers the information appears in a form which seems to be closer to the speaker's intentions. When he says "John built this mobile", the speaker intends to express the fact that the goal of the building action is the mobile (and not John). It makes less sense to state that he intends "mobile" to be the NP of the VP. We think about our environment in terms of relations, not of noun and verb phrases, and therefore relations should figure as hypothetical constructs in a model of the speaker and the hearer.

Suppose for a moment that the above argument is wrong, and that it is the grammatical categories which appear in the performance model. Then, the question arises how they got there. For lexical categories, such as N, V, M, there is little difficulty, since these can be viewed as classes of words. No similar solution is possible for the major categories, like NP and VP, which appear higher up in the phrase structure tree. By contrast, the relations in the I-marker present no obstacle for an account of how grammar is learnt. When Johnny builds a mobile, the situation is perceived in such a way that Johnny is the agent of the activity of building, and the mobile is its object. This way of viewing the world—which finds its expression in the I-marker—is the only thing that must be claimed to be innate. Surely this is a far cry from the claim that specific linguistic constructs (or rules of inference from a corpus) are innate. The latter assumption is far stronger than the former, and the former should therefore be preferred.

Let us look at a much simplified example of an I-marker in Fig. 1. The figure is simplified through omitting some information (viz. the fact that "Johnny" is singular, "build" occurs in the past, etc.) all of which must be assumed to be contained in the speaker's intentions and in the I-marker.

Two important points must be mentioned in connection with this I-marker. First, the I-marker is hierarchically arranged just as the corresponding P-marker is. This is so, because the concepts in question are also hierarchically arranged in the speaker's intentions. In the I-marker of Fig. 1, the mobile and not John is modified in a certain manner (which is expressed in speech by "this"). Similarly, in "Tommy eats a big apple", it is the apple which is big and not Tommy. The second point is that the I-marker does not contain any information as to the temporal order in which the words appear in the utterance. There is of course a logical order of elements, in the sense that the relations in question are not symmetrical; the mobile is the object of the building activity, and not vice versa. But the speaker's intentions in themselves do not determine the temporal order of words or concepts, and therefore this order has no place in the I-marker. In the resulting utterance, order of words will be determined by a rule of grammar, which has to be learnt. Formally, this rule is a transformation, but to avoid confusion I prefer to call it a *realization rule*. The realization rule states, e.g., that in Fig. 1 the branches a and b of the object node are to be realized in the order b + a: "built" is uttered before "this mobile". It may be helpful, therefore, to look at the I-marker as a mobile rather than as a tree (this has been suggested to me by Dan Slobin): the branches

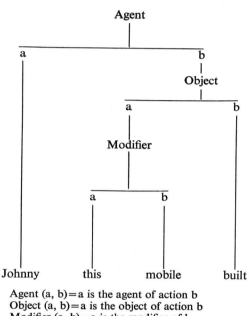

Agent (a, b)=a is the agent of action b
Object (a, b)=a is the object of action b
Modifier (a, b)=a is the modifier of b

FIG. 1. A simplified figure of the I-marker of "John built this mobile".

can revolve freely around the node, as it were; and, if you will, the branches are labelled a and b in order to keep track of the logical order, when they revolve around the node.

Speaking is the process of realizing an I-marker through speech sounds. Understanding is the process of assigning an I-marker to the heard utterance. Both are based on rules which pair meanings with utterances, and it is these rules which the child must learn. Learning takes place when the child hears utterances in a meaningful situation. He perceives the situation in terms of concepts and relations, i.e. in terms of an I-marker, and associates it with the heard utterance.

D

In some nativist discussions of language acquisition, a model is described, the input of which are the linguistic data, i.e. utterances, and the output is a grammar, i.e. a set of rules relating utterances to meanings. It is argued that the linguistic input does not contain the deep structures which are the bearers of semantic information, and that this raises the problem for learning theory of how the acquisition model arrives at the meaning-utterance rules from such an input. The present proposal suggests that the input contains not only utterances, but utterances coupled with their meanings. The task of the model is to derive from these meaning-utterance pairs a set of rules which show how utterances and meanings are paired. Surely this should not be beyond the scope of learning principles. If the input would be no more than linguistic data, there might indeed be a problem. But children do not learn grammar by listening to speech without reference to the situation, just as they do not learn the meaning of words by listening to a mere list of words.

There are differences between I-markers and P-markers in addition to those mentioned above; since these do not affect the main argument of this presentation, I shall mention some of these only in passing (see Schlesinger, in press, for a discussion). It seems to be necessary for the functioning of the production model that the I-marker should not contain words, but rather concepts which are neutral as to grammatical category. The terminal string in Fig. 1 should be conceived of as consisting of such concepts. Thus, "build" stands for a class of words which includes also "building" (noun), and "built" (past form). A realization rule determines which one of the words belonging to this class is chosen for the utterance. Syntactic features, such as "count", "common", "animate", and "human", also belong to the concepts as they appear in the I-marker, and presumably some selectional rules belong to the I-marker. ("John frightens sincerity" is ruled out by the speaker's intention and not by an acquired realization rule.)

Note also that there is no one-to-one correspondence between P-markers as currently conceived of and I-markers. In "I smell the flower" we have an agent-action relation, but this is not true of every case where the sentence consists of a noun-phrase followed by a verb-phrase. For instance, "the flower smells" exemplifies a different relation. Fillmore (1968) has discussed this problem at length, and has arrived at a linguistic solution which has influenced the present formulation.

Instead of going on to discuss I-markers, let me try to show how the child learns to map these into utterances, i.e. how he acquires realization rules. I shall limit myself here to the learning of word order, since I have nothing new to contribute to the learning of other aspects of grammar.

The realization rule which the child finally comes to use must accord a relative position to the terms of a relation. If A is the object of B, the English-speaking child must learn that the corresponding words, a and b, are to be uttered in the order b + a. However, such a rule is probably not learnt directly, but by some detours. Here I want to suggest one plausible route by which the child arrives at the rule which functions in the adult speaker. This route is implied in the name of this paper: from pivot to realization rule.

My suggestion is that before he acquires realization rules, the child makes use of concepts, such as *agent* or *object,* and these concepts figure as pivots in his two-word utterances. In other words, the English-speaking child learns that the word representing the agent appears in the first position, the object-word in the second position, and so on. And, of course, if one word acts as a pivot in the two-word utterance, the position of the second word is also determined thereby. For example, the child says "Tommy eat", rather than "eat Tommy", because he has learnt that the word expressing the agent ("Tommy") comes first, without having had to learn any rule concerning the position of the action-word.

Concepts like "agent" and "object" are rather abstract, and one might question whether a small child is able to master these. However, there is plenty of evidence that the child perceives his environment not just in concrete terms: thus, "more" is a word which appears very early in many children; but what is its concrete reference? In the literature on child language you find "more apple", but also "more wet", "more outside", and many others. The child seems to refer by this word to something which has been and is no more, and/or something which he has had and wants still more of. The verbal definition here is very complex, but apparently the environmental and external cues which trigger the response "more" are not too complex for the child. Likewise, the child will have no trouble in identifying the agent or the source of an action. From examples in adults' speech he then learns that the word referring to the agent always comes first.

The pivots suggested by Braine (1963) refer to individual words. It may be the case that conceptual pivots—like agent, object, modifier, and others—which I am proposing here have their origin in Braine's pivots. The child first learns that several words are P_2. Next he observes that these words figure as object, and generalizes from these instances to the rule that all objects are P_2. This would be an instance of concept formation. If this is so, we should predict that, at a certain stage, when the child learns a new word and then uses it as an object of an action, this word will appear in the second position. Braine's pivot theory would predict this for a newly learned word only if it appears together with a P_1 word. Further, if the *same* word is used as agent it will appear in first position. To test this prediction one would have to analyse an extensive and fairly exhaustive corpus of the child's speech. At any rate, the assumption seems plausible that pivots of individual words are learnt first, and that conceptual pivots are generalized from them: the latter will be called, therefore, *generalized pivots*, or GPs.

GPs are operative only in two-word utterances. "Tommy eat" may result from the rule that agent is a GP_1, "eat apple" may be due to the rule that object is a GP_2. But these two rules are not sufficient to determine the word order in "Tommy eat apple". For structured utterances of three words or more, the rule must be such as to relate two terms to each other, and these are the realization rules of the mature speaker. Realization rules are learnt on the basis of GPs. For instance, after having learnt that the agent comes in first position, the child learns the rule that the agent precedes the action belonging to it. Table I illustrates how "Tommy eat apple" may result from two such

TABLE I. EXAMPLE OF TWO REALIZATION RULES MAPPING AN I-MARKER INTO AN UTTERANCE

Relation in I-marker	Object (apple, eat)	Agent (Tommy, eat apple)
Realization Rule	Action + Object	Agent + Action
Utterance	Eat apple	Tommy eat apple

realization rules. These rules may be applied in either sequence, and at present we do not know anything about the sequence of steps in the performance model.

In conclusion, let me show you some data which seem to accord with the explanation which has been sketched here. But first notice one important point about GPs. Among the GPs we find agent, object, modifier, location, and possibly some others; but "action" cannot be a GP, because in the two-word utterance it sometimes comes in the first place—when coupled with an object—and sometimes in the second place—when coupled with an agent.

Table II presents translations from the Hebrew of two-word utterances of a boy between the ages 1 : 8 and 1 : 11. I used to jot down his utterances sporadically, usually not more than five to eight a day, and

often much less. Such a small corpus cannot of course provide con-
clusive evidence, but the data are suggestive. At least my recording was
not biased by my hypotheses, because at the time they were made,
though I had some ideas about realization rules, I had none about GPs.

The relations which are expressed by utterances in Table II are
agent with action (in the left column), agent with object, and action
with object (in the middle and right columns respectively). In this
period I recorded many more utterances which did not express any one
of these relations, and these are not presented here. A full agent-action-
object combination first appeared in the 11th week and such utterances are also not included in the table. Utterances which do not follow
the adult word order are marked with an asterisk. Further, introducers,
like "Mummy", "Daddy" (i.e. the name of any person whom the child
addresses), have been omitted. (The utterance on "Week 1" actually
occurred about 3 weeks before those of "Week 2".)

The agent-object combinations deserve special mention. It seems that
we have here a stage which precedes that of the action-object combinations. While there are few such utterances reported by other writers,
I have found many agent-object combinations also in another Hebrew-
speaking child. The appearance of agent-object utterances supports the
notion of generalized pivots, which according to the present proposal
are the basis for the development of realization rules. For the mature
speaker there is no place for a realization rule agent + object. Instead of
assuming that the child learns such a rule and then unlearns it, it seems
more plausible that the child learns a GP_1. In the present case, "agent"
appears as GP_1 in (a) utterances constituted of an agent and its action;
and (b) in utterances where the agent appears in combination with an
object.

Looking at the words which exemplify the various GPs, we first of all
note that the agents which appear in the agent-action utterances are for
the most part the same as those appearing in the agent-object utterances: "Daddy", "Eve", "Jimmy", etc. Likewise, largely the same
objects occur with the agent (middle column) as with the action (right
column). This is in line with the claim that the child learns the concepts
"agent" and "object" as GPs. By contrast, none of the action words
which appear with an object occurs also with the agent: the left column
contains mainly intransitive verbs and some vocal mimicry which serves
instead of verbs, whereas the right column contains transitive verbs,
or combinations like "give-me", "put-on", which always appear as a
unit at that period. There is no single "action" class apparent in these
data; this is to be expected since, as stated, "action" cannot be a GP,

because it must appear sometimes before an object and sometimes after an agent.

In Table I there is hardly any overlap between the class of nouns which serve as agents and the class of nouns which serve as objects. The latter are inanimate (water, tea, slippers, radio, etc.), whereas the former are mostly animate (Daisy, Mummy, Daddy; "a car" is perhaps also animate for the child). Perhaps the child first acquires two classes —animate nouns and inanimate nouns—instead of one noun class, and thus learns from the outset to make a distinction which is essential in

TABLE II. SOME TWO-WORD UTTERANCES OF A CHILD AGED
1:8–1:11 (TRANSLATED FROM HEBREW)

Week	Agent with Action	Agent with Object	Action with Object
1		Daddy water (Daddy has given me water)	
2	Eve sh . . . sh . . . (Eve sleeps)		Give-me grapes
3		* tea, Daddy Daddy (Daddy shall give me tea)	
5	Daisy bye-bye	* tea Eve, Eve tea (Eve drinks tea)	
6	Daddy noo . . . noo . . . (Daddy threatened me saying "noo, noo") Daisy bye-bye Eve hee . . . hee . . . hee . . . (Eve laughs)		
7		Daisy dessert (Daisy shall give me some dessert)	
8	Eve comes		
9	Mummy comes Daddy hit	water, Jimmy water (Jimmy drinks water) (?)	
10	Mummy, Jimmy, Eve, all bye-bye (they are all going away) car drive (the car is driving) Daddy hit		

TABLE II—*continued*

Week	Agent with Action	Agent with Object	Action with Object
11	house fall (when playing with building blocks) Mummy, Eve . . . all bye-bye	Eve juice (Eve gave me juice)	
12			* beigel don't want
14			give-me, give-me cookie * cookie give-me
15	Daisy comes		* tea give-me put-on slippers put-on sweater switch-off radio * pants take-off
16	* ahhn . . . car (mimics noise of car) car fell yes, who comes? Daisy comes		bring-me car put-on shoes Daddy, take paper? * Daddy, paper take, yes?

the grammar of the mature speaker. In general, it may turn out that the first grammatical categories are learnt as classes of words which are associated with a given GP, like agent, modifier, or location. Other categories, like "verb", cannot be learnt in connection with the GP, and would have to await the appearance of a realization rule like "agent + action".

At the beginning of this paper I made a plea for more work on explicitly formulated theories. Now I would like to add another plea: what we need just as urgently are extensive transcripts of utterances made available to workers in the field, against which theories can be tested. The data published so far may be sufficient to support the respective writers' explanations, but they certainly do not suffice to evaluate these against rival explanations. If the transcripts are to be useful for testing the explanation presented here, which involves semantic concepts and relations, then the child's utterances must be accompanied by a description of the situation and a guess at the meaning of the utterance.

Discussion

BEVER: What you have done is to take the traditional concepts of logical grammatical relations, which Chomsky has articulated in the form of the basic P-marker, and to place them in something which you call an I-marker. But that does not solve the problem, it merely changes the nomenclature.

SCHLESINGER: I am not claiming at all that the relations proposed here are new. The trouble with the current conception seems to be that it looks at grammar as a two-backed beast with deep structure and surface structure. Then you have two interpretative components: the semantic component gives the semantic interpretation, and the phonological component gives the phonological interpretation. The problem now is the relationship between deep structure and semantic interpretation. According to Katz (1966) there is a one-to-one correspondence between these two: this means that there is redundancy in the system, which is obviously an undesirable feature. According to a more recent approach, deep structure is somehow identified with semantic structure; the work of Fillmore (1968) and Lakoff (1965) is relevant here and so is that of Tesnière (1959). What I am saying is that I-markers already represent semantic interpretation.

The issue I am raising is: what must be taken as innate? No doubt, something or other is innate: the organism comes equipped with something. But I think it is methodologically unsound to make assumptions which are not absolutely necessary. Only the very minimum should be assumed to be innate. For instance, nobody has shown how the knee reflex could have been learned, and the consensus of opinion is that this is innate. The relations I have discussed here are also what I take to be the bare minimum. In *John builds*, it is not the building which "does" John, but John who does the building. We cannot even conceive of an organism which sees *John builds* in any way which is different from the one where *John* is a source of the action and *builds* is the action. On the other hand, I do not believe it necessary to assume that major categories, like NP, VP, are innate; of course I cannot prove that they are not, but I think it is methodologically unsound to shove everything under the carpet of innateness. If you suspect that I am taking issue here with the proponents of nativism, you are quite right. It is very difficult to quarrel with them, because they have never been very explicit in stating what it is that is innate. Occasionally, they talk about innate propensities, and I am not satisfied with that either. What all this amounts to is a challenge to all of us to try to specify the conceptual relations which the speaker operates with.

MEHLER: I would like to take up two points with you. There are various kinds of logical relations, and some of them linguists are good at analysing: actor, action; statements with *have*, statements with *be*. But there are other relations, such as the relation *of*; as in *he's the father of*; there are *than* relations: *he is older than*; there are the rest of the comparatives. Now if you look at these, do you think you could get away with just action and actor being innate and the rest derived from these?

SCHLESINGER: No, of course not. I am sure that the actor-action relation is basic, but I cannot state which are the other necessary relations. However, the relations represented in the phrase marker according to current work are not sufficient either. For instance, the subject-of relation (i.e. the relation between NP and S) semantically probably contains several relations. Thus, in *I smell the flower* you have actor-action relation, but *the flower smells* exemplifies a different relation, though in both cases you have a noun phrase followed by a verb phase. Semantically these are clearly different things. As you know, Fillmore suggests that subject-of and object-of are not relations of deep structure.

If you challenge me to explain how deep structures are learned, I cannot answer. I don't think anybody else can either. But, once the deep structure is "given" as a conceptual, cognitive structure, it is easy to see in principle how it is coupled with the surface structure. Here the transformations of the generative grammarian enter the picture, and I think everybody will agree that these are learned. How they are learned—for instance, how the inversion of the interrogative is learned—is a different question, but it seems fairly obvious that they are learned.

MEHLER: Maybe you don't need any translation from deep structure to surface structure. It may be that it is possible to compute both things in parallel. J. P. Thorne's data in Edinburgh (Thorne *et al.*, 1968), and the data I have gathered in perception suggest that there are not two analyses but rather that these two processes are going on in parallel all the time; so maybe we don't even need a translation system. The next point I want to raise is this: if you set to work, within the framework of generative grammar, you accept that describing a cognitive phenomenon can be done best through an axiomatic system. One can argue that each level of the axiomatic system must have some components which are innate.

Suppose you say that only axioms are innate and the rules of formation and the vocabulary are learned: how would you learn a vocabulary? Since we accepted the need to work within the framework of a generative system, we have then to propose an axiomatic system for the vocabulary too; which will have, in its turn, a vocabulary and so you will have a regression to infinity. This will happen unless you accept that at each level of the axiomatic system there are some cognitive, innate parts; for instance, an innate part which allows you to set up axioms, and rules of formation. Now once this is said, it is true that we don't know how to characterize what the innate parts are. But you are not going to solve the problem by saying that the sentence is in a one-to-one relation with its meaning, because it is precisely the meaning that we want to account for. The sentence *John is taller than Bill* comes not only as a phonological representation, it has a meaning attached. Where does that meaning come from?

CHURCH: I have the feeling that we are up against a basic confusion here between what is innate in the structure of language, and what is innate in visual perception. This leads us to the problem of how far we can take language as some kind of replica of what is perceived. The basic problem, and probably the unanswerable problem, is how man first started trying to translate his perceptual experience into symbolic form.

This could be very different from the problem of how the child uses the linguistic materials around him to translate his perceptual experience into the linguistic forms. Now, there are many things in the development of perception which make it perfectly clear that we cannot take for granted that a child of 18 months sees the world as we do. Take the field of causation among adults in a given culture—there is usually good agreement about what causes something else to move, in a situation where two abstract forms join up and then move away together. Adults see one form pushing on the other form, but children often see one form as passing at the back or the front of the other. That is something which adults never see, so we cannot take it for granted that there is going to be consensus on the most objective kinds of perceptual experience. Now, in your example, *John builds the mobile*, you can phrase it in two ways: you can say that John will be motivated to build the mobile, in terms of the motivating effect of his environment, or you can say that the demand qualities of the environment motivated John to behave in such and such a way.

SCHLESINGER: But can you perceive it in such a way that it is the mobile which builds John? Isn't that the question really?

CHURCH: Certainly the locus of the question is different.

SCHLESINGER: It is John who is doing the act, and grammar doesn't tell you whether he is the originator of the action as well as the actor.

AMBROSE: I think we should be careful not to be led into the position of appearing to regard "innate" and "learned" as dichotomous. A lot of time has been wasted in the past by assuming such a dichotomy. I think it's fairly clear now that when one attributes innateness to some aspect of behaviour, it doesn't mean that this aspect cannot be influenced by the environment in its development. Similarly it makes no sense to consider something as being learned without taking into account that inevitably the so-called innate aspects of the organism will have influenced the course of learning.

Simplification in Children's Language

URSULA BELLUGI

Salk Institute for Biological Studies,
San Diego, California

INTRODUCTION

MOST OF THE language learning process takes place between the ages of 2 and 5 years. By 2, children are just beginning to combine single words into rudimentary two-word utterances. By 4 or 5, the normal child's syntax is already extremely complex and intricate, and his language bears a strong resemblance to that which he hears around him. The early two-word utterances often resemble sentences of the adult language with a very large number of omissions. The sentences of the 5-year-old are often indistinguishable from correctly formed sentences of the language. What happens in the periods in between? We have found several periods where the child's sentences show systematic deviations from the adult language, as if they were constructed according to a different set of rules.

We have found in fine-grained studies of the language development of three unacquainted children, Adam and Eve and Sarah, as we have called them, that the order of emergence of constructions is quite regular across children, and that there seem to be specifiable periods in the language acquisition process (see for example, Brown, 1968; Bellugi, 1967; Brown and Hanlon, 1970). We have also found that the children produce sentences at various periods which are frequently of particular structural types, and are characteristic of child speech.

It seems that the child's language at various periods is systematic, rule-governed, and not necessarily directly imitative of the adult language at all periods. Here we will consider evidence that the child is using rules in forming sentences, that these rules do not always correspond to the rules presumably underlying the adult language, and that certain types of syntactic simplification may be represented by the systematic deviations from adult speech.

We will consider three types of systematic regularities which we found in the speech of the children. These regularities share the following characteristics:

(a) They occurred in the speech of more than one child (and have been observed in others since).

(b) They occurred with considerable regularity and frequency during the period under observation, and with some evidence for productivity; that is, these are not idiomatic forms, but regular creations.

(c) They occurred in a form which is characteristically deviant from the syntactic form which occurs in the language the children hear.

(d) There is some evidence that these are "transient hypotheses"; that is, they are later replaced by more mature forms.

(e) They are fully specified semantically. These are not structural types which are anomalous or ambiguous.

Where there is evidence, we will discuss efforts to correct the child's slightly deviant forms. We will attempt to characterize (in totally non-formal terms) the nature of the child's systematization, and to suggest the types of simplification of rules of the adult language which are presumably represented by the child's limited sentences. Most of the examples are from Adam, since he is the most prolific of the three children in terms of regular syntactic "errors". We will concentrate on the time when the children's mean utterance length in morphemes exceeds 3·5. Table I presents the periods of language development for Adam.

Out of the set of constructions we could use to illustrate the general points we want to make, we have picked three problems: (a) auxiliary inversion in children's questions; (b) the relationship of negatives and indefinites; and (c) the development of case-marking in children's pronouns. In each case we will be interested in the child's systematization and simplification of the language he hears and in his reconstruction of the underlying regularities of language.

AUXILIARY INVERSION IN QUESTIONS

Yes/No Questions

Auxiliary verbs begin to appear in children's speech in abundance after the sentences are longer than 3·5 mean utterance length (roughly after 3 years). These auxiliaries occur in declarative sentences, negative

TABLE I. LANGUAGE DEVELOPMENT OF ADAM

Period	Sample[a] numbers	Mean age (year and month)	Mean utterance length[b] (in morphemes)
A	1–5	2 : 4	2·0
B	17–19	2 : 11	2·5
C	24–26	3 : 2	3·5
D	32–34	3 : 6	4·0
E	40–42	3 : 11	4·7
F	49–51	4 : 6	5·2

[a] Samples were transcriptions of two-hour tape-recorded conversations between mother and child taken every 2 to 3 weeks.

[b] Mean utterance length is based on 100 utterances per sample.

sentences, *yes/no* questions and *wh-* questions during the same period (see Klima and Bellugi, 1966). The occurrence of these forms in children's questions, however, is not equivalent over the two major types of questions in English: *yes/no* questions and *wh-* interrogative questions.

Yes/no questions are ordinarily formed by inverting auxiliary verb and subject noun-phrase (and providing *do* support where necessary). But this operation is not required, and rising intonation alone can signal a *yes/no* question with complete adequacy. For example, "You went there yesterday?" and "Did you go there yesterday?" are paraphrases and equivalent. One might expect that non-inverted questions would occur in child speech before inverted questions, but this does not seem to be the case. Table II presents the occurrence of modal

TABLE II. MODAL AUXILIARY VERBS IN YES/NO QUESTIONS
ADAM

Samples	Affirmative		Negative	
	Non-inverted	Inverted	Non-inverted	Inverted
1–16	—	—	—	—
17–24	1	—	—	—
25–34	7	198	—	3

Examples:
Inverted: *Shall I put this this way?*
Won't you have some monkeys in my house?
Non-inverted: *He might get sick?*

auxiliary verbs in inverted and non-inverted form in Adam's *yes/no* questions. We see that modal auxiliary verbs do not begin to occur in the child's speech until Period C and beyond, and once they occur they are overwhelmingly inverted in *yes/no* questions. Notice that only *8* are instances of non-inverted types as in *He can see me?* and *201* are inverted as in *Can she do it?* in Adam's speech. There is an occasional mixed form in the early part of that period, not frequent enough to discuss in detail:

> Can they should go down that Mass Avenue?
> Did I didn't mean to?
> It is was a snake?
> Do she don't need that one?

We notice that in terms of communication and grammaticality the inverted and non-inverted forms of the question are equivalent. *He's going out?* is just as acceptable and conveys the same information as *Is he going out?* In terms of the adult grammar then, the inversion rule is optional. The children, however, almost invariably produce questions with the auxiliary verb and the noun-phrase subject inverted in *yes/no* questions, once they begin using auxiliary verbs with any regularity.

Wh- questions

Well-formed *wh-* questions in English involve two grammatical operations (leaving other complications and special considerations on one side). An interrogative word (*what, where, when, who*) is associated with a missing element which is being questioned. In normal questions, the interrogative word is located initially in the sentence, and there is inversion of noun-phrase subject and auxiliary verb (with *do* supplied if there is no auxiliary).

> When *is he* going?
> How *did she* manage?
> Who *did the boy* push?
> Where *did she* hide?
> What *was he* looking at? etc.
> (See Klima, 1964; or Brown, 1968, for further details.)

Roger Brown (1968) has pointed out that there is an intermediate form of *wh-* question in adult speech which does not require inversion of auxiliary verb and subject (what we might call the *prompt question*), *He said what? She can do what?* However, these do not begin to occur in the children's speech until much later than the period under discussion, and even then they are rare. When children construct *wh-* word questions before the period we are considering, the interrogative word is *initial* (not: *He said what?* but *What he said?*). There is some evidence that the *wh-* interrogative represents a missing constituent in the child's question, and that the child understands that the interrogative word refers to a missing constituent in the adult questions. The child responds appropriately to these questions in the speech addressed to him. For example:

Mother. What do you hear?
Child. Hear a duck.

The special characteristic of children's *wh-* interrogative questions at this later stage is that it is some time before the auxiliary verb and noun-phrase subject are inverted (see Table III). The child produces a

TABLE III. MODAL AUXILIARY VERBS IN *WH-* QUESTIONS
ADAM

Samples	Affirmative		Negative	
	Non-inverted	Inverted	Non-inverted	Inverted
1–16	—	—	—	—
17–24	3	—	2	—
25–34	22	8	9	—
35–42	5	33	5	—
43–51	4	27	—	5

Examples:

Non-inverted:	What you will do?
	Why we can't find the right one?
Inverted:	Where should we put them?
	Why can't they put on their diving suits and swim?

set of questions that communicate perfectly adequately and yet they are syntactically deviant from the questions he hears. The children asked questions like these:

Where I should put it?
Why the kitten can't stand up?
Why you won't let me fly?
What she will do with me?

These forms persist even though they are never heard by the child, and even though the child at this period inverts noun-phrase subject and auxiliary verb in *yes/no* questions. We found at the same period many questions of this form:

> Shall I put the light on?
> Can I put those goats in there?
> Won't you come and have some whale fish?
> Will Robin help me?

We see from Table III that in samples 25–34 there were 31 non-inverted *wh-* questions as compared with 8 inverted *wh-* questions. When we compare this with the same child's productions of *yes/no* questions (considered above), we see that it is not the operation of inversion of noun-phrase and auxiliary verbs which promotes the immature form, but it may be the *combination* of inversion and *wh-*question in a single string.

There were, incidentally, also some doubling of auxiliary verbs, but these were not frequent enough to consider as a persistent type of structure. During this period the child asked:

> What shall we shall have?
> What I can should put there?
> Why was I did break it?
> What we will shall have?

The children's most frequent version of *wh-* questions is not an imitation of the speech they hear around them: an adult would not say "Where I should put it?" During this period, in experimental sessions, we asked the child to repeat sentences. We found he would often repeat the utterance, but filtered through his own rule system:

> Adult: Adam, say what I say: "Where can he put them?"
> Adam: Where he can put them?

We should note in Table III that, while the numbers of negative questions are small, there seems to be a tendency for inversion in negative *wh-* questions to occur later than for comparable affirmative questions. During the period when affirmative questions tended to be inverted and negative ones not (samples 35–42), we made another intervention. (Since this was an extra experimental session, these figures are not included in the table.)

Since in indirect questions, normal declarative word order is preserved, we decided to elicit *wh-* questions by using the indirect question form.

One of us had the glove-puppet figure of an old lady, and responded to the child's questions with the quavering voice of an elderly puppet. The other adult gave the child instructions in the form of indirect questions (which preserve word order). We had a set of twenty questions, half affirmative and half negative, which we mixed randomly and interspersed with other games and conversation during the session. The game went like this:

> Adult: Adam, ask the Old Lady what she'll do next.
> Adam: Old Lady, what will you do now?
> Old Lady: I'll fly to the moon.
>
> Adult: Adam, ask the Old Lady why she can't sit down.
> Adam: Old Lady, why you can't sit down?
> Old Lady: You haven't given me a chair.

In the course of the game, Adam inverted all the affirmative questions (*What will you do?*) and did not invert any of the negative questions (*Why you can't sit down?*) although they were presented in random order. This confirms our observations from spontaneous speech, that affirmative *wh-* questions had subject-auxiliary inversion before negative questions.

What linguistic mechanism can we suggest for the occurrence of these immature forms, and for the types of linguistic simplification which may be represented here? As in other cases, Adam gave us the clearest picture of consistency and change, but we found the same phenomena occurring in Sarah and Eve, and other children we have observed since. Lack of inversion in *wh-* questions occurs concurrent with inversion in *yes/no* questions. From the view-point of adult grammar, one rule is missing from the *wh-* questions: the auxiliary inversion rule. There have been various formulations of the question transformation in recent literature, the details of which are not important here; we can suggest that perhaps there is a limit on the permitted complexity of a string at various periods. This would be a performance limit in terms of grammatical complexity. That is, if inversion and *wh-* preposing are both required as in *wh-* interrogatives, only the latter operates on the string.

It seems clear from recent psycholinguistic work that we cannot equate adding grammatical rules and psychological complexity in any direct straightforward way (Fodor and Garrett, 1966; Garrett and Fodor, 1968). We have no real basis for predicting, in any case, that an inversion rule would be omitted rather than a preposing rule, for example. We should expect, if one explanation were on the basis of number of rules of the grammar only, to find *Didn't we do what?* as often as *What we can't do?* and we have already shown that the first alternative does not occur frequently in the child's rule system, while the second does. Also a straightforward notion of a limit on number of rules which can be applied to a string of any one period would predict many "immature" forms which do not occur. On the other hand, the fact that affirmative *wh-* questions invert before negative *wh-* questions suggests some form of complexity limitation operating to determine the shape of the string.

These characteristic immature forms, which drop out of the child's speech in the next period and are replaced by the mature form, are considered as representing limits on the permitted complexity of sentences in the child's grammar. We see that the child analyses the sentence he hears, and reconstructs his responses in accordance with his own rule system, preserving the semantic nature of the message.

RELATIONSHIP OF NEGATIVE AND INDEFINITE

The relationship between location of negatives and indefinites in a negative sentence gives rise to a complicated set of rules with interlocking restrictions in English (see Klima, 1964). Consider the following set of sentences:

Someone gave John something.
Something was given to John by someone.
John was given something by someone.

The forms of indeterminate (*someone, something*) are the same throughout. Now notice what happens when we negate the set of sentences:

No one gave John anything.
Nothing was given to John by anyone.
John was given nothing by anyone.
or
John wasn't given anything by anyone.

Notice that it is no longer the case that the forms are the same from sentence to sentence. Consider the affirmative sentence *Someone gave John something.* There are various ways of forming a negative sentence from this string: *No one gave John anything.* or *John wasn't given anything by anyone.* On what does the particular form depend? Each sentence has only one negative form, which can combine either with an indeterminate *or* an auxiliary verb. This option can be taken only in case there is no indeterminate before the tense of the verb. Even then the negative must combine with the first of the indefinites if there is more than one (not *John was given anything by no one).[1] If in the position before the tense of the verb there is an indeterminate, the negative must combine with this; all other indeterminates in the string are pure indefinite forms. The location in the surface structure of the sentence is the determining factor, not whether or not the constituent is subject or object of the verb.

In general, then, the presence of a negative promotes the occurrence of the indefinite (any) form, rather than the indeterminate (some) form which is common in declarative affirmative sentences. In standard speech, there is a limit of one negative formant per main verb (to rule out No one said nothing). In addition, there are special restrictions on the location of the negative formant. Negation tends to occur as early in the sentence as possible, so that if there is an indeterminate form located before the tense of the main verb of a negative sentence, it is obligatorily negated. Thus, we have No one said anything, and not *Anybody didn't say anything. The passive form of this sentence is not *Anything was said by no one, but rather Nothing was said by anybody, indicating again the restriction that the negative must combine with the first indeterminate if it is before the tense of the verb. These, then, are the facts of the location and occurrence of the negative formant in a sentence, the particular shape of an indefinite in a negative sentence, and the restriction and relationship between them.

How does the child approach this complex set of rules? The first approximation is by way of ignoring the dependency relationship altogether. Negative sentences and affirmative sentences do not differ for the child in terms of indeterminate/indefinite forms. The second approach is by way of simplifying the rules to a single generally applicable rule. Finally the child's sentences match the adult system in syntax.

Before 3 years, indeterminate forms in the speech of the children we studied occur only as modifiers in noun-phrases. We will start with the period when the negative formant begins to combine with the auxiliary verb of a sentence, when the child has mastered basic sentence negation, and indeterminate forms occur more freely in the child's speech. For Adam this is Period C, when Adam is just over 3 years old. Consider the occurrence of negative sentences with indefinite/indeterminate forms in the speech addressed to Adam, compared with the sentences he uses, in Period C.

[1] An asterisk indicates that a sentence is not a grammatical sentence of English.

Adam's Mother	*Adam*
You don't have anything to pour it in.	You don't want some supper.
This car doesn't have any lights.	Mommy don't let me buy some.
I don't see any fish in here at all.	I don't like some.

What is the difference between these two sets? In the mother's negative sentences, indefinite form *any* occurs with a negative sentence: *He doesn't have any arms.* In the child's sentences the corresponding form is the indeterminate *some*: *You don't want some supper.*

We can see the relationship between the two sets of rules in the following dialogue:

> Adam: Can I shoot us all?
> Mother: No, then you wouldn't have any more Ursula.
> Adam: Why I don't have some more Ursula?

Let us consider the source of this systematic regularity in his speech. During this period we find that indeterminate forms are occurring in all the major grammatical functions for the first time in affirmative sentences and questions. He uses them as subjects: *Somebody took the telephone*, as objects of verbs and prepositions: *I took something from him; I looking for something*, as adverbials: *I dream sometimes; Can I put it somewhere?*, as modifiers of mass and plural nouns: *There are some bottles; Here's some tea*, and as modifiers of singular count nouns: *Here's some plate for you; We got some birthday today*, as well as in negative sentences: *You don't want some.* Generally indeterminate forms are correctly used. There are, however, two types of over-extension: indeterminate *some* is used as a modifier of singular count nouns, and in negative sentences.

> Here's some plate for you.
> They gonna throw some baseball in the park.
> We got some birthday today.
> I gonna put some leg on the funny man.

At this period, then, indeterminate forms occur in all major sentence functions for the first time, and extend over into negative sentences.

The child's rule persists even when his utterance is based on his mother's previous one, as we have shown. The child then clearly is constructing (and in this case reconstructing) according to his internalized system of rules. What is the nature of the simplification? For the negative sentences he has produced, what is missing is the relationship between negative formant and pure indefinite *any* forms. The simplification eliminates an entire set of rules from consideration. Notice, before we continue, that the two sentences communicate equally effectively—there is nothing semantically missing in the message. The child's sentence *I don't want some supper* is fully specified semantically and lacks only the appropriate adjustment of *some* to *any* following a negated auxiliary verb. What is required is the addition of a rule (or rules) which relates the shape of indeterminate forms to the occurrence and location of a negative formant.

If we look at the system in Period E, 9 months later, we find that there has been a wholesale replacement of the child's rules by another system of regularities. The mother's sentences are formed as before; but the child's system is quite different. Here is a sample of Adam's negative sentences in Period E:

Adam's Negative Sentences. Period E

> I'm not scared of nothing.
> He's not doing nothing but standing still.
> Little puppies can't bite no one, right?
> Don't never leave your chair.
> Don't let him cut none of mines.
> He can't have nothing.
> He never had no turn in that.
> I never have none.

We notice that the child has replaced the indeterminate *some* forms from before with negative forms in a negative sentence wherever applicable. During the time that we were observing, mothers rarely corrected their children explicitly on matters of grammar. The mother did, however, sometimes repeat what the child said, and make the grammatical adjustments necessary to change the child's sentence to a well-formed adult English sentence. During the period we have been discussing (Period E) there were five such interchanges, presented below. Perhaps the most interesting aspect of these interchanges is that they produced no effect whatsoever on the child's system. In these samples, and for many months afterward, multiple negation persisted in the children's speech.

Mother's Corrected Repetitions of Adam's Sentences

Adam	Mother
I can't punch no more.	You can't punch any more?
I don't have no more.	You don't have any more?
I don't want no people to recognize me.	You don't want anyone to recognize you?
Have no paint on.	It doesn't have any paint on?

In each case, the mother repeats what the child says, but with syntactic changes in the direction of the adult system. Perhaps the most interesting aspect of these interchanges is that in no case did the child change his rules to accord with his mother's "correction". The child's system seems quite impervious to this gentle prod towards grammaticality. Sometimes his next production followed immediately after one of her well-formed sentences. For example:

Child: Have no paint on.
Mother: It doesn't have any paint on?
Child: I didn't put no paint on.

Mother: You don't have any more flats.
Child: I don't have no flat tire.

McNeill (1966a) reports an even more dramatic case with another child where correction was direct and pointed:

Child: Nobody don't like me.
Mother: No, say, "Nobody likes me".
Child: Nobody don't like me.
    (eight repetitions of this dialogue)
Mother: No, now listen carefully; say, "Nobody likes me".
Child: Oh, nobody don't likes me.

This resistance to correction of the children's system is certainly worth further study. It does not seem to be the case that there is much external pressure for change in our samples, but even when it occurs the child's own rule system is relatively impervious. Eventually, of course, the child's system does change, and in the direction of the adult model.

We might point out some other implications of these interchanges. In the previous period we had examples of the child repeating at least portions of the mother's negative sentence but filtered through his own rule system. In this period we find the same phenomena. The mother's sentences are formed by a consistent set of rules; the child's sentences reflect his changed internalized grammar. As his system changes, it is reflected in these near "imitations" of the mother's sentences.

Period C

> Mother: Then you wouldn't have anymore Ursula.
> Child: Why I don't have some more Ursula?

Period E

> Mother: You don't have anymore flats.
> Child: I don't have no flat tire.

What type of simplification is represented here by the child's grammar? We need to look at a further set of sentences produced by the child. So far, it may seem that the child has an alternative rule, not a simplification of rules. That is, wherever in a negative sentence we would use a pure indefinite form, he uses a negative pronoun or adverb instead. But the problem is further clarified if we look specifically at the child's sentences which *begin* with some negative pronoun or adverb:

> No one's not going to do what I'm doing.
> No one can't even find me.
> Nothing won't scare me.
> He never won't scare me.
> But nobody wasn't gonna know it.

Now it becomes clear in what sense the child's system is a simplification and not just an alternate route. He accomplishes in one rule (colour indeterminates negative everywhere in context of negative sentence) what must be presumed to be a more complex set of interlocking rules in the adult language. It is, however, more complicated than in the preceding stage where the occurrence of indeterminate (*some*) forms in a negative sentence did not affect their shape. Here there is clearly a dependency relationship in a structural system between a negative in a sentence and the indeterminate forms which occur in various grammatical functions: subject, object, adverbial, modifier. It is, however, a less complex relationship than that required for the correct generation of English sentences. Its simplicity lies in substituting one rule for several rules which have special locational restrictions and optional routes.

CASE MARKING IN PERSONAL PRONOUNS

The development of case marking in children's language has not yet been studied in detail. We will consider here only one aspect, which occurred in the children's speech in an immature form and persisted over a rather long period of time. Noun-phrases which contained at least one pronoun and were joined with *and* were produced in a number of grammatical functions; the pronoun was nearly always first person reference, and invariably in objective case. Thus, Adam asked *Can me and Paul share?* and said *That me and everybody's colour.* We will look at this structure first from the point of view of self-reference in the adult grammar, and then developmentally in the children's language.

The class of personal pronouns has been called "shifters" because the reference changes with the person speaking. We will not deal here with this aspect of the problem, but another which is intricately tied with syntactic processes. Assuming that a child has developed a notion of self-reference in his own speech and that of others, it is still the case that this reference changes in form depending upon its logical grammatical function in the sentence. If *X* means self-reference, notice the changing forms we fill in in the following sentences:

    (a) *X* see him.
    (b) He sees *X*.
    (c) *X* sees *X*.

In (a) we fill in *I*, in (b) instead *me*, and in (c) with two variables, first *I*, and then *myself*. We notice that *I* directly precedes the verb, is the subject, and is sentence initial in these examples, but this is not always true. *I* occurs within utterance boundaries in sentences like *She asked if I could go*; as grammatical subject in sentences like *I was hit by the car*, and precedes non-verbs in *I who was alone asked him*. The objective form *me* occurs before verbs in a number of structures, as in *He made me do it*, and *Everybody but me tried it*. No simple straightforward analysis of positional elements in adult English, then, will be adequate to determine the occurrence of *I*, *me*, *myself*, in various utterances. A number of grammatical rules intervene between assignment of case and the final position in the superficial structure of an utterance.

Let us look at the development of this phenomena in child language. Because this has not been outlined in previous reports, we will include a glance backward at the early stages before looking at later syntactic regularities in the child's mastery of this aspect of the grammar.

Period A. In the early stages, there were at first no occurrences of an accusative case pronoun *me*. Self-reference was by way of *I* as sentence initial, and much more frequently the use of the child's name in various positions. Occasionally, both name and pronoun appeared in the same sentence.

I like hit.
I laughing.
I Adam like that.
Adam home.
Adam painting.
Like Adam bookshelf.
That Adam.
Pick Adam up.

Period B. A few months later, the use of the child's name as self-reference had nearly disappeared. The child's sentences were still quite simple. *I* was used by the child in initial position, and *me* when the self-reference was within the utterance boundary.

"I" in Declarative Sentences

I like drink it.   I here.
I give him kiss.   I making coffee.

"Me" in Declarative Sentences

It's for me.   Wake me up.
One for me.   Don't leave me.

This set of sentences is apparently correct according to the adult model. However, self-reference also appeared in *wh-* questions, and we note that the form is consistently *me* whether in subject or object function.

Wh- Questions: Object Function

Why you waking me up?
Why you knocking me off?
What funny about me?
Why laughing at me?

Wh- Questions: Subject Function

Why me spilled it?   Why not me careful?
When me want it?   Why not me can't dance?
Why me going?   Why not me get hit?
Why me break it?   Why not me sleeping?
Where me sleep?

This suggests the possibility that the base form of the pronoun for self-reference at this period is *me*, and that when sentence initial, it is marked for nominative and becomes *I*. The child's hypothesis follows general statistical regularities in the language he hears. The self-reference *I* is far more frequent at the beginning of sentences than internal to sentences, and *me* does not occur as sentence initial except in non-sentential responses, as *me too*. We are excluding here vocatives, rejoinders, exclamations as part of the basic sentence structure. We find in the child's speech, *Mommy, I want that*, or *Yep, I do it*.

What of the systematic regularities of self-reference in *wh-* questions? Often the child's questions are based on previous statements of the mother. The mother makes an utterance or explanation and the child creates a question based on this utterance. Brown (1968) outlines discourse relations for these questions in consecutive utterances.

Discourse Relations for Why and Why Not Questions

Adult	*Adam*
Because you are not sleeping.	Why not me sleeping
Because you aren't careful.	Why not me careful?
I think you broke it.	Why me break it?
You got some chocolate on it.	Why me get some chocolate?

The child in constructing his question transposes *you* to self-reference; but the self-reference is not initial in the question, and does not occur in nominative form. Instead we find: *Why me break it?*

Period C. By 3 years, or at the 3·5 mean utterance length level, which has been the starting point for the rest of the discussion, there is a general change in the child's system. Now there are some complex sentences and auxiliary inversion in *yes/no* questions. The immature structures from the previous period no longer occur. Here are some occurrences at Period C of nominative self-reference which does not occur at the beginning of the sentence.

I used to wear that when I little baby.
All those I got to play.
When it gets dark I can keep this.
That what I do.
Can I help open it?
Can I put them on when I go outside?
What I play with?
Why I can keep them?

We may infer that the child no longer uses a positional hypothesis based only on occurrence of self-reference initially in the sentence.

Period D. By Period D we find still more complex sentences, and the correct underlying application of nominative to logical subject. In addition we find the first use of reflexive pronouns, somewhat over-extended at first, and not confined to reference back to the subject of a proposition.

Reflexives

I hope so myself too.
One for myself.
It's myself.
Who broke it? Myself or you?

We also find the occurrence of conjoined parallel sentences, with appropriately nominative subject markings.

Conjoined Parallel Sentences

He going in and I going in too.
You push one and I push one.
You have some and I have some.
You got your spears and I got my spears.

There are the structures that would permit "gapping" or conjoining in various ways. One way is as follows:

Possible Conjoined Sentence in English

He and I going in.
You and I have some.
You and I got spears.

It is the occurrence of these conjoined noun-phrase structures that we will turn to next. There are no such occurrences (that is, with pronouns) until beyond Period E, when the child is 4 years old.

Period E and beyond. Between 4 and 5 years of age, we find the first occurrence of conjoined pronouns in the child's utterances. We have noticed that self-reference is appropriately marked for nominative for some time before this, even when the relationship of grammatical function and the position in the surface structure of the sentence has become quite indirect. The relationship of nominative case marking and the positioning of elements in the surface structure has now become more indirect than before, as more rules intervene between location of grammatical function and the final shape of the sentence.

In addition to more complex occurrence of *I* in non-initial position:

Can I keep this if she says I can?, we find the following indicators of
the relatively deep assignment of case marking:

I; in utterance final position:
> Where were I?
> Got lots of them, don't I?

I; not directly preceding verb:
> He say I better not do it.
> What did I almost run into?

Me; directly preceding verb:
> Watch me do it again.
> Ursula let me share her paper.

Other accusative case pronouns preceding verbs:
> All of them did.
> Now I know all of them are the same size.
> Leave him standing.
> I hear him crying.
> I didn't have her make any.

By this period many rules must intervene between case marking and the
ultimate string of formatives—adverb placement, negative placement,
interrogative inversion, among others. Assignment of case marking is at
a relatively deep level of abstraction in the grammar and not dependent
on the position of the pronoun in the surface structure of the sentence.

When combined noun-phrases begin to occur, the shape of the structure is quite consistent. The pronoun is in the accusative case regardless
of the grammatical function it serves.

Conjoined noun-phrases with a pronoun in Adam's speech:
> Me and Paul have string, huh?
> Me and Robin are friends.
> Were me and Paul there?
> He wants to do everything that me and Robin do.
> Can me and him play with this?

The examples given are in subject function. There were also sentences
like *That's for me and Robin, One for me and Paul, She gonna take a
picture of you and me.*

In terms of corrections and frequencies in the mother's speech, these
constructions occupied a unique place. In 52 hours of mother–child

interchange, there was not one example that could have been a model for these constructions. The mother used conjoined noun-phrases, but the pronouns were limited to *you* which does not have different forms for nominative and accusative. The mother occasionally repeated the child's sentence; but because these personal pronouns are "shifters" the interchange did not function as a correction.

Adam: Can me and Robin share?
Mother: Yes, you and Robin can share.

For these constructions on the part of the child, in terms of our records, there is no model in the mother's speech, and the child's utterance is never an imitation of an adult sentence. We can certainly say that in terms of input data, the construction seems grossly under-determined.

Notice the change in form of the verb which occurs when we conjoin the subject noun-phrases of two singular sentences:

John *works*
Paul *works* $\Big\}$ John and Paul *work*.

When sentences are combined by way of conjoining subject noun-phrases, the singular verbs combine to a plural verb form, although each noun-phrase retains its singular status. This suggests, as a description of the child's rule, a plural noun-phrase node in the phrase structure which has a plural marker. This special noun-phrase could also in general account for the occurrence of sentences like *Me and Robin are friends* where presumably there is no underlying form *I am a friend*, *He is a friend*, or *John and Mary met*, where there is no corresponding *John met*, and *Mary met*. We note that in the child's sentences the requirement of plurality is always met, as in *Me and Diandros are working, aren't we?*

Most of the conjoined noun-phrases in these sentences have the form "self-reference and Y" where "Y" is a proper name. It is plausible that the location of the pronoun and its separation from the verb promote the lack of nominative form. We have already made many arguments against this notion in the rest of the child's grammar; there are additional examples within this set which argue against this interpretation. In *Me and him are drum makers* and *Can me and him play with this?* one of the pronouns is adjacent to the verb and still in the accusative case. In *Me and Diandros are working, aren't we?* and *Could we have juice, me and Ursula?* the conjoined pronoun is related to its substitute pronoun in the nominative case, *we*. It seems appropriate to suggest then that we can describe the child's speech by considering noun-phrase conjoining as a part of the deep structure of the sentence. It would seem that nominative case marking does not yet apply to this type of noun-phrase.

In terms of the general progression of case marking in first person reference, we have seen the following steps:

Development of Case Marking Personal Pronouns

Period A

I like hit.	Self-reference is *I* in sentence
Adam painting.	initial position and child's name
Pick Adam up.	in any position.

Period B

I here.	*Me* within utterance boundary;
Wake me up.	*I* when sentence initial (excluding
Why you waking me up?	vocative rejoinder, but not *wh-*
Where me sleep?	interrogative as part of sentence).

Period C

That what I do.	First person pronoun marked for
Can I close it?	nominative if located before
What I laughing about?	finite verb, otherwise *me*.

Period D

He going in and I going in too.	More direct relation between case marking and final position in
One for myself.	string; first occurrence of reflexives; conjoined sentences without "gapping".

Period E and Beyond

I never eat it.	Subject function pronouns
Where were I?	marked for nominative
All of them did it.	regardless of position unless part
Me and Robin are friends.	of conjoined noun-phrase. Many
Me and him are drum makers.	rules intervene between case marking and final form of sentence.

By this interpretation the language system develops in the child by ever increasing (and sometimes over-increasing) conditions on the applicability of rules. We suggest that we may consider that the base form of *I/me* self-reference is *me* (since this is the direction of intrusion of errors in the child's speech). In a growing set of environments, this base form is marked for nominative. At first a positional interpretation is adequate, i.e. first person pronoun is marked for nominative if initial in sentence; then it is nominative if initial in sentence, excluding rejoinders, vocatives, adverbials. Later first person pronoun is marked for nominative when it precedes tense (a finite verb). Gradually the relation becomes more complex as more rules intervene between case marking and the surface form of the sentence. The positional interpretation no longer holds as adverbs intervene (*I always do it*); a complex noun-phrase can promote accusative case (*All of them did it*); interrogative inversion comes after case marking (*Where am I?*), etc.

At the latest stage discussed, first person pronouns may be considered as marked for nominative everywhere as in the adult grammar, at a relatively abstract level. There is still an exception: when self-reference occurs in conjoined noun-phrases, the accusative form still prevails.

DISCUSSION

We can now make some tentative suggestions about children's simplifications of the rules of language. We find in general that the order of emergence of certain types of structures is remarkably similar across children who have heard different sets of sentences as input. We find, moreover, that the same types of "immature" forms or transient hypotheses occur across children during periods of the language-learning process. The children's sentences are not directly modelled on the speech the children hear, at least in the data we collected. They occur rather consistently over a period of time, and are subject to change, as the child's system changes. Thus, the children seem to develop similar autonomous systems, independent in certain ways from the language of the adult community.

When changes in these systems occur, they are in sets of structures, rather than in patterns of individual sentences. The structures represented here seem to be rather impervious to attempts at correction by the adult. The changes in children's language at various periods seem to be quite general and systematic. Sometimes the change is to another type of simplification, still not giving rise to sentences like those the child hears. These developments are not directly predictable from the input data.

It seems that the child extracts regularities from the speech he hears, and that the sentences he produces are more like reconstruction than

E

imitation. We have presented a number of examples in which the mother asserts something, and the child repeats it. The child does not reproduce exactly what the mother said, however, but rather produces his *reconstruction* of what was said. It is as if the input sentence were processed by the child, and then reconstructed according to his own rules.

Beyond these general remarks on mechanisms of development, we have made an attempt to characterize a few of the linguistic dimensions in terms of types of simplifications, which might underlie the regularities we find in children's speech. We have made several tentative suggestions about the characteristics of children's simplifications.

Auxiliary Inversion in Questions

Perhaps there is a limit on the permitted complexity of a string at this period which may account for the lack of inversion of auxiliary verb and noun-phrase subject. This may represent a performance limit, since the operations presumably involved seem to be part of the children's linguistic competence at this period.

Negatives and Indefinites

In the children's early sentences with indeterminates (*some*), the form did not change from affirmative to negative sentences. In adult English, sentential negation (auxiliary plus negative) would promote a change to indeterminate (*any*) forms in a sentence. The child omits the dependency relationship required by the language and produces both *I want some* and *I don't want some*. In later versions of sentences with indeterminate forms, there is a layer of negative colouring in the child's negative sentences. This is in place of the complex set of restrictions on location of the negative and indefinite forms which are a part of the underlying grammatical regularities of standard adult English. The child's system seems to substitute one general rule for a set of several interdependent rules.

Case Marking in Personal Pronouns

We have outlined the history of case marking for pronouns (nominative and accusative cases). The accusative form: *me* occurs in all but one context at first; when self-reference is first in the sentence. Then we find marking for nominative: *I* in an increasing number of environments. The case marking appears to be based largely on position in the surface structure in the early stages. Later, as more rules intervene, case marking is based on grammatical/logical function in the underlying structure.

In general terms we are interested in the child's analysis and synthesis of the underlying grammatical regularities of language. It is this capacity to reconstitute or reconstruct a complex underlying system of rules from the language around him, that basically characterizes the remarkable achievement of the child during the period of language acquisition.

Discussion

BELLUGI: The interesting thing about repetition is that even when the utterance is so short that you could expect an exact repetition, what you actually get in a child's utterance is some sort of reliance on basic rules. Our material was not gained through formal experimental situations— most of it was spontaneous. But even at the age of 5 or 6 we found that to ask for a repetition was an excellent way of confirming something which was found in spontaneous production. When we asked for a repetition of a passive, for instance, what we got back reflected the child's own linguistic system, at each particular stage.

ERVIN-TRIPP: I rather like the notion you have about the difficulty of applying several rules at once; but there is one problem about it, it would leave you unable to predict which of the things will not be performed—unless you have some kind of complexity notion about the particular operations that are being combined.

CHURCH: It seems to me that the phenomena you have described here represent the child's problems in learning the rules of redundancy in English. I can't help wondering if the two things you describe, with respect to interrogation and negation, occur simultaneously or occur maybe in sequence. It sounds to me as if it is at least hypothetically possible that the child first learns that a single feature will discriminate between declarative and interrogative, or that a single feature will discriminate between affirmation and negation, so that the difference between *Will he play with me?* and *What will he play with?* sounds as though he has found a single feature that will transform the sentence from a statement to a question and that does the job for him. Then, when it comes to negation, it looks as though he's piling on the redundancies, *Nobody don't want do nothing with no string.* In these two cases he seems to be following quite different principles. On the one hand a single feature will do to draw the distinction, on the other you need a whole lot of features to be correct. So I wonder if these things appear simultaneously or whether, in fact, they come at different stages in the child's development. If I had to guess, I would guess that the need for a lot of redundancy would come later than the need for a single feature that could draw the discrimination. This is something that I just don't know, and I wonder if your data showed anything. Maybe here a French–English comparison would be helpful. Of course in English negation you generally get by with one feature; in French you almost invariably need two. Does the child begin by saying "je + ne + vais" and does it take him a while for him to say "je + ne + vais + pas"?

SINCLAIR: In colloquial French the *ne* disappears; now even adults say *je vais pas*.

BEVER: What about children?

SINCLAIR: Children don't use *ne*, just the *pas*, since it has disappeared in adult speech.

ERVIN-TRIPP: Is there any evidence that what happens in memory is different depending on what you ask the child to do? For example, you ask him to imitate a sentence and then try to find out whether he could understand it. That is, is understanding concomitant with imitation? If you ask a child to comprehend, what happens about the loss of information that would be necessary in order to imitate? So do you set him, in a sense, to attend to different features of the input depending on what you ask him to do?

MEHLER: I think children always imitate idiosyncratically. If you give them a sentence they spontaneously transform it very much in the way that Ursula Bellugi has been telling us about. There will be inversions of order, there will be elements that drop out and there will be shortening of the sentences. But comprehension precedes correct production; even when they do things like that in production, they may very well understand the sentence.

On the other hand there are many ways of forcing production. Mme. de Bardies and I are trying out a new method. We have pictures, for instance, of a little girl and a dog. If we put the picture of the girl down first and then the dog, and ask the child to produce a sentence, we get: *The girl is carrying the dog*. But if we put down the dog first, we get: *A dog*. And then if we put down the picture of the girl, the child has really only one way out, he must produce a passive sentence: *The dog is being carried by the girl*. This is a method of persuading a child to use certain forms which one might not find in spontaneous utterances.

E. INGRAM: If the child has seen the girl first in a previous experiment and then you show him the dog, what happens?

MEHLER: Then you would get: *The girl carries the dog*.

E. INGRAM: What happens if you put the dog down first and the child doesn't have the means to use the passive productively, what do you get?

MEHLER: Then what you'd get would be the repetition: *The dog, the girl is carrying the dog.*

SINCLAIR: In one of our experiments where children were asked to start their description of an event by naming the patient, we also get that formulation. But depending on the age of the child, we also get expressions like *the dog and the girl are walking together* or *the dog is there and it is the girl who is pulling him along* or *the dog gets pulled by the girl.*

Sensorimotor Action Patterns as a Condition for the Acquisition of Syntax

HERMINE SINCLAIR

Ecole de Psychologie, Université de Genève

IN PSYCHOLINGUISTICS, as in other fields, the issue of empiricism against rationalism has once again become the topic of many controversies. Though the title of this paper might seem to indicate a plea for empiricism, this is not the case; rather it is a plea for an intermediate position as outlined in Jean Piaget's epistemology. In fact, Piaget has for many years argued against the restrictive choice between rationalism (a structuralism without active construction by the subject) and empiricism (the assumption of acquisition processes without structures). His proposal of a third possibility is nearer to the rationalist than to the empiricist hypothesis, since it involves innate functioning; but it does not presuppose innate structures with biogenetic programming. Every structure comes from a simpler structure, and it is possible to go back not only to reflex mechanisms, but to spontaneous movements of the organism from which reflexes stem as stabilized differentiations, and perhaps even further back. Piaget's point of departure for his study of intelligent functioning is what he calls *co-ordination of actions.*

Elementary co-ordinations of actions have functional properties: a behaviour pattern has a tendency to repeat itself and to extend to new objects: the new-born baby sucks the breast, and the sucking scheme[1] will repeat itself on other objects: his thumb, blanket etc. This Piaget calls *assimilation* and it is the cause of the establishment of new relationships and correspondences. Assimilation of new objects into the action scheme goes together with a differentiation of the action: this is called *accommodation* to the new object. The baby does not suck his thumb in exactly the same way as he sucks the breast; moreover, thumb sucking necessitates a bringing together of hand and mouth.

[1] For an account of Piaget's theory and terminology see Flavell (1963). (Editors' footnote.)

Elementary co-ordinations also have structural properties: even in a reflex there is an ordering of movements, as there is in an acquired movement, or at a later stage, in the attaining of a goal. There is also a hierarchical subordination, e.g. the touching and then the grasping of an object are subordinated to pulling the object towards one. The co-ordinations of actions are continuously subject to adjustment and at the end of the sensorimotor period, i.e. before the semiotic function permits the representation of objects and events in their absence, they result in action structures that are the beginnings of later thought structures. A gradual, oriented development takes place through active interaction between subject and environment. Similar views are held by present-day biologists and ethologists. Biologically, the organism does not develop in a strictly pre-programmed way, nor is it passively submitted to the influence of environment; there is a constant interaction and, most importantly, there are endogenous self-regulatory mechanisms which assure the organism's adaptation. Ethological studies have made it clear that evolution in behaviour can only be understood by taking into account the total environment in which the animal lives. In particular, animal communication systems have to be studied in the context of their adaptation to the biological needs of the species and to the requirements of their habitat.

Matters are no doubt immensely more complex for human beings, who have emotional, social and cognitive needs as well as physiological ones; but it seems reasonable to suppose that their communication system is also adapted to these needs. Consequently, since modes of interaction with the environment change as the infant grows up, it would seem artificial, to say the least, to ignore them in the study of the acquisition of language. Rationalist psycholinguists tend to make a cut between subject and environment, just as they make a cut between competence and performance, the former being, at least partly, innate, and the latter subject to external influences. For example, according to J. Katz (1966), the full set of linguistic universals is part of the genetic endowment of human beings. He argues as follows (p. 271):

"We cannot assume that the presence of some feature in every natural language is merely an accidental correlation. . . . We must find something in the context in which natural languages are acquired which is invariant from one such context to another and can plausibly be regarded as the *causal antecedent* for the existence of common features in different natural languages. (Accordingly, we ignore such invariants as the fact that all speakers of natural languages live close to the earth's surface, that all breathe air, that all walk on two legs, etc., since these invariants cannot plausibly count as causally sufficient for the acquisition of a natural language.) This context includes, besides a non-verbal infant and fluent speakers of a natural language speaking their language, geographical, cultural, psychological, and sociological factors."

Katz goes on to argue that no environmental factor is invariably present wherever natural languages are spoken. There is no cross-community regularity in psychology, sociology and anthropology. Child-rearing patterns, rituals, social structure etc. differ greatly from one culture to another. Thus, concludes Katz, the one constant feature amid all the differences is the common innate endowment of human language speakers. This last point is where a Piagetian psychologist disagrees. Far from there being no common psychological factor, the basic functions and structures of human intelligence, from the practical sensorimotor intelligence to the later concrete operations of thought, are universally present among human beings who do not suffer from severe mental defect. Wherever Piaget's tests for operational thought have been applied, exactly the same structures with exactly the same succession of stages have been found. (This does not mean that the time at which they appear is necessarily the same in every culture, or necessarily the same for every individual in a given culture.)

Our contention would be (a) that the infant brings to his language acquisition task not a set of innate linguistic universals, but innate cognitive functions which will ultimately result in universal structures of thought; (b) that linguistic universals exist precisely *because* of the universal thought structures—and these are universal, not because they are inborn but because they are the necessary outcome of auto-regulatory factors and equilibration processes; (c) that since intelligence exists phylogenetically and ontogenetically before language, and since the acquisition of linguistic structures is a cognitive activity, cognitive structures should be used to explain language acquisition rather than vice versa.

What are the cognitive acquisitions which the infant has made before he utters the first sound-combinations which are meaningful in the sense of communication by language? And in what way has the infant changed cognitively, emotionally and socially, so that he begins to need language? Among the acquisitions referred to in the first question there should be a set of structures and functions to account for the linguistic output (in comprehension as well as in production) at that period. In other words, the child must possess cognitive structures which make it possible for him to assimilate the base rules, since it can be assumed that much of the structure of the base is common to all languages. The second question refers more to the dynamics than to the structural properties of the child's behaviour. What pushes him at a certain time to begin to use language which resembles adult language and which can be interpreted as having a meaning?

We usually take language proper to start when a fair proportion of the child's utterances can be interpreted meaningfully, usually at about 15–18 months. But obviously before this there has been a long preparatory babbling stage, during which the child has acquired many of the phonetic and melodic characteristics of his mother tongue. Well before the first "meanings" become clear, the infant can produce many speech sounds and is able to imitate words. Why does he not use language to communicate at this stage? Once again, the explanation should be sought in the total development of the baby. He has gone well beyond the elementary co-ordinations of actions. He can differentiate between goals and means: that is to say, no longer does the sight of an object simply trigger an action scheme; when he wants something, he will execute a series of ordered actions which enable him to do what he wants with the object he wants. According to Piaget, two structural elements underlie the achievements of the sensorimotor period:

(a) a first "group-structure" of *spatial displacements*: the child can come and go in his familiar environment, returning to his point of departure, and he can make detours, realizing that the same point can be reached by different paths;
(b) *object permanence:* objects no longer cease to exist when they disappear from the visual field, and the infant can find an object again if it is hidden in various places while he is watching. Object permanence is the invariant which underlies the group-like structure.

The child now lives in a world where he is an active person, distinct from the objects he acts upon; and he is now ready to become "a knower of things", as well as "an actor on things".

At this point, an important new feature manifests itself: the beginnings of the semiotic function. So far, his cognitive discoveries were directed only towards practical success, and involved immediate action; from about 18 months onwards, we observe problem solutions which are prior to actually carrying out the act, which implies the ability to represent reality mentally, to recapitulate actions in the past, and to anticipate actions in the future. A good example of such a problem solution is given by the following observation (J. Piaget, 1946):

"Jacqueline, at 1:8, arrives at a closed door—with a blade of grass in each hand. She stretches out her right hand towards the door knob but sees that she cannot turn it without letting go of the grass. She puts the grass on the floor, opens the door, picks up the grass again and enters. But when she wants to leave the room, things become complicated. She puts the grass on the floor and grasps the doorknob. But then she perceives that in pulling the door towards her she will simultaneously push away the grass which she placed between the door and the threshold. She therefore picks it up in order to put it outside the door's zone of movement" (Flavell's translation).

She had represented to herself a picture of what would actuall happen when she opened the door.

In another case a child was actually seen to perform a motor act of representation. Lucienne (1:4) had been playing with Piaget who put a small chain inside a matchbox which was half closed. Lucienne, who had already practised filling and emptying pails and other receptacles, had no difficulty in retrieving the chain either by turning the box over, or by poking a finger into the box. Piaget then made the opening so small that the chain did not fall out, and Lucienne could not get her finger into it. As she was manipulating the box, she suddenly stopped, then she opened and shut her mouth several times, at first slightly, then wider and wider and then suddenly, she pushed the box open. Piaget sees this as an example not of verbal symbolism but of motor symbolism; a representation of an act by a movement which is not part of the act.

During this same period, an affective development takes place which is in many ways parallel to the cognitive development. Without going into details, the infant's relationship to persons and things changes from a state of not differentiating between the self and the environment to a differentiation which allows, and calls for, communication rather than contact. The comparatively late start of language proper has to be seen in the light of this development. Many cognitive discoveries have taken place, and the child (of one and a half years) is already so clever in dealing with his environment that it may well seem surprising that it is still impossible to teach him "to talk". However, his cognitive acts are, as we have said, only directed by the search for success, and limited to the immediate present. From the point of view of communication, affective states linked to the outcome of his acts are what the baby wants to communicate, or can communicate, and not cognitive acts as such, on which he cannot yet reflect. It need not surprise us then that the aspects of adult language which express affective states—stress, melody, intensity, duration—are already present in his language. These non-segmental features have already been interiorized by imitation before the first discrete, meaning-bearing elements occur. Non-vocal means of expression are, of course, also used.

Thus it is not until the beginnings of the semiotic function appear, as seen in the use of motor-symbolizers (Lucienne) and in symbolic play (where one object can stand for another, and where sounds are imitated), that language can begin to play the role of a semiotic system which represents reality. This system is in a sense ready made, but obviously the child cannot use it immediately. Once again, we have to take into account his total development: the child will use language to express *his* reality, he will construct verbal expressions according to *his* needs (cognitive and social); moreover, to process the data of the ready-made system, he can only use the operative patterns he already possesses; in other words, he will reconstruct the input according to *his* cognitive capacities. The human communication system is not, as is the case for certain animal communication systems, immediately present, but it will be slowly built up to fulfil its function, that is, to represent and communicate events and thoughts in the language of the community.

It seems evident that if we assume the child of one and a half years old to have acquired no more than what associationist psychology credits him with, that is to say, an unorganized conglomerate of habits and bits of learning, then there is no way out but to introduce innate linguistic structures in order to explain his language acquisition. But the achievements of sensorimotor intelligence may provide the infant with just those cognitive structures that allow language acquisition. Moreover, functionally speaking, at this point the child's cognitive and affective needs require the use of objective, communicable signifiers.

Speaking in a general and theoretical way, it is possible to show the similarity between Piaget's descriptions of sensorimotor structure and Chomsky's description (1965) of deep structure. The child at this stage can order, temporally and spatially; he can classify in action, that is to say, he can use a whole category of objects for the same action, or apply a whole category of action-schemes to one object; and he can relate objects and actions to actions. The linguistic equivalents of these structures are concatenation, categorization, i.e. the major categories (S, NP, VP etc.) and functional grammatical relation (subject of, object of, etc.). These are the main operations of the base of the syntactic component which characterizes a highly restricted set of elementary structures from which actual sentences are constructed by transformational rules. Finally, these base rules have a particular formal property, namely that they may introduce the initial symbol S (sentence) into a line of derivation, so that phrase-markers can be inserted into other base phrase-markers. A psychological parallel to this so-called recursive property of the base can be found in the embedding of action-schemes one into the other, when the child can put one action pattern into another pattern. This can be traced back to the simple circular reactions of a much earlier stage.

Let us stress that with such parallels between linguistic theory and psychological theory there is no question of treating generative grammar as a performance model. All that is being argued is that the child possesses a set of co-ordinations of action-schemes which can be shown to have certain structural properties which will make it possible for him to start comprehending and producing language. These same structural properties will later develop into the interiorized logical operations.

In the light of these theoretical speculations, what actually happens when a child says its first recognizable "word" in a meaningful way? To take another of Piaget's examples (1946), Laurent, at the age of 17 months, says *aplu*—which first means somebody's departure, then the act of throwing something on to the floor, then the fall of an object, then the game of handing over a toy and getting it back from the other person, and finally, at 19 months, it simply means "to start over again". What is new in this kind of behaviour? And why does it happen? Until now, gestures, mimicry, pointing, crying, moaning, crooning and babbling were sufficient for his needs; the persons around him reacted adequately. He himself also reacted to the sounds and gestures made by his family, and seemed to interpret them as signalling wishes, approval and disapproval—mainly of himself. But something new happens when he produces the expression *aplu* in an appropriate situation. Before the child can utter *aplu* in a meaningful way, something very important must have happened. When he heard somebody say *il n'y en a plus* or *tu n'en as plus* he understood that this did not refer to an affective state, but to a non-affective, external state of affairs, known to both speaker and hearer. In fact he credited the speaker with an act of symbolization. Without the prior realization that a succession of non-imitative sounds can refer to external reality, the child could not have produced such a meaningful sound sequence, which an adult could understand.

Thus a true symbol (or sign) is produced, which like adult words is conventional and not produced by onomatopoeia (a device he has been using for a long time); but this sign still retains the characteristics of personal symbols in that its meaning is fluid, attached to an action scheme, and that it changes its meaning in the course of the following weeks according to the different assimilations of the action scheme. From now on, the advent of the semiotic function, which has been heralded by imitations of models in their absence, and by symbolic play, will allow rapid development of "vocabulary". The elements of the vocabulary are of two kinds, the one just mentioned, which gives a personal interpretation to parts of adult sentences, and the other kind, words which the child is actually taught by the people around him: *papa*, *maman*, *au revoir*, etc. However, he is not yet putting words together into phrases; *aplu*, though it stems from two adult words, is obviously an indivisible expression. As yet, we cannot speak of syntax. As soon as combinations of two or more "words" appear, matters become complicated. In the first place, there is again the distinction to be made between on the one hand combinations that are almost certainly taught or at least imitated as a whole, like *i va 'nir* (il va venir), and, on the other, combinations that are the result of active construction on the part of the child. It is of course the second kind that we suppose to be made possible by the general co-ordinations of the action patterns of sensorimotor intelligence.

I should like to quote a few examples, all taken from Grégoire (1937) for one child between the ages of 1:10 and 2:0.

boum popote   (said when a door slams shut)
boum sonèt   (said when a bell rings)

It is tempting to suppose that *boum* (or *poum*) is a kind of VP and *popote* and *sonèt* a kind of NP. This is supported by other utterances at the same period, e.g.:

pati bet   (partie, Berthe
pati kème   (partie crème)

But shortly afterwards came

jiji poum   (*jiji* from *lit*; meaning that the child fell from the
                 bed in a kind of game)

Here *poum* occupies a different position, and the meaning is different, it is not the bed that falls, it is the child who falls off the bed. In

se poum bate   (said when a boy falls to the floor)
se poum   (said when the child fell, meaning "I hurt myself")

poum is preceded by *se* which might be assimilated to either *fait* or *c'est*; in either case *poum* seems to have changed to an NP. A new expansion, but still of the same order of an apparent VP followed by an apparent NP, occurs a few days later: *cassé aussi bodome* (*bonhomme:* the little man made of paper is also broken); at the same time we find: *zampe cassé* (lampe), *bodome cassé*, with the order NP–VP. But VP–NP is again noted a little later: *pati pti chfal* (cheval), for example.

The resolution of the difficulties presented by these utterances might be found in the distinction between the surface structure relation, topic/comment, and the deep structure relation, subject/predicate (adopted by Chomsky, 1965). In *boum popote* and *poum bate*, *poum* is the topic, that is, the event which strikes the child, but the deep structure subject is still *popote* and *bate*, and *poum* is the predicate.

Another point raised by these utterances touches also on categories and functions: the examples cited seem to suggest that relations are more fundamental than categories, in fact, that relations direct the assigning of words to categories rather than the other way round. From the point of view of cognitive development, this is not surprising (see J. Piaget *et al.*, 1968), but from the standpoint of linguistic theory it may be doubtful. However, it is remarkable that in all the early utterances I have found, none seem to express only the pseudo-grammatical relation subject/object; whenever two NP's are linked together, the relation is that of possession, like the "*jiji maman*" (*le lit de manan*), used in a deictic way. Relations are there from the beginning, and no pseudo-relations need to be explained away.

In conclusion, it seems that there is a remarkable convergence between the types of base rules as described and formalized by Chomsky (1965) and the types of sensorimotor co-ordinations and later pre-operational structures as described and formalized by Piaget (1947 and 1936). In particular, "recursiveness" as the basic factor that explains the potentiality of producing infinite number of utterances from a finite set of rules, i.e. the creative aspect of language, has deep-rooted psychological parallels in the very early circular reactions and the embedding of schemes to which they lead. The new formulation of the concept of transformational rules within the framework of generative grammar has made the parallel much closer than it was before. Finally, the introduction of the principle, formulated by Katz and Postal (1964), that transformations do not affect the meaning relations of the base components, which are thus invariant, adds an important link with psychology, since it supposes an invariant for the system of transformational rules. One of the most important acquisitions of the sensorimotor period, inextricably linked with the structures we have discussed, is precisely a first invariant, namely the permanency of the object.

Discussion

CAZDEN: I have two questions. Am I correct in gathering that you are using the term "imitation" to mean both imitation from a present model, and imitation from something stored in memory, with the model not there?

SINCLAIR: Yes, the latter would be called deferred or delayed imitation.

CAZDEN: Do you have any evidence at all of the role of immediate imitation in language learning? Is new verbal behaviour coming in in this way?

SINCLAIR: I wouldn't know.

FOSS: There is some evidence that in birds which mimic, delayed imitation occurs before immediate imitation.

CAZDEN: Delayed imitation seems to me to be almost a meaningless term, because, in a sense, you can say any new behaviour is delayed imitation. Whenever the child does anything new, can't it be described in that way? Anything that the child says, which is like an adult utterance, could be called delayed imitation!

SINCLAIR: That is really why I took *aplu* as an example, which in itself, of course, is meaningless to an adult. The great difficulty is that at a certain age you get interiorized imitation, so that a child who repeats something 3 hours later may have done some sub-vocal imitations earlier on.

BEVER: We tried one situation for eliciting passives in which the experimenter acted out what was going on with toy animals. We found that between $3\frac{1}{2}$ and 4, when children can understand the passive sentences, they work very hard not to produce them, although they could if pressed. We would for example make an elephant kiss a cow. If we just said: "What happened to the cow?" stressing the semantic object, they would then say: "The cow, the cow, the elephant kissed the cow". In a few cases they produced the passive, but only after we had repeated the experiment with other animals and other actions. With other children we tried to get them to produce passives straight off, but they just wouldn't do it. They would always produce active sentences; but after they had gone through the experiment in which they had been exposed to some passive sentences and seen them acted out or had to act them out themselves, then they would produce a few passives, but very reluctantly.

SINCLAIR: We had quite a few subjects of 6, who said: "Now you're going to ask me to start the sentence with the cow." But round about 5 and 6, we got a whole number of strategies to avoid the passives which also satisfied what we wanted them to do; which was to exchange the agent and the patient.

E. INGRAM: We found, in an informal setting, playing with toys, that there was an enormous fluctuation in the children's ability to use passives. One day the child seems to be able to handle the passive, you think she has got it; the next week it had all gone again.

HUXLEY: Of course it depended very much in that case on the type of verbal material which we were using. Animates as actors were much more easily coped with than inanimates in a passive structure.

SINCLAIR: And it also depends on the types of verbs you were using. Some verbs have far easier passives. Anything which involves an irreversible situation like *breaking* is much more easily understood than *pushing*, for instance, which can work both ways.

MEHLER: I would like to suggest that there are some Piagetian terms which we have used in development for too long. These are sometimes not very helpful, like *accommodation* and *assimilation*, which are too general at this point of the game. They fulfilled an important purpose when Piaget used these terms many years ago, because, in a way, they stressed the biological aspect of the problem of development. Much of the work of Lenneberg can be seen as an improved development of this. But today we won't get anywhere if we use terms which are obscure and difficult to pin down. I would say that it is much more interesting to make errors of commitment; that is, to present a precise model that can mimic the stage of development in more than one dimension and then be wrong in this or that respect. This would be better than to continue to use terms like *assimilation* and *accommodation*. Would you agree with this statement?

SINCLAIR: I agree in the case of language development.

BEVER: What is the general cognitive correlate for the linguistic relation which you referred to; that of *actor-action-object*? I got some of the correlates clear from what you were saying, but this particular one seems to me to be one of the critical characteristics of language and I did not understand what the link is with a cognitive strategy.

SINCLAIR: I'll try to link it up, but I'm not too clear about it in my own mind. First of course, there is the feedback of the baby's own action on something. I think we are all agreed that it exists at an extremely early age. The next steps are still well before language; that is when the child notices and reproduces the effect of one object upon another. For instance, he will tap the table with a stick, he will look at the table and he will do it again. Now he has the stick and the table in relation to each other. If he has two objects he can handle, he will reverse it and make the other one do the tapping, he will perform the action the other way round. This stage represents a step further than the first simple step of his own action on something else. Now he can look at an object and make it perform an action in relation to something else.

BEVER: That is the step that interests me. The first step that you outlined, in which the child bangs things and notices that banging against different things makes different noises, seems to me to be the kind of activity that most young primates indulge in, not just humans. The crucial step seems to me to be the inference which is that somehow the child decides that it is not just that objects have different properties when he does something to them, but that they might in fact do something themselves in an active way. But I don't see what general cognitive properties this follows from, or what the analogue is in Piagetian theory of the conception of a semantic-logical relation like actor-action-object.

SINCLAIR: My idea, more or less, was that *poum popote* was a statement that was partly expressed by onomatopoeia—*poum* is sound echoing sense. The sound is clearly linked to the object that made the sound, and this can be considered as bringing together an object and its effect. I'm not saying that there is direct immediate relationship; but rather that something which seems to develop into a relation between objects, as being agent or patient, can be traced back quite a long way in the baby's behaviour.

BEVER: What you are really saying is that the basic cognitive relation is *cause and effect*, and that this has one manifestation in the child's motor development and another in the notion of actor-action-object. This in itself is a hypothesis, a theory which is not explained by anything that goes before. What exactly do you mean by "trace back"?

SINCLAIR: An example of what might be called "tracing back" is what happens in imitation. One can see how the baby first only imitates when you do a movement which is already in its own repertoire. When he does something, you do it and he then will do it again. A little later he will make a movement he hasn't done yet himself; if you make a new movement, he will be able to imitate that. Still later, he imitates with a slight time lag; that is to say, you may go to the kitchen and you come back and you find that he is doing now what you did before. Next, you find he will imitate something which has gone on quite some time before. Now this is getting further and further away from the direct presence of something to imitate. This seems to be an indication that the baby's capacities for evoking something without it being there are developing. Of course, recognizing is there from the beginning.

BEVER: The capacity for memory, of the sort that you are talking about, evoking something which is not there, already presupposes the capacity for symbolization. You can't remember something unless you have developed the symbolic form for it.

SINCLAIR: Yes, because the symbolization is sought in the imitation.

BEVER: What I am trying to ask you is this: is the change in the capacity for symbolic behaviour emerging from these earlier forms to be taken as an explanation of the symbolic behaviour, or is it the case that symbolic behaviour is viewed as resting on the achievements of these earlier developments, but not explained by them?

SINCLAIR: The latter.

BEVER: That's an innatist hypothesis.

SINCLAIR: Piaget's theory comes much nearer to the innate hypothesis than to the empiricist.

BEVER: I think it is not a question of nearness; that is a nativist hypothesis.

SINCLAIR: Except that the behaviour is not just triggered by good external circumstances, but develops by slow interaction between the subject and his surroundings. That is the only difference.

MEHLER: I know that Bruner's sequence of events, the enactive, the iconic and the symbolic, is not accepted in Geneva as anything real or meaningful. I tend to agree with this, but I really don't understand where your disagreement with his position comes in. It seems to me that you are still trying to translate action into, say, perception, and perception into symbolic systems like language, without saying much about the translating system itself. This is precisely why I do not like Bruner's theoretical position (Bruner, 1966). Isn't this sensorimotor into group structure, and group structure into propositional logic doing essentially the same thing? That is, talking about these disconnected stages and not talking about what makes the translation from one stage into another?

SINCLAIR: The first point where we disagree with Bruner is that he seems to view *change* in symbolization systems as the basic model for cognitive development, whereas we would see the change in symbolization systems—if such change exists—as the *result* of cognitive development. The second point would be that we doubt whether you can see actual stages like enactive, iconic and symbolic because it seems that everybody up to adults may use any one interchangeably.

MEHLER: Bruner doesn't deny that. He says you acquire a new stage by incorporating the old stage and expanding it, say, from the enactive to the iconic: you don't lose the enactive, but you gain the iconic. Let me put the question somewhat differently, without talking about Bruner. Do you think that actions *as such* can become a structuring component of language?

SINCLAIR: Not action, in the sense of having a lot of things to play with, but action in the sense that every baby, having a few things to handle, somehow or other extracts from his actions a kind of pattern. In that sense, yes. But not in the sense of needing a lot of objects to handle.

MEHLER: Yes, but couldn't one look at the reverse way, and say that certain very general rules pre-exist and therefore permit some relations to be extracted from actions? Rather than that actions structure cognitive or linguistic relations? That is the question I am really asking; because you could be led to predict something very false. Imagine a child born with a paralysis or some neurological illness which makes him incapable of moving. Your theory should predict that he would be incapable of thinking or talking.

SINCLAIR: No, that wouldn't be the position at all. At an extreme case where he could only move his eyes and perceive moving objects, you would still have co-ordination of ocular movements and abstraction from the co-ordination. As long as the organism survives there is some kind of feedback and abstraction from action going on. Don't take "action" too literally. This is a very very extreme case, but there is nothing in the theory that would predict that this baby would not go through the same stages as any other child though probably with much more difficulty and much more slowly. But this is totally extreme and totally hypothetical.

MEHLER: But then "action" is being used as a hypothetical construct.

SINCLAIR: No, because "action" is anything that transforms reality. Any action on the part of the subject, with the knee, or the chin, or moving the eyes so that you get a different view, has the ability of transforming reality. Actually, as far as I know, the thalidomide children, who have been followed in Montreal, have been found to go through exactly the same stages as far as object permanency is concerned. What I really want to get across is that it is not the hands that make for the action, but it is anything that can produce transformation of reality.

BEVER: The action simply happens to be, for biological reasons, the first level of expression of a set of internal structures. Although in an epigenetic view it may be necessary to go through this period before developing a symbolic function, it does not *cause* the symbolic function. Bruner's empiricist position, as far as I can understand it, is trying to show that the higher symbolic functions actually follow from the earlier developments. He is making certain very simple empiricist assumptions and not nativist assumptions which is quite a different viewpoint.

Sentence Completion Tasks

INFORMAL TALK

J. MEHLER

Centre Nationale de la Recherche Scientifique, France

IT IS VERY difficult to control sentence production. What we did was to adapt methods of sentence completion for use with the children which have been in use in experimental psychology, with adults, for a number of years. We tried to find methods of tracing the stages of development which children underwent in the task of supplying meaning in sentences. These sentences had the nouns, or the verbs, or both removed. This meant the children had to supply meaning, but in a controlled setting. We have been fairly successful, particularly with one of our methods, and it might be interesting for others to try it out. I will now describe all three of the methods which we attempted.

In one set of experiments, the children were presented with pictures and a message, where white noise replaced some of the semantic content. The children were told that the person speaking the message was on the seashore, which was why the message was somewhat indistinct. We said: "Here is a picture and the person who is on the seashore will tell you something about this picture." In another set of experiments, we used the white noise in the same way but the children were given no picture to help them with the task. In a third set of experiments we used a telephone connected to a tape recorder. The child received a message through the telephone. He was told that the person at the other end of the telephone was near the sea, so some of the words might be made inaudible by the waves. This meant that he would hear something like "The *mm* is being *mm* by the *mm*", if the sentence (before white noise was introduced) had been "the sound is being heard by the man" for instance. Then the child had to tell us what he heard over the telephone. I think the use of the telephone makes the task more realistic and interesting for the children.

137

One of the limitations in eliciting sentence production from children is that it is very difficult to adapt such tasks for 2-year-olds. It just doesn't work; even 3-year-olds sometimes have problems with it. Maybe we could discover some slight modifications which would make the method applicable to even younger children, but the data we have so far start at 3:6 years or 3:7 years at the earliest.

I will first describe the experiments in which the children were presented with pictures and sentences with white noise. For the first sentence, "Les *mm mm*", the child sees a picture of two rabbits running. For the second, "La *mm* est *mm*" he sees a coloured car. For the third, "La *mm* donne des *mm*", a fruit tree bearing some fruit. For the fourth "C'est la *mm* qui *mm*", a chimney which is smoking. For the fifth he sees one of two pictures: "La *mm mm* de la lumière', either a lamp that is lit, or a lady turning on or off a light switch. For the sixth, "La *mm* est aimée par la *mm*", the child sees a girl with a cat in her arms or a little girl who is licking a lollipop. I will analyse these sentences in the order in which the child shows some success of completion.

The first sentence in which the child shows some success is sentence (4). The fact that the verbal introduction there is "c'est la *mm* qui" makes it easier for the children. The simple replacing of "qui" by "que" makes it still easier. Three children out of 9, of less than 4 years, were successful in this task. Eighty per cent of the children between 4 and 5 years were successful—that is to say they completed it grammatically and respected the syntactic constraints given by the instructors. For example, "c'est la cheminée qui fume" was a successful number-(4)-type sentence. The typical error we found in analysing the production of this sentence was that "qui" was replaced by "il" or "elle"; so we find sentences like:

"C'est la cheminée, elle fume."

SCHLESINGER: It is more or less equivalent.
MEHLER: Semantically it is more or less equivalent but syntactically it is quite different.
ERVIN-TRIPP: This is the kind of result you get in imitation, too.
MEHLER: Right, exactly. Maybe we will have time to go into comparing these results with imitations and with repetitions in comprehension and so on. Take sentence (3) now:

"La *mm* donne des *mm*."

We get some success at 3:5 years but not much and 100 per cent success at $5\frac{1}{2}$ years. The typical errors in this sentence appear to occur because it is adapted to the structure of sentence (4): "c'est la *mm* qui donne des *mm*". We had enough controls to be fairly confident of this. Some of the children received sentence (3) first and the others sentence (4) first, so there was no possibility of one syntactic form being generalized to the other.

SCHLESINGER: Is sentence type (4) the more frequent form?

MEHLER: It is, for these children, in production.

SCHLESINGER: I meant in adult speech.

MEHLER: I have no idea.

SINCLAIR: I am afraid it seems that your results are somewhat linked to the fact that you show a picture. What they are doing is saying "this is" or something like that.

MEHLER: That is possible; I am doubtful, however, because even if we ask for repetition only, without showing pictures, we get the same type of answer "c'est la *mm*" more often than you would expect. For instance, if you give a child a sentence "la vache donne du lait" or something like that, you receive "c'est la vache qui donne du lait" even if there is no picture.

SINCLAIR: Yes but that is very understandable, even from an adult's point of view, because "la vache donne du lait" is a general statement. It is as if you were saying "it is cows that give milk".

MEHLER: I am trying to make the point that if you ask a child to repeat a sentence, he can repeat some sentences without worrying about whether it is a general sentence or not, or what its range of application is. In other sentences, he makes systematic modifications. It seems that almost any sentence you give at an early age—at about $3\frac{1}{2}$ or $4\frac{1}{2}$—is perceived as "it is + noun phrase + verb + noun phrase". This happens whether or not you have a picture. In some sense it is a basic structure.

SINCLAIR: Yes, but you do run the risk of the other interpretation that I suggested, since you are presenting the children with pictures.

MEHLER: We did this experiment with pictures first because we were not very confident about how well the children could perform without some semantic constraint. Since then we have done further experiments without pictures, in which the results are exactly the same. If you compare these results with an experiment which we have in press now, which deals with sentences under comprehension, repetition, recall and completion, you will find the same general pattern of changes, so that I think the reason is more basic than simply that the child is presented with a picture.

Let us look now at sentence (2):

"La *mm* est *mm*."

This appears to pose enormous problems for the children. You will notice that the length of the sentence does not correlate at all with its complexity. You could even argue that the longer the sentence, the more the syntactic content is redundant, so the easier it should be. However, if this were the case, sentences (5) and (6) should be the simplest; and they are not. This means that accounting for different performance is much more complex than anything to do with either length or meaning alone. As I said, sentence (2) poses enormous problems for children and their degree of success in completing it shows little stability. A child might be successful at a certain point, and then the next time not successful at all.

SCHLESINGER: Is this picture about an adjective? What should this sentence be completed with?

MEHLER: If we show a cow; the cow may be a certain colour.

SCHLESINGER: Would you say that the need for an adjective might be part of the reason for its difficulty? Dr. Sinclair just mentioned that adjectives were hard to grasp.

MEHLER: Well, in this case "*mm*" could be an adjective, a participle or an adverb. These are the three acceptable possibilities. The errors we get, however, show that the complexity is due to one very frequent completion. They simply say "it is a cow" or "it is the cow which is in the field", or something. From about $5\frac{1}{2}$ years we get sentences such as "the cow is the cow" or "it is the cow which is in the field", or something. From about $5\frac{1}{2}$ years we get sentences such as "the car is a car" and "the cow is a cow". It is odd that this is a very late form, which one might have expected very early, as a way out for the children. It never turns up before $5\frac{1}{2}$ years of age.

SINCLAIR: Did you get correct gender here? "La vache est une vache"?

MEHLER: Yes, and "la voiture est une voiture". Let us look at the first sentence now:

"Les *mm mm*."

The results here are rather interesting. It generally turns out that there is subject-verb-object regularization at $5\frac{1}{2}$ years. The type of error you find rather depends on whether the child gave a transitive or intransitive verb. But it seems that the child is always referring to subject-verb-object strategy. He frequently introduces "c'est . . ." at the beginning.

ERVIN-TRIPP: Could one say then that errors are in the direction of using a pronoun subject?

DE BARDIES: No.

ERVIN-TRIPP: It looks as though it is a replacement of the noun phrase by the "c'est *mm*" structure, the pronoun structure. When you give a sentence, do you ever set a more complex noun phrase in the response? MEHLER: In some later cases, yes. I have examples, later on, of some different types of sentences which complicate the picture. What you suggest was, in fact, what I expected to be able to show but it didn't work out—I wish it had! Because in fact the subject-verb-object as the primary strategy for children is a very interesting hypothesis. It would simplify our views enormously. The children are more complex than the hypothesis we can make about their behaviour.

Let us look at sentence (6):

"La *mm* est aimée par la *mm*."

This is a passive sentence and we get little success for this type before 5 years of age—say 5 and one month. We find that with this type only the sentences which the child completes with two animate nouns are successful. So in "la petite fille est aimée par la maman" you have to have two animate nouns and the child will be successful. If he uses an animate and inanimate noun he gets into syntactic trouble.

BELLUGI: In what direction?

MEHLER: "Le petit garçon (verb) par la bross", "La maman est (verb) par la banane" or something like that. There are not many others. At $5\frac{1}{2}$ years you get 100 per cent correct with the two animates. This experiment goes up beyond $6\frac{1}{2}$ years and we still don't receive many correct responses with animate/inanimate.

KLIMA: How can a child interpret from the picture what is really going on. With double animate, if you have "aimer" for example, let us say "La jeune fille est aimée par la maman", how do you know who is doing what?

MEHLER: Well, that doesn't seem to pose any problems for the children with a picture of a girl and a mother.

KLIMA: How do you interpret the response?

MEHLER: Which response?

KLIMA: They could answer either way; how do you define it?

MEHLER: We don't. We are just interested in whether they are structuring a passive sentence which is related to the picture or not.

KLIMA: Related in any way?

MEHLER: Yes, in any way. In one example we have a picture of a girl sucking a pacifier and if you give the correct verb as support and the correct structure there is still no success. Maybe it is that you allow two ways of completing the first and only one way of completing the second.

I would have thought, from some very preliminary work we did in ambiguous sentences two or three years ago with Mrs. Sinclair, that the more ways there are in which it is possible to complete a sentence presented, the more likely the child is to produce a correct response rather than the reverse; but I do not want to push that, since we are going to start all over again on ambiguous sentences.

BELLUGI: Dr. Sinclair, didn't you use some passives with the possibility of reciprocal action?

SINCLAIR: With certain passives in reversible sentences, young children cannot decide who is the actor or the patient and they give an interpretation which is ambiguous, in the sense that both are actors and both are patients.

BELLUGI: Yes, "laver" for example.

SINCLAIR: An example with *laver* would be: "show me what happens when I say 'the boy is washed by the girl'." They would do a reciprocal action, that is "the boy washes the girl" and "the girl washes the boy". It is the same with *"pousser"* (push). The child does not make one thing push the other, both things push each other.

MEHLER: We have some tables in which Mme. de Bardies gives the typical error for all these sentences for children about $5\frac{1}{2}$ years old. For example, "C'est la *mm*" at a later stage gives us sentences with suppression of "c'est"—you get the canonical form subject-verb-object. For "le *mm* donne des *mm*", "c'est des *mm*" is the most common error and the addition of "qui": "c'est le *mm* qui donne la *mm*"; that is, first the addition of "c'est", then finally the addition of "qui", then success. The second typical error is the definition of place where the action takes place, in the road, or in the field, or something like that. For the passives you get this animate/inanimate distinction; animate/inanimate leading to more errors than animate/animate.

I will now describe the telephone experiment which we did with children between 4 and 11 years of age. They were presented with five sentences:

(1) Le *mm* a mange la *mm*.
(2) Il *mm* que tu joues.
(3) Demain je *mm* le *mm*.
(4) La *mm* que je *mm* est *mm*.
(5) Le *mm* qui *mm* est *mm*.

These sentences were given to older children, so it was possible to give much more definite instructions, like "You are going to rephrase the *mm*'s within the sentence so that the sentence will mean something, will say something". We give some examples for training, for instance: "Le *mm* a *mm* le cheval" and we explain "You could say: 'le garçon a monté le cheval', 'le monsieur a vu le cheval' and so on". So the child understands what he is to do. He is allowed either to choose his own words immediately, or to ask the instructor to repeat the sentence frame; he is quite free to ask for a repetition of the sentence several times. This is one of the reasons why we are not presenting these experiments as real experiments but as pilot data. We are trying to find out what the responses look like, but we still cannot control how many presentations per child we make. Some children did not require any repetition of the sentence; some children required two or three presentations—this is in fact influencing our results. Since we are not really interested in finding out how we can put production under control we allow quite a free situation.

With the telephone experiment, of course, no pictures are presented. The first sentence "Le *mm* a mangé le *mm*" has 100 per cent success at 6:5 years. "La *mm* que je *mm* est *mm*"—sentence (4)—has 50 per cent success at 6 years, 80 per cent success at 8 years, and 100 per cent success at 10 years. The second sentence "il *mm* que tu joues" at $8\frac{1}{2}$ years has 10 per cent success and 20 per cent success at a later age, but never more than that. "La *mm* qui *mm* est *mm*" has 0 per cent success at 8 years and 90 per cent success at 9 years, which is a very dramatic change.

The typical error in the first sentence is the addition of "c'est qui". This is the typical completion we find, the addition of "qui" and the replacement of "le" by "un, une, le, la". The omission of the past participle is the other main error, combined with a number of possible additions which would complete the sentence semantically. For the second sentence the main errors are of a semantic nature. "Il joue que tu joues." The child has difficulty in dissociating the two verbs here. For "Le *mm* qui *mm* est *mm*", the reason for the errors is that they lose the "*mm* que est *mm*", so that one of the parts is not completed. Finally for the third sentence we get errors of transitive/intransitive verbs and never a future tense. The greatest difference in the results is between "le *mm* que je *mm* est *mm*" and "le *mm* qui *mm* est *mm*". I will repeat the results. When you have "que" you have 50 per cent success at 6 years, 35 per cent success at $6\frac{1}{2}$ years, 50 per cent at 7 years, 80 per cent at 8 and 100 per cent at 10. Now the change "que" to "qui" gives you 0 per cent success at 8 years and 90 per cent success at 10. The greatest reason for failure is that the child replaces "que" by "qui".

Discussion

SINCLAIR: The frame for the telephone situation seems a bit unreal. If you are speaking on the telephone you do not say things like "my desk is red". Also the present tense is difficult for young children, usually a past or future is easier to understand. With the verb *donner* for instance you must say "*he has* given" or "*will* give".

SCHLESINGER: You could perhaps give more constraint, more focus. You could say: "this sentence is going to be about a cow". Or you could have a very compelling picture with a mother fondling her baby and a cow on the grass and a broken cup; then you could say: "now tell us something about the picture". As for tense, you could have somebody say "this sentence is about something that is going on right now", with that constraint built in from the beginning.

SINCLAIR: You could do that for the picture and the sentences about the smoking chimney, but it is not very natural with *donner*.

MEHLER: Yes, maybe we have to give some reality to the conversation itself.

E. INGRAM: Did you try to get the future? What do you get when you say "demain"? In English you get "going to" used before a proper future is used: "They are going to get crashed", for instance.

MME DE BARDIES: The same thing happens in French. You find the immediate future used by the children.

BELLUGI: Was there any special reason for picking singular nouns? It seems to me that they are twice as hard.

MEHLER: Why should that be the case?

KLIMA: Because if you use a noun in the singular, you then have to decide whether it is masculine or feminine. I would choose plurals, which leave out this other variable.

MEHLER: That is a very good suggestion.

KLIMA: I suspect if I was given your task I would stall just as much as the children.

MEHLER: I must confess that I myself had the same feeling.

KLIMA: And that applies particularly to the second sentence. I had to think a long time before I could decide what was going on in the "il *mm* que tu joues".

MEHLER: I must explain. One of the premises of this experiment was this overall belief that a subject-verb-object primary strategy would show up. Since this primary strategy has not shown up very strongly, the rationale of the experiment and the contents of the sentences have been changed a bit.

SINCLAIR: I think that the fact that it does not show up may be due to something utterly different.

MEHLER: Exactly, we think we over-simplified it. But it is not clear that complicating the content of the sentences and the story, and so on, would be better to show a subject-verb-object order.

E. INGRAM: Some of your sentences have only closed-class items in them, whereas some have open-class items in them, *donner*, *la lumière* and so on. You said you were controlling for syntactic and semantic constraints but this seems to me to be compounding these two variables.

MEHLER: Yes, I agree with you. In our more recent experiments we are being much more precise about this particular factor. It is very difficult to control for this entirely, but we are trying to construct sentences where we can piece out these factors. It seems to me we have two possibilities: either we drastically simplify the material or drastically complicate it. I think what we will do is try both lines and see if one pays off better.

KLIMA: Another complicating factor in perceiving sentences might be just at what point the article is perceived if there is no noun after it. It could be in some of your sentences that the preceding article is just not perceived when there is no noun after it. Take the third sentence for example, "Demain je *mm* le *mm*". If they substituted an intransitive verb for that I would not be surprised to get "Demain je viens".

MEHLER: Yes and then drop the rest of it. This is in fact one of the errors we do get. If this is so, I mean if the perception of certain factors is affected by dropping out some words, it might be a good thing for us. We might get a very much more regular order of comprehension, much more solid than we have.

KLIMA: This could be the explanation of your errors rather than the subject-verb-object strategy.

MEHLER: Yes, although the tape is constructed in such a way that there should theoretically be no problem, acoustically, in distinguishing "le". We constructed the tape artificially. You read the words one by one. "Demain", "je" and we put a verb in when we do the tape, "Demain je (verb) le". Then we cut out the verb and there is enough space, at least 70–120 milliseconds, between the end of one word and the beginning of the other. We cut out just the verb, and replace an identical amount of tape by a wave of white noise, so that when you listen to the tape you have no trouble in hearing the "le"; it is very well isolated. If it is true that the children in fact do not hear the "le", I don't know how we could prove this, it would be very interesting.

BELLUGI: When they were older they could be asked to read it. That would be one way of finding out how much they could do.

MEHLER: I don't like that very much as a method. I know one or two people in France who tried to get sentence completion by writing, with 8–10-year-old children. The variability you get is enormous, much larger than you get with other means.

ROBINSON: One possible control which you could apply is to ask them to repeat these sentences in a little more noise, showing to what extent their alterations of what you give them are functions of choosing words together.

MEHLER: We did think about this and this is how we got round to inventing the telephone situation. But under the circumstances you describe, children just won't perform at all.

The Requirements of Model Users

ELISABETH INGRAM

University of Edinburgh

FOR THE FIRST time in history, probably, there exists a model for language acquisition and language behaviour created by linguists and derived from linguistic theory. It is of Chomskyan origin, and has been elaborated by various authors, e.g. Katz (1966), Lenneberg (1967), McNeill (1966a, b).

However, a proportion of people who come to child language from an interest in child development in general find themselves unable to base their work on this model. They are very much aware of the need for a theoretical framework for their predominantly pragmatically oriented studies, yet they feel that there is a lack of fit between the model they are offered and what they need. Why? I would suggest that there are some quite general characteristics that a theoretically conceived model must possess in order to be of value to people who are more interested in accounting for empirical phenomena than in model-making as such. The model must be relatively *stable* and it must have a degree of *plausibility*. Further, in interdisciplinary fields it must be seen to be *relevant*, and it must be *compatible* with the basic assumptions the user makes about his own field.

1. *Stability.* The high rate at which emendations of the model are produced, within the same general theoretical frame, creates difficulties, particularly since most of the work circulates in cyclostyled form for years before it gets published. The result is that people not on the mailing lists plan their research and describe their findings in terms which have long been abandoned by the originators. The concept of underlying kernel strings as proposed by Chomsky in *Syntactic Structures* (1957) was used by outsiders long after Chomsky and his group had discarded it. There are respectable linguists who hold that *Syntactic Structures* which includes kernel strings, is not markedly inferior to *Aspects of the Theory of Syntax* (Chomsky, 1965), which rejects the

F

concept; but people who are not primarily linguists do not have the necessary background to make and to trust their own judgements on points of theory, and when they see people being clobbered in print for being out of date, it does not exactly encourage them to tie their work too closely to the twists and turns of theoretical linguistics.

2. *Plausibility*. If a model is to be useful it must incorporate concepts that one can believe in. It is not sufficient that the model is conceived of as accounting for a wide range of phenomena—or, to use the current terminology, that it is powerful—nor is it sufficient that it is capable of being successfully formalized. Consider for instance one of Chomsky's least ambiguous statements of his position on the acquisition of language:

> "As a precondition for language learning, he [the child] must possess, first, a linguistic theory that specifies the form of the grammar of a possible human language, and, second, a strategy for selecting a grammar of the appropriate form that is compatible with the primary linguistic data" (Chomsky, 1965; p. 25).

I do not find it plausible that a child is born preprogrammed with a set of hypotheses concerning all possible grammars and with a fully operational and efficient logical apparatus for deciding which grammar actually obtains locally. So the whole of the notion of the innate Language Aquisition Device is useless to me.

3. *Relevance*. The assumptions that are presupposed and the concepts that are built into models must be seen to be relevant. We have heard (Hymes, this volume) how unhappy the sociologists and sociolinguists are with the notions of "the idealized native speaker-hearer" and "the homogeneous speech community". These platonic conceptions do not, apparently, seem very relevant to people who are interested in the study of communication between individuals within and across groups. Labov, for instance, found that New York negroes do not invariably say "he crazy", sometimes they say "he's crazy". The realization of the copula is more likely under certain conditions: if the following word is a verb, or the preceding sound is a vowel, or the subject is a pronoun. This is an indication that language usage does vary in ways which are systematically influenced by linguistic factors, but are not fully determined by them. Neither obligatory rules nor optional rules will account for this; so Labov proposes a different sort of rule —variable rules—which incorporate the notion of probability (Labov, 1966).

Nobody, probably, would maintain in so many words that the assumptions made by linguists for the purposes of developing abstract linguistic theory are necessarily the same set of assumptions that one might think it useful to make in working out a model relevant to a given area of empirical research. But the model for language acquisition and usage that I am discussing does presuppose exactly those assumptions that are presupposed for abstract linguistic theory.

4. *Compatibility.* The concepts underlying a model borrowed from another field must be compatible with the general concepts of the larger field that one is working in. The original formulation of the notion of competence seems to be an example of conflicting underlying views concerning the basic notion of knowing. According to Chomsky, competence includes (a) the categories and rules of the grammar which enable the individual to assign a structural description to all possible sentences, and (b) the native speaker's implicit *knowledge* of the grammar. In psychology generally, knowledge of an abstract concept may be postulated only when it can be demonstrated (i) that the individual can *act* systematically in terms of the rules, or (ii) that he can *formulate* the categories and rules in question. Nobody, however, claims that the native speaker can formulate the rules of his language—the linguists themselves are still struggling. And according to the theory, the responsibility for acting on the linguistic knowledge is explicitly excluded from the competence component, and explicitly attributed to the performance component. So, knowledge in Chomsky's sense is quite different from the usual sense in psychology. When there is incompatibility of this sort two things may happen. The intruding model may be so persuasive that it is the whole general field which is restructured, rather than the particular disturbing concepts. This is what seemed to be happening at one stage: most of the papers by psychologists in *Genesis of language* (Smith and Miller, 1966) and in *Psycholinguistic papers* (Lyons and Wales, 1966) reflect a faithful acceptance not only of Chomsky's grammar but also of his notions concerning language acquisition as set out in *Aspects*, chapter 1 (Chomsky, 1965). The other possibility is that the intruding concept, provided it has lasting value, will be adapted to fit in with the total purposes of those who try to employ the model. In this conference it seems that, though the performance/competence dichotomy in its canonical form is accepted by some, it has also been reformulated, directly attacked and even ignored by others.

These reflections on the acceptability of theoretical models for pragmatic purposes are, I believe, generally applicable. Now I want to turn to some of the basic assumptions of the Chomsky-derived model of language processes, of which language acquisition is a part. As I understand it, the assumption is that the model for language behaviour is, in one way or another, to be found in the general theory of the transformational linguists. The major postulates of the linguistic theory, and in particular the postulates concerning the nature of grammar, are consequently taken to concern also language behaviour.

One basic postulate of the linguistic theory is the centrality of the syntactic component. One basic postulate concerning the syntactic component is that it has two quite distinct parts: a base component in which the major syntactic relations are represented by a phrase structure grammar and a surface part in which the various necessary transformations are effected.

In addition it is often—not always—explicitly or implicitly assumed that the processes underlying language behaviour must to a significant extent mirror the formal rules of the grammar. This means, since the rules are set up so that the sentences they generate can be tested for correctness by an algorithm, that people are supposed to function like logical machines.

While some people have found these assumptions a fruitful source of hypotheses (e.g. Miller, 1962), others have found it inhibiting to have proposed strategies to mirror rules; and others, like Braine (1963), have found themselves criticized among other things for proposing an independent model of very early language acquisition on the grounds that in terms of the Chomskyan model all he accounted for was surface structure, not deep structure (Bever *et al.*, 1965). However, as Schlesinger has pointed out, the force of this criticism depends on the assumption that, because the grammatical formulation proceeds from deep structure to surface structure, the learning strategies must proceed in the same direction. But it is entirely conceivable that as a matter of strategy "... the acquisition of underlying structure would occur as a second stage, by the way of 'inductive' inference from an already acquired stock of surface structures" (Schlesinger, 1967; p. 398).

There have been indications recently that some of the basic postulates of the linguistic theory, as one gleans them from the literature, have been taken up for review. As a non-linguist, my impression of this has been very vague, but it has become rather more definite during this conference.

1. *The centrality of the syntactic component.* Already Slobin (in Smith and Miller, 1966) has suggested that a model of language acquisition which did not take meaning and context into account was not very convincing. It seems to me that there has been an increasing realization

of the centrality of semantics. This has fundamental consequences for a model of language acquisition.

2. *Deep structure.* For years the apparently inviolable position has been that the deep syntactic component is represented by phrase structure rules. However, Thorne, Bratley and Dewar (1968), at the conclusion of a 5-year project to programme a machine to analyse English sentences, reported that their most successful programme was based, not on a phrase structure *plus* transformational rule operation, but on a finite state *plus* transformational rule operation. Theirs was a recognition grammar, set up for a limited purpose, and they did not claim any universal significance for their work. But to me it is very interesting that, for a job where practical considerations had to be taken into account, they found that they needed to change something as fundamental as the nature of the rules of their deep grammar. Other linguists have more directly doubted the necessity of accepting that the nature of deep structure has been determined. Fillmore for instance (1968) maintains that subject and predicate do not belong to deep structure, as the standard transformationalist theory asserts, but that they are relatively surface concepts.

3. *The dichotomy between deep and surface grammar.* I was under the impression that one of the main arguments for distinguishing sharply between deep component phrase structure rules and surface component transformational rules was that this represented the best chance of axiomatizing the syntactic theory. But according to Thorne, "Given the present formulation of transformational rules in linguistic theory, it is doubtful whether a generalized axiom is possible" (Thorne *et al.*, 1968; p. 296); and it appears that Thorne is not alone in this view.

Obviously this does not necessarily mean that one should give up the distinction between deep and surface structure, but one is led rather to speculate on the nature of the distinction and whether it is sharply dichotomous or not.

These new developments, if I have understood them right, open up the whole field again. This is very confusing, but also liberating. I have at times had the feeling of being up against some monolithic, immovable set of assertions and dogmas, which I could neither fully assent to nor get round. Now, it seems, everything is wide open, and it is possible to question, to re-evaluate, to shift models around so that they can be made use of for particular purposes, such as trying to reconcile and make sense of the information we have about developmental psychology and the statements that linguists and psycholinguists make about the processes of language development in children.

Discussion

BEVER: The extreme form of the argument concerning the distinction between deep and surface components was perhaps by way of over-reaction to the linguistics of the '40s and '50s, but the distinction is still worth observing. I think we all adhere to the assumption that the under-standing of the sentence is closely related to the information which is represented in the deep structure, and that this is distinct from at least some of the superficial properties of the surface structure. I'd like to withdraw from the position that it has to reflect the underlying structure as specified by transformational grammar, because who knows what that is? The underlying structures that we must look for are "thought groups". I don't want to claim any originality here, since anybody work-ing on child language in the Continental tradition around the turn of the century was concerned with logical relations and perception and reten-tion of sentences in terms of what I've called "thought groups".

HUXLEY: You would say that in the click experiments (Fodor and Bever, 1965) the clicks indicated breaks between two thought groups?

BEVER: Yes; that we have since verified. We originally thought it had to do only with surface phrase structure. But we have since obtained evi-dence with critical instances like

"John will defy Bill to go",
"John will desire Bill to go".

The object of these two verbs are different; the object of *defy* is just *Bill*, but the object of *desire* is the whole clause *Bill to go*. And we found that there is a greater tendency to misplace the click into the break between the verb and the object when the object is a whole clause, than when it is just the noun.

The more experiments we do and the more we think about it the more obvious it becomes that particular lexical choices are important. Know-ledge of *defy* and *desire* for instance can short-cut or guide the listener away from having to pay attention to surface structure at all and simply direct him to the organization at the level of deep structure.

So we have become interested again in the specific psycho-linguistic properties of particular words; and also linguists have become interested in how to specify the properties of individual words. This interest is with respect to the roles that these words could play in deep structure, and this does imply a rather different view of deep structure, one which would more easily be compatible with "thought groups".

KLIMA: I'd like to put what is going on about deep structure and surface structure in a slightly different way. At first it looked as if you could take some sort of base structure reflecting deep syntactic relations and then use transformations to rearrange them as required with certain limitations built in from the start. Now the interest is more in trying to work out some of the formal restrictions which limit the amount of rearranging you can do. That is, given the nature of structure, what can you do with it? For instance, when can elements from one clause be displaced and put into another, how complex can you make a deletion, how far can you push it through a sentence? How complex can the interrelationship between surface structure and meaning be?

Another point is that it is wrong to think that the formalization of the grammar was ever intended to have anything directly to do with the understanding of sentences; it is not even a copy of whatever form the internalization of grammar takes in the mind.

E. INGRAM: But linguists have expressed themselves in such a way that people have believed that they make claims about the understanding of sentences.

BEVER: Yes. The notion of strong adequacy has been invoked every time a reformulation of syntactic structure has been proposed. All along, such notions as ambiguity, synonymy, logical relation and functional relation, have been invoked as part of the set of facts that a linguistic grammar is intended to account for. It is not intended to account only for the particular sequences which occur, but also for intuitions about surface structure and deep structure of those sequences and the ambiguity of derivation that is possible. So in a sense the kind of facts that a grammar is intended to account for are not just sentences but the set of intuitions that native speakers or semi-trained native speakers can call up from their feelings about sentences.

SCHLESINGER: Why is it that nobody makes any serious attempt to put these intuitions, that linguists talk so much about, to an empirical test? It is usually the linguist who provides you with the intuitions, and he also does the analysis. You can always criticize any particular experiment, if you don't like the results, but ultimately you expect *some* experiment to come out according to your theory. There are experiments which show that people will accept sentences with one central embedding, but not with two. Now if an experiment on grammatical intuitions comes up with results that go against your theory, what would you say?

BEVER: If an empirical test shows you what you know is true, is false, then there is something wrong with the empirical test.

SCHLESINGER: But how do you know that something is true—this is exactly what I am aiming at.

BEVER: We are in a formal bind at the moment. If we allow one embedding we see no natural way of not allowing two embeddings. I think, though, that there is a difference between coding a sentence, which can be done with two embeddings, and the phenomenology of a sentence. If you view the grammar as studying sentences which seem to linguists to be decodable by some scheme, then this should be included. If you view the grammar as something to describe those sentences which have phenomenological reality, then centre-embeddings for instance should not be included. But I am not convinced at all that the linguistic tests tap phenomenological reality either. They tap people's understanding of the word "grammatical", which of course is totally variable.

MEHLER: I have two points; first about experiments. Experiments in developmental child language can show you what children *can* do at various ages, but you can never conclude from them what children *cannot* do. Because a better method could always bring out other things. I am reminded of something Mimi Sinclair and Tom Bever and I did together. We first gave children straightforward acceptable passive sentences and then we gave them sentences that were not acceptable, like "The policeman was eaten by the apple". And we got non-acceptance of sentences like this at a much earlier age than we expected. When children notice the anomaly of such sentences it means that they can, however precariously, use the passive voice, and this was at an age where previously it was supposed to be totally absent.

The other point is that I cannot see any difference between a linguist having an intuition about a sentence being grammatical and a sentence having phenomenological or psychological reality. You have some sentences which you rule out because they are non-grammatical, and you have some other sentences which are not sentences in the phenomenological sense but you accept them. Now, is this acceptance only motivated because you don't know how to block that sentence without blocking an enormous amount of other things, or is it that you make a difference between intuition and a phenomenological reality?

KLIMA: It is certainly a combination of both.

E. INGRAM: If you say it is a combination of both, then you haven't solved either problem, have you?

BEVER: That's right; it's a big mess.

KLIMA: It is a bit of faith too; you hope that a principle will sort it out.

BEVER: We are waiting for a principle to come along to help us do better.

CHURCH: It sounds to me as though people are saying that you can't keep psychology and linguistics apart, but you can't find any real way of getting them together either.

BEVER: The problem is that they are inextricably together.

MEHLER: But we are trying to sort some things out. There is quite a lot of stuff around about sentence-processing. It isn't all consistent unfortunately. We have quite a lot of evidence, the work reported by George Miller (1962), my own dissertation, if I may mention it (Mehler, 1964), and so on, which on the whole fits in with the syntactic model. But we must also say in all honesty that there are some data that we have gathered which don't seem to fit in very well—at least as I understand it. For instance we once did an experiment—several of us at M.I.T.—on predicate adjective versus short passive, things like "the cat was red" versus "the car was passed". So you give ten sentences of one type and then the eleventh sentence of the other type and measure whether there is any delay in the perception of the eleventh sentence; we found there was no difference between the sentence types whatsoever. Well, there is a negative finding—we didn't publish it; you generally don't publish negative findings, you just talk about them in conference.

BEVER: Well it could be that these short passives are so frequent in the language that they acquire some sort of surface reality which is relatively independent of their derivational status. That way you could still salvage the general rule.

MEHLER: Now you are using the frequency argument that we have rejected when it was used against us.

BEVER: No I'm only saying that we will have to take account of other factors than just the syntactic ones. There is other stuff around; Slobin (1968) studied memory with passives and found that memory was better for truncated passives than for full passives—even though truncated passives are supposed to be derived from agentive passives.

KLIMA: Well, there is another interpretation of that, not exactly like yours. The difficulty is not in specifying the agent in the "by + noun phrase". The difficulty comes because in the agentive passive what you are doing is to separate the subject from the agent, in the active form the subject and the agent coincide, and in the truncated passive you are not concerned with the agent at all. This is perhaps more a semantic interpretation but it is still a linguistic one. The lexical category of the verb would be important; for instance, "the glass was broken by the boy" should be easier than "the glass was hit by the boy", because with *break* the more important thing is what it was that broke, so the natural order would be deep object-verb, but with *hit* the agent is more important, so the natural order is agent-verb.

BEVER: That should make a nice little experiment.

MEHLER: I think that much of our discussion has revealed differences in our approach to psychology in general. So that we can have more profitable discussion, I think these differences should be characterized now.

If you look at any history of science, say the one by Kuhn (1962) on the structure of scientific discovery, you will find that there are several stages in science, one of which can be characterized as botany. This is the stage of finding differences, you look at the leaves on a tree and you try to determine whether one leaf is different from the other. Then you move on to the stage when you are trying to find similarities. Eventually you get into a hypothetico-deductive system where it is all right to grind out predictions—a little bit like a machine. These predictions are probably rather arbitrary because your system is, in general, rather arbitrary too. Finally you get the fourth stage, let me call it for the time being the generative model-making stage.

Unless it is possible to go from botany to the generative system, it seems to me that we pile up pieces of interesting, probably useful data which are left like a dictionary. You have data A, data B, data C which are not being related to anything whatsoever. A case in point, for instance, is Skinner who has had pigeons pecking at keys now for 20 years, and has been piling up data with computers. As far as we know, no general principles have come out of this work, because one of Skinner's ruling principles is to avoid making hypotheses about data. On the other hand there is another school which says: "make your hypothesis first, formulate your intuitions clearly and specifically and see whether nature fulfils them or not".

These two different approaches influence your data-gathering system. If you avoid making some very general but well formulated hypothesis, you gather data and you collect what will look interesting and significantly different, you follow up the differences between, say, children who behave differently in different tasks. On the other hand, when you have a guiding hypothesis, you are testing and looking for invariants; that is, you are trying to find the stages through which all children go, trying to predict the main parameters which are the same for everybody. This approach will eventually allow you to make an axiomatic statement. An axiomatic statement will permit total derivation of behaviour from a very economic system. This requires a totally different methodology from the search for differences. Although people following the two approaches are both psychologists, they are looking for different things. It seems to me that some of the people interested in the social aspects of language are presenting us with differences which come from the parental way of responding to questions, of talking of moral and socio-economic questions etc., whereas the cognitive psychologists have talked about invariants.

BEVER: Many kinds of data will turn out to be relevant once there is a theoretical framework to interrelate them. Specifically, the problem is to find the mechanism which describes the interactions of social and linguistic development, a general mechanism which will show how *social* generalizations are transformed by the child into parts of the structural systems for linguistic capacity. Without that mechanism, at the very least, the two enterprises of structural linguistics and socio-linguistics are doomed to remain distinct.

HYMES: I think people's different feelings on these issues are conditioned by the historical experience of their disciplines. Now, in anthropology, we constantly have the feeling that in other aspects of social science there are people applying precisely these deductive models with horrible consequences. That is, they take for granted that they already have enough botany, and therefore derive consequences. I think we have seen this in some of the theoretical discussions about the Vietnamese war.

BEVER: A bad model is better than no model if one insists on solving a problem.

HYMES: I think the question of what position you choose to approach certain problems or interests from is a very complicated one. I don't think it can be "either-or". I think it is still an open question whether or not, given a particular interest and body of data, one could approach this body of data by means of a generative model.

MEHLER: Let me clarify one point. When I talk about botany, I am not talking about this scientific strategy in a critical manner necessarily. I mean, there is a type of botany which can be criticized, like Skinnerian botany which I think is useless. On the other hand there is a type of botany which serves the purpose of presenting us with data which might lead to a fruitful hypothesis. Now, what is the difference between one and the other? Good botany results in making provisional hypotheses to order the world around you, not in a dictionary fashion but in a rationalistic system.

BEVER: In this specific case, the hypothesis would transfer from socio-linguistic facts to linguistic facts. Without that provision it is not clear at all how to use the facts that are being gathered.

ROBINSON: I think it is a question of where you start. If you start with sociology or if you start on individual differences, your initial data are going to look very different from the data collected by people who start with a 0-year-old child and study him. All I was trying to suggest was that, at some point, these would meet and eventually one has got to account for both.

MEHLER: Yes, but isn't it the case even when you say: I am going to look at the world naively, doing botany without hypotheses, that you are in fact bringing to the situation your covert hypothesis? And that means that you are not overtly expressing it, which can lead to a further confusion of the situation.

HYMES: I think part of the problem is that people doing botany appear to have a somewhat *ad hoc* approach and their critics are afraid of eternal irrelevance. Skinner is the example of failure to make data relevant. On the other hand some people are afraid that many cognitive psychologists reach premature conclusions because of their closure of the theoretical system.

E. INGRAM: I think it is not the dichotomy between theorizing and data-collecting that matters. What is important is the level of generalization at which one makes hypotheses. There is a tendency to think that the more abstract the level at which you make a hypothesis, the more respectable that hypothesis is. But, from the other point of view, if you make a hypothesis that is terribly abstract and general, requiring an enormous amount of organization of data, an enormous amount of information to validate and invalidate, you may waste an awful lot of time testing and rejecting premature models.

MEHLER: I think the characterization of hypotheses into levels of abstractness is a very good one, and I agree totally. But I myself come to some rather different conclusions. Almost any hypothesis which is very concrete can be invalidated by some data. For instance, association can be invalidated by any experiment which is very restricted. But it is true that association can handle a number of problems. If you make your hypothesis too narrow in abstractness, too concrete, you will be unable to decide the range of validity it has, or even determine its accuracy. It is only when you stick your neck out with a broad enough hypothesis that you can be shown to be wrong.

ROBINSON: But how do you begin to account for the enormous difference in performance of children when they leave school at 15? How do you begin to account for the differences in what they are apparently able to perform? These are the educational facts one starts with. You have to develop some sort of explanation for this. If you find you can break the mass of children into social class groups and you find that the working class are, in general, performing much less well than the middle class, then you go on to develop hypotheses as to why this may be so.

One thing that we think might be relevant is what is made available for the child to learn.

CAZDEN: I think this kind of discussion about basic differences in research methodology is very important and I am delighted that we have got on to it. I certainly will be the first to agree that *ad hoc* selection of miscellaneous data is not going to add up to anything; but I do feel that Peter Robinson has been put in a difficult position by some of us. The one piece of research in this area that does have a theoretical perspective behind it, coming from sociologists, is the whole Bernstein project. The idea that this just consists of a whole mass of correlations (in the hope that something will come out of it) is very far from the case.

BERNSTEIN: I was just thinking that maybe, within the so-called human sciences, one must make a distinction between hypotheses which are concerned essentially with variations and hypotheses which are concerned with seeking universals. It may well be that hypotheses concerned with variations will be particularly weak in instances relating to universals, in exactly the same way as hypotheses concerned with universals may be weak when it comes to dealing with variations.

BEVER: It isn't clear what "variation" means without explicit variables which are being varied. When you talk about variation, are you talking about variation on dimension X or dimension Y? The point is that the theories which have to do with variations, or the sets of arrangements of facts or hypotheses which have to do with variations, tend to draw on the theories that have delineated the structure of the material that varies. A separation of these two approaches, I think, is in principle impossible; therefore I do not think we can tolerate the two theories existing side by side, without a theory of their relation to each other.

Early Utterances

ERVIN-TRIPP: Dr. Bever pointed out that, prior to the one-word utterances, there was evidence of sentences uttered by the child that seemed to have intonational properties like later utterances, although these early utterances didn't seem to have an English word in them. This agrees with many observations in the literature, although they have never been reported in enough detail. Nakazima (1962) tells us that, after the period of repetitive babbling, about 9–12-month-old children tend to use intonations as if they were in a conversation, that speaking was more often addressed to people and dolls, that understanding of parental speech developed, that it is "connected to certain objects", and that the spectrograms begin for the first time to allow differentiation of children in Japanese and American milieux. That this differentiation is not posessed before 9 months is supported by R. Weir.

These early "utterances" have several interesting properties. The child behaves in very much the same way as he does when he is saying sentences that you can interpret because you recognize English words. He acts as if to him there is nothing different in the two kinds of sentences. In the cases I have observed these utterances are still continuing to occur several months after the child has developed two- and three-word sentences. Occasionally a single word from the normal vocabulary of the child will occur; but for the most part they seem to be quite separate, structurally, from the other utterances. You don't have several words that you can recognize and then something you can't interpret; it is as though they are produced through some kind of separate device. It seems to me that one of the reasons why we don't know much about this, is that it is very difficult to transcribe. The early diary reports round the turn of the century refer to the appearance of this phenomenon, but the utterances are not written down. And you need a fairly large corpus of utterances in order to investigate what might be going on at this stage. Our observations suggested that something may happen rather dramatically in comprehension to allow a switch from perceiving an utterance as some kind of whole—identified by intonation, timing, and some few salient features one can see on spectrograms, but without any component morphemes—to the stage when the child first identifies words as isolatable units and separates out words we can recognize as English. Anecdotally, parents have sometimes reported that these unanalysed units are more characteristic of younger siblings. If it were the case that the input by older siblings tends to be short sentences, but that language-conscious parents train the older child with isolated words, such a difference might well be expected. But of course one needs to tape family interactions to test this notion. Dr. Bever says he spent some time working on one of these funny "sentences", which appeared recurrently and he was able to find a meaning for it.

BEVER: The meaning was something like *Can I touch it?* It wasn't terribly complicated, it was just the kind of thing which kept occurring over and over again.

HYMES: How did you decide that was what it meant?

BEVER: By looking at all the situations in which it appeared, tracing little bits of its development. But it didn't really grow, it just sort of was there, and then disappeared and was replaced by other forms of asking.

HYMES: Roughly how long was the utterance?

BEVER: Three quarters of a second, or a second, something like that. It had a rising intonation, which was one of the clues that we paid attention to at first, but it also had some internal articulation, which didn't seem to have any obvious relation to anything in the adult language that we could work out.

HYMES: Once you discovered that it meant *Can I touch it?*, could you recognize it in any language element that might have meant *Can I touch it?* or could have been related to it?

BEVER: No.

MEHLER: I wonder whether this question is not related to the sort of experiment that the Dutch phonetician Tervoort is said to have performed. Apparently, what he claimed was that children learn to speak first of all by grasping the intonation patterns in the language of the community. The way he did it was by testing non-Dutch and Dutch children, he would gather samples of both groups of children and then see whether, before there were phonological distinctions, these children were distinguished by their babbling. It turns out—he doesn't say how he did it—that before you can establish phonetic differences, you really *can* recognize the children from different language communities. This seemed to imply that the first acquisition the child makes is to learn some general intonation patterns.

HYMES: I heard Jakobson saying that about Czech children.

BEVER: Well, in person he claims that about all children. One problem has been raised by recent research in Haskins Laboratories; they have evidence that certain language-specific phonetic properties emerge very early—maybe by 9 or 10 months. So what we perceive as intonational development might really be developments in articulation. These basic phonetic properties have to do with co-articulation effects. What they have worked on most thoroughly is the co-articulation of the onset of voicing and the release of the tongue in a plosive consonant. Apparently, across languages there are three kinds of relations between voicing onset and release: either the two are co-incidental; or voicing comes 50 milliseconds before tongue release; or 50 milliseconds after. Of course, most languages use just two of these possibilities. The Haskins researchers find that at 8 or 9 months there begins to be a noticeable differentiation in the infant's vocalization of plosives, that is he starts to follow the regularities in his native language.

There seems to be a related belief that intonation patterns represent global semantic feeling; I am not sure that this is true. In adult language, intonation patterns are crucial for certain basic *structural* decisions, which you have to make perceptually. For instance, probably most of the information that we get about how to segment a sentence into basic thought groups, apart from the information that we get from semantic structure, is from where the speaker puts his pauses and how he shapes them. In a sense this is purely structural information. There is no affective content involved. It may or may not be true of the child that these long melodic phrases are affective; but I think it is possible that they may well not be.

SINCLAIR: I think Grégoire (1937) has a nice example of a child like that, where the child tries out several intonations. If I remember rightly it was *a; ba ba, bababa* which was later transformed into: *ababa, baba, bababa* and then *a; baba, ba; ba.* There are some structural properties there, without any doubt. The circumstances were simple, the child was playing by himself all alone.

MEHLER: I got somebody to send me some recordings from Argentina of children from English families, so there would be no difference between the children; I got recordings in the States too. But I haven't done a real psycho-physical experiment to see whether recognizability, by English people, of the children who were raised in an English culture versus a foreign culture can be distinguished. But as early as 6 months, to my ear, there are clear differences in intonation.

BEVER: The way to test it would be to put it through a drastic filter so that the articulation information was mainly lost. That is dangerous because, as I mentioned, what might be relevant to the perception of intonation patterns could be the relation between the articulation and the intonation, so a negative finding would not prove much. But if you found effective differences in recognizability, after it was filtered, that would be convincing.

MEHLER: You have to take several steps in an experiment like that, namely, first make your psycho-physical experiment without any masking at all, then introduce a white noise.

SINCLAIR: The peculiar thing about the Grégoire study, if I remember rightly, was that these patterned sound sequences were always the sounds that the child had already had for a long time in his repertoire. On the other hand, any new sound being introduced at that period would not give rise to longer sequences with this kind of intonation pattern.

MEHLER: From the tapes I listened to I tend to doubt that. One of the curious cases that we had was the sound we got from one of the babies who suddenly started making very interesting intonational patterns with guttural sounds at 6 months and 2 weeks, but who hadn't been doing this, or using these sounds, at any of the previous sessions.

ERVIN-TRIPP: I would like to hear more discussion about how one can get some independent way of assessing the meaning relations in so-called "two-word sentences". I think there is a serious problem with these early sentences. Some of the work that Gruber (1967) has done, using video tapes of children, gives us more information than we've had before, about the behaviour of the child at the time the speech occurred. Do you have any further thoughts about this problem?

SINCLAIR: The topic/comment distinction seems important here. In my example, *poupée cassée* was said just after *tasse cassée*; so here it was fairly clear that not only was it the cup that was broken, but also the doll that was broken. In the other case *boum popote*, I think the striking event, or the topic, was *boum*, that is the action, the *slamming* of the door, with the noun here as comment.

SCHLESINGER: I want to refer back to what Dr. Ervin-Tripp said about the problem of identifying which meaning relation has been exhibited. It is more difficult to identify relations than to assign categories like "noun", "verb", etc. to the words in an utterance. What would be required to analyse relations with any degree of confidence (certainly not 100 per cent confidence) would be records in which each utterance is annotated not only by a guess at its interpretation, but also by a description of the situation which has triggered the utterance. In this way, another researcher can evaluate how well this fits his own scheme. Now, when I went over the published literature, I found many cases where I wasn't sure how to analyse the utterance because it consisted of just two words, which could be categorized as nouns or verbs, but there was no way of discovering the meaning relation between the two. It was just two words, and the words were quite clear and could have been categorized as nouns, or verbs but there was nothing else. There was no way of discovering the meaning relations between the two.

SINCLAIR: May I just ask something about ordering? In all the cases where I could confidently establish a possessive relationship between two words, the relation was in this order: *lit maman*, as it would be in French surface structure. I didn't find any example of *Maman lit*. Do you ever get this reversal in English? Do you get something like *comb Daddy*, with possessive meaning, instead of *Daddy comb*? I think that the English word order appears to be in normal form from the beginning also.

ERVIN-TRIPP: It certainly does appear very early in the correct order. I remember that in some cases we were in doubt as to whether it was really two words or one. It was often treated, as far as we could see, as if it was a single word.

SINCLAIR: Without any exception, all the examples we have are like *lit maman*, *auto papa*, and never never the other way round. In studying these utterances I think one must bring in the situation in which they occur. There seems to be rather a difference in structure between utterances which describe a past event, even if it is only just past, like *papa parti*, and utterances that are accompanying an action, where the child is doing something; and finally utterances which are more an expression of desires, or commands. These three categories seem to render slightly different parts of the total structure dominant. I don't really know, but I think the distinction between them is important. Actually, the utterance describing past events seems to be always of the *poupée cassée* or *cassée poupée* type, at least in French, whereas the commands and desires sometimes look like two NPs together.

ERVIN-TRIPP: Instances where the same word seems to be used ambivalently as either noun or verb seem to present problems for this kind of analysis. This is why criticism is frequently made of assigning the category of noun or verb to early forms. Take the word *tea*. The word could be used interchangeably for a cup of tea, or for the action of drinking. It seems to me very difficult to establish whether it is the object, or the action, the child is referring to.

SINCLAIR: I think that at that level action and object and the total scheme form so much one whole that it is not a good idea to try and assign categories to these words. To try and find meaning relationships is a totally different matter.

ERVIN-TRIPP: But I don't see how you can divorce them; if you have a statement like *Daddy tea*, as in one of Dr. Schlesinger's examples, how are you going to assign a grammatical relation and make this decision?

SINCLAIR: I don't know; it depends on the situation. Was *Daddy tea* taken to mean "Daddy give me tea"?

SCHLESINGER: No, certainly not. It was *Daddy drinks tea* or *Daddy gave me tea*. That was the agent-object example. Whether *tea* means the tea itself, or the drinking of the tea, I think that is almost unanswerable. This fits in with the idea that the concepts in the I-marker are not really words, they are not identified as to grammatical category, but are more global concepts. Take *John eats*; it is not the word *eat* which appears in the intention, in the idea the child has of the sense before he speaks, but a whole set of words which include *eat, food, meal* and so on. Which word is chosen from the set is determined by the grammatical rules which he learns, and therefore he chooses *John eats* and not *John food*. But there may be a stage, and this fits in with what you said, that at a time when he doesn't know whether it should be *Johnny drink*, or *Johnny tea*, he will produce either.

BEVER: Some of the things that have been said bring out one problem, that it is not clear that the child views what he is doing as putting together two separate words at all. The very fact that the child's mastery is holistic, has intonation and stress and so on—or at least, appears to at about 1 year old—indicates that this may be his first view of what language is—big blobs of acoustic mess. For him an utterance may not be a series of distinct words put together.

SINCLAIR: But there must be something in the Tinbergen experiment with dummies (Tinbergen, 1951) where there is a whole category of dummies and only certain properties which will elicit the response. This means that already at the animal level the organism does not look at all the perceptual characteristics of a configuration, but somehow or other has a categorization of those to which it responds. Now I feel this is relevant to your big blobs, as against more discrete units.

BEVER: Yes. I am just attacking the blind assumption that our problem is to explain how the child, having discovered words, then discovers the relations between them. That is all.

E. INGRAM: This is a fairly traditional problem, not only in the study of child language but in the study of unknown languages. It is a long time since the principles of commutation were proposed. You must assume that it is one unit unless you can show that the two parts actually attach themselves to other parts in a meaningful way.

CHURCH: Another test is whether the units correspond, in their sequences, to the way they occur in adult life.

BEVER: We are talking here about phenomenological problems in children and adults, which makes it doubly difficult, since we don't know much about phenomenology of adults and certainly not about children. It is entirely consistent with this problem for the child to utter a sequence *a b* and also *b a* without carrying out the internal differentiation of the sequences into two sub-sequences. And it is also entirely possible for the child to say only *a b, c d, e f, g h,* and to think that each separate utterance is made up of two segments, where there is no overlap and no commutation.

E. INGRAM: What you are saying is entirely possible, both ways. What I am saying is that commutation is a minimal criterion for the investigator before he can credit the child with segmentation. The child has to utter *a b, a c* and *d b* before one has any justification for thinking that he is segmenting.

BEVER: What should concern us is not necessarily how the child discovers ways to put words into relation with one another, but how he discovers the separate pieces that make up the relations in the sentences that he hears. It is worth considering the view that the child starts out with a holistic set of utterances and then applies internal cognitive analysis to these whole global utterances and portions out their pieces.

SCHLESINGER: Are you talking about his own utterances, or the other persons?

BEVER: I'm talking about both of them.

Comprehension and Grammaticality Judgements

ERVIN-TRIPP: I would like to see more done on the comprehension side of development; it seems to me that this is one thing that we are still in very serious ignorance about.

BEVER: At 2 years, the child seems to be capable of acting out simple declarative sentences. Now he certainly isn't saying simple declarative sentences, or most children are not. Practically everybody in the field has tried to see how young children can perform on this acting-out task. It seems that one cannot go very much below 2, maybe 1 year 9 months, then capacity begins to disappear very sharply. Now that may be a methodological problem, I don't know. The comprehension of declaratives is a discontinuous development which is in itself important. It is rather baffling that the capacity is so good at this young age. I agree with you that we have to trace the perceptual capacity as far back as we can. A very striking phenomenon in our studies is that no child who succeeds in learning to act out intransitive sentences like *the dog is lying down*, fails to act out transitive sentences like *the cow kisses the horse* without semantic constraints involved. That in itself struck me as rather like the question whether three-dimensional perception precedes two-dimensional perception in children. It may be the case that intransitive sentences are psychologically *more* complex than transitive sentences: this is indicated by our assumption that all the underlying grammatical relations are in some sense innate. So it might be the case that young children can act out simple declarative sentences with subject + verb + object, sooner than they can act out intransitive sentences with just a subject and a verb.

SCHLESINGER: Why should this be so?

BEVER: The explanation would draw on the claim that the differentiation of sentential relations into actor/action implies immediately to the child the distinction actor/object as opposed to actor/non-actor; so once the child achieves the relations involved in *actor*, he automatically acquires those involved in object. We claim that the child is initially prepared to deal with sentences with actors, actions, and objects. The notion of actor and action without any object for the action might be something which actually comes later.

CHURCH: A look at receptive language, which we see late in the first year, in fact involves actor-object relations.

BEVER: You mean, the object relation would appear first?

CHURCH: I don't know whether it should, theoretically, or not. In fact, you usually find it easily if you say to the child, just casually, *hand me my socks* and he picks up the socks and hands them to you. You can get a lot of this kind of thing in everyday situations where the child apparently comprehends quite well, at much younger ages than 2.

BEVER: Yes, I agree, but what we are discussing here is the view that the subject-verb relation is to be distinguished from the verb-object relation and is distinguished by the child as two separable components. At least, that is what Dr. Schlesinger implied in his presentation. Now, if that were the case, one might expect that subject + verb comprehension would be prior to subject + verb + object comprehension, as a whole. What I am suggesting is that that should be looked into; there is a possibility that it would not be the case and that actually intransitive sentences are the more complex.

SCHLESINGER: What about production?

BEVER: In production there is the same performance problem as with line drawing; the development of the full productive mechanism is independent of the development of the capacity for appreciation of the structure.

HUXLEY: I understand, Dr. Bever, that you are suggesting that transitives are prior to intransitives.

BEVER: Yes.

HUXLEY: That puzzles me because, within linguistic theory at the present moment, there are very strong suggestions from several people, in Great Britain at least, that intransitives are prior to transitives.

BEVER: Yes; in America Postal, among others, suggests that a sentence like *John hit the ball* really comes from *John hit + the ball hit* and that their co-ordination transformation then marks one of them as the subject of this activity and one of them as the object. However, this formal analysis says nothing about acquisition.

SINCLAIR: I have two tiny bits of evidence to put in here. One is the preference of many children, round about 4 or 5, for verbs that can be both transitive and intransitive like *break—the chair breaks—I break the chair*. When we ask children to describe certain actions they even make up words like that. They use verbs which in ordinary French are not of this kind, as if they were.

HUXLEY: I would like to distinguish between these verbs that have been mentioned, because in the case of *break* transitive and *break* intransitive you can argue that *break* transitive is in fact a causative type of verb and there is a good argument that causative verbs are a separate class and children use these relatively early. I don't think *smoke* is necessarily the same sort of verb.

KLIMA: If the real distinction is between causative and non-causative verbs, that could argue against the co-ordinative transformation. In a derivation from a causative verb you would first get an intransitive, and then the transitive would have to be derived from that.

BEVER: No; in fact quite the contrary, because *the glass breaks* is derived from *something breaks the glass*.

KLIMA: Not semantically. And this interpretation has the advantage that it would include verbs like *fall*.

HYMES: It seems to me that we have two lines of argument here. One is: how would you analyse it if it were just a linguistic problem? Would you say the one came from the other, or not? The other thing we are talking about is what we are willing to suppose happens psychologically, in the real life of the child. Let us look at these two lines of evidence and the relationship between them. If you convince yourself that something is developmental, would you then be prepared to argue with the linguist about his analysis?

BEVER: No. Ontogenetic priority does not imply formal priority in the description of adult structures. It would be entirely consistent with Postal's formal analysis that the first structure the child discovers is one in which the verb is joined by two nouns, while it is only later that the child discovers that some verbs can join with only one noun.

HYMES: Conversely then, the argument about what the structure was, in the language as a whole, would tell nothing one way or the other about development.

BEVER: As far as I can see, that is correct.

SINCLAIR: Has anybody tried to find out about grammaticality judgements in children? I have tried this, but I get the most curious things.

KLIMA: That is not surprising, if they are still learning the language.

SINCLAIR: We have a sorting task in which the children have to put together white chairs and other objects. We use *white* and *chairs* because in French adjectives agree with nouns: *chaises blanches*, not *blancs*. First we ask: *What is the colour?* The children will answer: *Les chaises sont blanches.* Next they are asked to sort the objects, and when they are asked what they are doing, four out of ten children will lose the correct form *blanches.*

We have two types of sentences uttered by the children:

> *Les chaises sont blanches*
> *Les chaises sont tout blancs* or *Les chaises est tout blancs*

When I ask them which sentence is right, I get this sort of answer: *If I talk about why I put them together, "les chaises sont tout blancs"; but if you ask what colour they are I say "blanches".* Now, what kind of intuition of grammaticality is involved there?

ERVIN-TRIPP: What were you putting together, other white objects?

SINCLAIR: Yes, there were white babies and brown babies and brown chairs.

ERVIN-TRIPP: Some may have been counting a more general category which included some object that would not fit the restricted grammatical description.

SINCLAIR: Cognitively, I don't think it is too difficult to explain. At the age of 4 or 5, once they have made a rough classification, they seem to see this as one unique object, which is totally white, since they have no idea of extension. Everything gets lumped together, the whole thing is *blanc.* Obviously, you wouldn't say *sont blanches* any more, in that case; but this is just an example of how impossibly difficult I find it to get any grammaticality judgement from children.

Cognition and Language

Methods for the Study of Early Cognitive Functioning

J. CHURCH

The City University of New York

MY PURPOSE is not to describe systematically the numerous techniques that have been devised for the study of cognition early in life, which I have done elsewhere (Church, 1970). Here I am more concerned to examine the relevance of such techniques for the understanding of human development and of linguistic development in particular. I see the central problem as how to understand the Whorfian hypothesis, how language relates to perceiving, thinking, learning, feeling, judging and development. Obviously, Whorf's formulation of the Whorfian hypothesis was incorrect. But the two sorts of different formulations that I see strike me as even less helpful. One position, perhaps best exemplified by the work of Furth, and explicit in the early thinking of Piaget, is that language is largely irrelevant to cognitive development, which is under the control either of autonomously maturing internal structures or of a veridically perceived environment. Many people within this tradition still study cognition with little reference to language: they *use* language but they do not investigate language.

On the other hand, there is "developmental psycholinguistics" exemplified by Fodor and McNeill in *The genesis of language* (ed. Smith and Miller, 1966), heavily influenced by Chomsky, which single-mindedly pursues the study of the development of linguistic structures without reference, as Dell Hymes has pointed out, to problems of communication or cognition or psychological functioning in general.

In my opinion, the kind of developmental psychology which segments learning, perception, cognition, language, to such an extent that these abstractions become practically reified, is a thing of the past. This is the kind of fragmentation which permits the writing of learned treatises on the effects of cognition on perception or of intelligence on cognition.

I would like to re-unite the various approaches to the study of cognitive development, and to bring the study of linguistic development into the same framework. What I am aiming at is a developmental phenomenology of infancy and early childhood, attempting to depict, analyse and characterize the life space of the child. The concept of life space I have taken from K. Lewin (1935) as the framework for the kind of study I have in mind.

The techniques for establishing the origin of early differences in cognition consist of a number of tasks which the child is set. Though I have found many of these in the educational literature, and in Piaget (with whom I share a belief in the importance of observation), my approach differs to some extent from both of these orientations. First, my approach is not psychometric, I do not wish to end up with a score. My conviction is that simple normative studies, unrelated to antecedent variables, are obsolete. It is now generally accepted that human cognition is inescapably relativistic; we know that there are important group differences as well as individual differences in the way in which self and world are perceived, categorized, thought and talked about, valued and acted towards. We need a new theory of intelligence, one which transfers the notion of intellectual differences from the organism to the environment. I want to plot out the characteristics of a stupid environment and an intelligent environment, which I believe can be done within the frame of the notion of life space.

Secondly, I do not completely accept the kind of structuralism, derived from Piaget, which is exemplified by Uzgiris and Hunt (1966). I am willing to grant only semi-autonomy to mental mechanisms and operations, and I would make them contingent upon the interaction of the organism with objects, human and otherwise. If we assume that there is some kind of structure, neural or whatever, corresponding to every sort of operation, we end up packing the child as full of structures as McDougall did with propensities. A model which gives the baby a set of "pre-wired" structures breaks down when we consider all the artifacts and processes, real or symbolic, which the child has to learn to adapt to; and cultural and subcultural differences make the picture even more complicated—unless we are willing to ascribe such cultural variations to genetic, that is, to racial factors. I prefer to think that the baby may be "pre-wired" with *sensitivities* to certain aspects of the world, and that semi-autonomous structures arise out of the direct and socially mediated interaction between the child and the world.

Thirdly, if we are going to be able to integrate the study of linguistic development with the study of cognitive development in general, we will have to persuade the linguists to give up some of their notions about language. The concept of the idealized speaker-hearer is not helpful. We have to examine language, not as if the child was developing in isolation, but in communicative, social and cultural contexts. We have to find what is fed into the child as well as what he produces, and we have to examine not only the formal aspects of language but also the kinds of functions that it serves.

I am looking for a description of the communicative acts and operations, where the primary classification is in terms of the kinds of points that the child is trying to get across, and where the formal description is subordinate to this. One instance of a communicative act is that of drawing contrasts, which is very clearly revealed when the child invents his own linguistic means: *This thing has an upper part and a downer part.* Only in this way can we hope to make sense of how language relates to the child's total grasp of the world around him, how language enters into the construction of his life spaces, and into their destruction and reconstitution.

In this context the notion of linguistic universals is useless and in any case the quest for them has proved largely futile. That is not to say that there are no cognitive universals; but they seem to be very basic, primitive, perceptual processes, of the kind that organisms need to survive. There must for instance be a kind of universal figure-ground organization, so that we do not constantly walk into obstacles on the assumption that they are spaces between objects. Without the visual cliff response (babies shying when approaching a real or apparent drop-off) real precipices would be a danger (though for some puppies and babies it seems to act as a positive attraction). But apart from such basic processes, most cognitive aspects are neither innate nor the simple product of maturation. Even when we assume that a given cognitive skill will appear sooner or later in just about everybody, there may still be marked cultural differences in the age of emergence.

I have now amassed something like 200 tasks from the study of cognitive development between birth and the age of 4. I have drawn on many sources and have found to my surprise that the literature contains a wealth of techniques. But it is not always easy to recognize the useful ones: for instance the Cattell scale (Cattell, 1940) has an item called "glass frustration" which makes one think of it as an emotional thing, and it was somebody else who pointed out to me that this was the same as my "ability to detour round a transparent barrier". By watching babies encounter and cope with objects, one can find a great many situations that are easily adaptable to formal testing. We tend to forget that the world is an intelligence test and that babies in normal environments spend much of their waking time exploring those environments and solving the puzzles they present. Some of these tasks ask the child to interact with stimulus objects, while others are questions designed to elicit information from the adult in charge of the child. For instance, I am interested in early manifestation of guilt feelings as an aspect of self-awareness. I have not yet found a way of eliciting guilt in the laboratory, but every mother I have asked has given me a sensible answer to the question, "How does he act when you catch him doing something he isn't supposed to do?" How verbal the tasks are depends, obviously, on the age of the child. At the earliest ages, it is the demand qualities of the stimulus objects that, quite reliably, tell the child what to do.

This set of tasks overlaps somewhat with those assembled by Bettye Caldwell (1964), by Uzgiris and Hunt (1966), and, most especially, by Audrey Little (n.d.) at Western Australia. At older ages, my tasks have much in common with the Early Childhood Inventories developed by Coller and Victor (1967). There are, however, some important differences. One, of course, is that the overlap among sets is far from complete. Like Charlesworth (1968), I place more reliance than the others on affective indicators of what is cognized and how. The baby's differential emotional reactions to strangers and familiar people can be taken as evidence that schemata of the known are being established.

My chief concern in using these tasks was to establish the early origins of cultural differences in cognition and, eventually, to relate these to cultural differences in child-rearing practices. We already have some evidence of early cultural differences in the sphere of motor and postural developments, as in Mead and MacGregor's (1951) observations on the early acquisition of styles of movement, and in Geber's (1958) observations on the remarkable precocity of African babies reared in the tribal fashion. Caudill and Weinstein (1966) have demonstrated sharp divergences in temperament between Japanese and American middle-class babies from a few months of age; it seems reasonable, then, to assume that early differences in cognition can likewise be demonstrated. One might also find some diagnostic uses for these tasks, singly or in combination. They may suggest some techniques in early education and provide a means of evaluating their effectiveness. Finally, they may be useful in studying the way non-linguistic aspects of cognitive development relate to the acquisition of language and the way language influences and fails to influence perception and thought at early ages.

I have grouped my cognitive tasks into six subtests, dealing respectively with (1) self-awareness, (2) social and personal awareness, and affect, with a subset designed to study the baby's developing reactions to medical personnel and preventive medical procedures—in short, learning to anticipate pain from his monthly check-ups, (3) imitation, (4) perception of space, spatial relations, and physical causation, (5) perception of objects and object attributes, and (6) perception of pictures and other two-dimensional arrays.

The usual difficulties in working with very young children are magnified when one is working with babies of a different race or subculture. To them everything about the experimenter may be wrong and terrifying, his skin colour, his accent, his smell. Particularly in medical settings, the examiner may take on the dreaded connotations of doctor. These problems can be solved—usually—with a bit of patience; it may be just as important to allay the stranger anxiety of the mother or accompanying adult as that of the baby.

SELF-AWARENESS

The earliest test of self-awareness with which I am familiar is to interrupt the baby's visual contact with the world by draping a cleaning tissue over the upper part of his face. There seems to be a fairly stable developmental sequence of reactions from no response, to vocal fussing, to whole-body activity, to head-wagging, to diffuse reaching in which the baby seems to want to use his hands but doesn't know where to apply them, to more localized but still ineffectual reaching in the vicinity of the head, to removal of the tissue by wiping it away, and finally typically by the age of 5 months, to reaching up, grasping the tissue, and pulling it off. This last, most mature response itself comes in three stages: the first consists in the baby's remaining still, and even tense, for as long as 30 seconds, as though trying to figure out what to do before reaching up to grasp the tissue; the second is immediate grasping and removal; the third is to remove the tissue and then put it back, as though initiating a game of peek-a-boo.

Another indicator of self-awareness is the baby's reaction to being tickled. A cleaning tissue is twisted to form a point which is then moved lightly back and forth across, in random order, the outer surface of each calf, the skin of each forearm, and the top of the baby's head. The developmental sequence in this case is from no response to a change of facial expression (typically a smile or a puzzled or quizzical frown), to generalized movement, to moving the tickled member, to looking towards the tickling, to touching the spot being tickled.

Although these reactions have been set forth in sequence, the range of

G

ages at which each appears is wide. It is not too surprising that 1-month-old babies should fail to react to this minimal stimulation; but babies as old as 3 or 4 months may also show no response. Responding in terms of a change of expression has been observed between ages 1 month and 4 months. Generalized movement occurs over the entire 1-to-6-month range. Movement just of the member tickled has been observed as early as 1 month and as late as 5 months. Visual orientation to the site of tickling seems not to begin until the age of 4 months. Manual localization—touching or rubbing or scratching the tickled spot—does not seem to occur in infants: I have not seen a baby under 6 months do it (although I have seen much younger babies scratching their eczema), and most babies older than 6 months are too active for this test.

One can detect the baby's beginning shift from almost total dependency to partial autonomy by asking the mother, "How do you know when he wakes up?" Characteristically, at about the age of 4 months, the baby no longer howls for attention as soon as he awakes, but instead spends some time amusing himself, crowing or cooing, playing with his fingers, exploring his surroundings, and in general being self-sufficient. At least some babies reach a point where this solitary interlude becomes an essential transition between sleeping and waking, so that they actively resent adult interruption. It would be interesting to find out whether this first autonomy is made possible by the attainment of visually guided reaching and grasping; it seems connected with the child's discovery of his hands, which is another interview item, as is the somewhat later discovery of the feet. I have not thought it worthwhile to ask about the discovery of his navel, a standard but often unnoticed event, or prudent to ask about the discovery of the genitalia.

The baby's ability to feed himself, and the differential timing for biting off mouthfuls from something held in the hand, like a biscuit or an apple slice, for soft foods which can be crammed into the mouth or licked off, and for picking up pellet-like bits, whether a pea or a piece of meat, and popping it into the mouth, is a potential field of study which I have not explored.

Stages in the baby's recognition of his own reflection in the looking-glass have been studied by Dixon (1957). In middle-class babies, recognition occurs at about 10 months. A report on the early education project in the Baltimore City Public Schools (1964), however, indicates that lower-class 4-year-olds may not yet recognize their own reflections. I have tried to verify this observation with a sample of lower-class 4-year-olds in Poughkeepsie but found that they all recognized themselves. I abandoned this approach, only to find that my wife, working with a group of disadvantaged Hawaiian and part-Hawaiian 3- and 4-year-olds, had observed in them a failure of self-recognition. The question is still moot.

Negativism is an indicator of autonomy and hence self-awareness, but I have so far found no way to study it in the laboratory. One can get at early manifestations of conscience, as I have said, by asking the mother, "How does he act when you catch him doing something he's not supposed to do?" This is, admittedly, a beating-your-wife kind of question, but so far it has always worked. I find the variety of behaviours described quite fascinating: no reaction; hurries to finish before he can be interrupted; tries to hide activity; flees or hides; stops activity and feigns innocence; cries woefully, cries angrily; acts fearful; proffers the forbidden object to the adult; or makes a lavish display of affection.

At younger ages one can ask the baby to indicate facial features and body parts that the examiner names, and at later ages one can ask the child to name parts of the anatomy that the examiner indicates. Striking social class differences exist in performance on these tasks. Bladder control is an index of self-awareness, and this attainment is signalled by whether the baby wears diapers or pants. Play-acting, pretending to be somebody or something else, would be a useful indicator if we knew how to elicit it.

What I have called the Cyclops effect (Church, 1966) is an interesting if transitory phenomenon that waxes and wanes between the ages of 1 and 2. One peers at the baby through a tube (I use the cardboard rollers from paper towels), saying "Boo!" or "Hi!" to make sure the baby is attending, and then when he has responded (typically with a smile), hand him the tube with a reasonable expectation that he will try to reciprocate. At its full flower, the Cyclops effect consists in the baby's planting the tube squarely between his eyes and being baffled to know why he cannot see through it. At ages younger than a year, babies seem not to try to look through the tube. When they first begin to try, they may place the tube in the midline of the head, but below eye level—most often over the nose, but in one case over the mouth (I discarded one 20-month-old who apparently was using the tube as a wind instrument). Whatever the baby's knowledge of his own binocularity, vision seems to be phenomenologically centred in a unitary field. By the age of 2, most babies fit the tube over one eye.

One can ask babies from $1\frac{1}{2}$ on to perform arbitrary, abstract actions of the kind that seemed to baffle Goldstein and Scheerer's (1941) brain-injured patients: "Open your mouth"; "Close your eyes"; "Touch your hair"; etc. One can ask children age 2 and over how many they have of various body parts: "How many ears have you got?"; "How many noses?" etc.—children seem to be neither amused nor disturbed by the plural designation of singular traits. The baby's knowledge of his own age is yet another useful index, even though he may have no idea of what the numbers and time designations stand for.

Somewhere between ages 2 and 3, children begin to apply trait adjectives (*big, strong, good, pretty, fat*) to themselves and to be able to specify some of their competences and incompetences ("I don't know how to read yet"), but I have so far not found any way to incorporate these self-verbalizations into a set of formal measures.

The final self-awareness item asks the child to talk about sensory functions. Notice that there are two sorts of questions. One kind goes from function to organ: "What do you smell (taste, touch) with?" and the other from organ to function: "What are your eyes (ears) for?" Most middle-class 3-year-olds can cope with this task, and they seem to do equally well on all five subtasks. Lower-class 4-year-olds do somewhat less well. (No statistical comparisons involving 3-year-olds were possible, since the 3-year-old data were collected by two students who graduated before the analysis was begun.) The lower-class 4-year-olds had difficulty with all the senses except vision. Several of our middle-class 4-year-olds had difficulty with taste (5 out of 16 subjects) and touch (6 out of 16 subjects).

SOCIAL AND PERSONAL AWARENESS

The chief stimulus material for the study of early social awareness is the experimenter, unless the child is afraid of him, and then one may use the mother, as long as she does not distract the child by over-empathizing, or actively intervening to help. One notes first of all whether the baby attends to the experimenter's face at close range. A surprising number of babies do not, and I suspect—without real evidence—that such inattention may be pathognomic. One then begins speaking to see if the experimenter's voice elicits a change of state. One finds out by asking the mother whether the baby smiles at people (I have had little luck making very young babies to whom I was a stranger smile), and, at a somewhat later age, whether the baby laughs. From the age of 2 months, one speaks in short bursts to the baby to see whether he shows any signs of trying to answer back—several times mothers have told me that the exchange of conversational babble is something the baby does only with his father.

From the age of 3 months on, one looks for signs of tension or reserve in the baby's reaction to the test situation, the examiner himself, or to the test materials. From the age of 5 months one tries to play social games with the child; saying "Boo!", pretending to be angry, playing peek-a-book, this little piggy, give and take, pat-a-cake, and waving bye-bye. One leaves a plaything on the table top to see if the baby will drop it overboard and then look to an adult to retrieve it. If the baby is able to creep, one asks the mother if he likes to be chased and if he himself initiates the chasing game. One also asks if he likes to hide and be found. One tries giving the child a plaything and then abruptly taking it away from him—this is a test of conservation, but it is also a test of how conservation is manifested emotionally and behaviourally, by puzzlement, woe, anger, or active searching or reaching. One asks the mother to reach out her arms to the baby to see if he responds in kind, and once he has been picked up what manifestations of affection—hugging, snuggling, kissing—appear. Logically, the question about early manifestations of guilt can be considered to belong here as well as in the category of self-awareness.

Reactions to Medical Personnel and Procedures

On the basis of observations of my own children, I hypothesized a developmental increase in the gradient of anticipatory fear that babies will show towards visits to the paediatrician. I later learned that this had been the topic of a somewhat abortive study by David Levy (1960). Here I must specify that in the United States babies are taken for monthly medical examinations during the first year of life, and receive an immunizing injection at almost every visit. On the first visit or two, the baby has no reason to expect pain, and he does not begin to scream until the needle actually goes in; it may even take him until several seconds after the injection to realize that something unpleasant has happened. Once the baby has begun to learn his lesson, he shows signs of fear at increasingly earlier stages in the process: the doctor's approach, being undressed for the examination, entering the examining room, entering the waiting room, approaching the doctor's office; by the age of 1 year, leaving home to go to the doctor's. As one mother told me, "We always take a taxi to come to the doctor's. Now, whenever he sees the taxi pull up to the house, he starts to howl."

Alas, my study aborted as thoroughly as Levy's. The reasons might be psychologically interesting if I could be sure what they were. I worked in the office of a paediatrician with a largely Japanese–American practice, and what I think I observed was the precocious development of a massive imperturbability, the babies stoically enduring without protest whatever was done to them. This observation is wholly consonant with Caudill's findings. It is still a moot question however, for the paediatrician gave the injections quickly and skilfully from behind, in a buttock, and the babies were given a lollipop which seemed to distract them from any pain or discomfort.

IMITATION

I had hoped to demonstrate, via a stable sequence of emergence of imitative behaviour, the origins of imitation in a general empathic capacity rather than in the reinforcement paradigm of various learning theories. Let me say immediately that I failed, but not without, I hope, learning something along the way. Following Zazzo (1957) the stimulus-action for the youngest babies was sticking out my tongue. Zazzo reports that babies 10–20 days old imitate tongue-protrusion, and I myself have observed it in a number of babies in this age range. However, with one part-Hawaiian sample (27 babies, aged 1–9 months), I could not elicit tongue-protrusion before the age of 2 months, and three of the five 2-month-olds who responded did so only inconsistently. Nevertheless, tongue-protrusion was the form of imitation that appeared earliest in this sample. As mentioned under the rubric of social and personal awareness, a kind of quasi-imitation that appears at about the age of 2 months in American middle-class babies is the infant's trying to speak back when spoken to—his reaction takes the form of twisting and squirming, miscellaneous mouth movements including smiling, and sometimes the production of a strangled sound or two. I succeeded in eliciting such behaviour from only three of 150-odd Hawaiian subjects; one was 3 months old and the others were 5 months old.

Some of the other stimuli used with varying degree of success and failure are: lip-smacking, arm-waving, head-wagging, sniffing, blowing and whistling (which are on Little's scale; obviously, one does not expect an infant to whistle, but I have observed a number of them trying to), vocalizations like ah-ah-ah and dah-dah-dah (which are on the Cattell scale at the 9-month level), slapping the table top (which Cattell places in the twelfth month but which my Hawaiian babies responded to quite reliably from the age of 7 months—obviously, one can test for this only with babies mature enough to sit up in a high chair or feeding table), making a great show of effort about picking something up, knocking over a plaything set in front of the baby, inverting a cup, hand-clapping, playing peek-a-boo, and waving bye-bye.

Other acts of imitation that I have observed adventitiously are copying the "ding" of a kitchen timer, the sound of an internal combustion engine, the squeak made by a squeeze toy, and dropping a block through a cardboard tube. A number of babies have been reported to croon to music from as young as the age of 3 months, but I have yet to settle on the right stimulus. (Two tasks in the area of spatial relations—pouring from cup to cup and using a stick to reach a lure—involve learning by imitation, and both work with children in the 14–24 month range.)

PERCEPTION OF SPACE, SPATIAL RELATIONS, AND CAUSATION

Several people have questioned why I consider the tasks that follow to be tests of space perception. I in turn have difficulty in understanding the question; these tasks all have to do with the location, orientation or direction of movement of objects with respect to other objects, to the concrete settings in which the objects are situated, or to abstract spatial co-ordinates such as up and down, and eventually, of course, to even more abstract ones such as north and south. Here we are dealing with everyday three-dimensional space, which I take to be the primary sphere of orientation. Some references to two-dimensional space come later.

Some aspects of spatial perception have been demonstrated so often that we need mention them only in passing. Everybody is confident now that newborn babies track moving objects with their eyes, and a few by moving their heads. From the age of a few weeks babies can track a moving person as far as they can swivel their heads, although this observation was treated as a major heresy just a few years ago. White (White, Castle, and Held, 1964) has studied visually guided reaching and grasping to the point where little seems to remain to be said. More in doubt is the age at which babies first orient visually to a source of sound. Wertheimer (1961) thought that he observed such orienting from birth, but later began to have his doubts. My own observations of 32 Hawaiian babies between the ages of 1 month and 7 months led me to conclude that 4 months was the turning point. One day, though, the mother of a 2-month-old spoke from behind him and he immediately twisted his head round in her direction. At that point I had almost finished running subjects, but I asked a few more mothers to do the same, and decided that, although the baby probably does not orient to inanimate sounds of moderate intensity until the age of 4 months, he turns to a familiar voice at 2 months.

I have already mentioned the next task, having to do with the development of the baby's ability to cope with a transparent barrier between him and some desired object, included in the Cattell Scale under the name of "glass frustration" (Cattell, 1940). It is one of Little's tasks as well (Little, n.d.). I have tried several forms of glass frustration, such as interposing a glass or a coarse wire mesh screen between the baby and the lure, and the one that I like best is dropping a coloured plastic clothespeg into a wide-mouthed, shallow, clear plastic container and setting it down in front of the baby. Up to the age of 8 or 10 months (Cattell gives the thirteenth or fourteenth month as the norm), the baby, if he responds to the clothespeg at all, tries persistently to grasp it through the side of the container. Notice that the container is visible to him—he may even grasp its edge in one hand while trying with the other to penetrate its side. He may also, in the course of his struggles, accidentally spill out the clothespeg, but he does not benefit from this experience: as soon as it is returned to the container, he resumes his attempted penetration. At the same time he is quite capable of taking something out of a container provided it is opaque. A related but somewhat more advanced task is to give the baby a lure in a transparent bottle with an opening too narrow to accommodate his hand. Here, of course, the solution is to invert the bottle and let gravity do the work. According to Cattell, babies can solve this problem imitatively in the thirteenth and fourteenth month, and spontaneously in the fifteenth and sixteenth month. In my sample, only three children older than a year failed to solve the problem spontaneously, and two 1-year-olds and one 14-month-old solved it.

Observing babies exploring space in their free play, it is striking that, though babies are highly sensitive not only to vertical drop-offs but also to the threat of surfaces that slope away from them, they do not seem to grasp spontaneously that the same laws apply to their playthings. I think I have seen babies try to set things down on a wall, like the comedian who hangs his coat on a non-existent coathook. It comes as a great surprise even to $1\frac{1}{2}$-year-olds that a toy car placed at the top of an incline should roll down it. To try to test for this effect in the laboratory, I built two low benches, one with a horizontal top and the other with a top pitched at 30° from the horizontal. These were placed so as to form a right angle, with a plaything on the floor near their junction, and then the child was placed by the toy, in the expectation that he would try to set it on one of the benches. The notion was that younger babies would choose at random between the benches, whereas older ones would show a consistent preference for the level top. But I never found out, since this seemingly innocuous partial enclosure proved to be so disturbing to babies that they either simply cried or fled.

Another task also included in Little's set, is to confront the baby with three playthings in a row. These must be objects small enough to pick up in one hand but not small enough to be picked up two to a hand. Reliably, the baby will want to pick up all three playthings. The discontinuity comes when he realizes that he has not got enough hands to go around, and that he will have to put down (or tuck under an arm) one of the two playthings he has already picked up before he can pick up the remaining one. In a sample of six babies, about the eighth month seems to be the turning point, although 8-month-olds may go through a period of bafflement, looking back and forth among hands and objects, before the light dawns.

Piaget has given us the interesting task of asking the baby to extrapolate the path of a moving object which disappears behind an opaque screen and then reappears on the far side. The least mature response is simply to lose interest as soon as the object disappears. A more mature response is to continue watching the point of disappearance as though in expectation that the object will reappear. The baby's response is scored only after he has observed where the object actually emerges from behind the screen several times. The most mature response, which seems to appear after about 8 months of age, is to swivel the gaze to the far edge of the screen in anticipation of the object's reappearance.

From the primate literature has come the task of securing a visible but out-of-reach lure by pulling on a string tied to it. This task has been used by both Little and Cattell; Cattell places it in the eighth month. There seem to be several developmental steps in the mastery of this problem: paying no attention to either the lure or the strings; trying to reach the lure but giving up; playing with the string but failing to notice that the lure moves when the string moves; discovering the correlated movement of string and lure and then capitalizing on the discovery to obtain the lure; and, finally, simply grabbing the string and pulling in the lure. Like Cattell, I find solutions to the problem appearing between the ages of 7 and 8 months. A variant of this task is the crossed-string problem, which adds noise to the system in the form of one or more extra lengths of string that lead nowhere. In my experience, every baby who solved the simple string problem was also able to solve crossed-string problems, which suggests to me that this complication tells us nothing further.

The next batch of tasks represents a failure in human engineering. I made the mistake of constructing a single panel containing a great many stimuli; as a result, my subjects were very easily distracted. The research needs to be repeated with only one task to a panel.

One group of tasks was designed to test the baby's ability to manipulate various kinds of latches to open doors in the panel: a simple pull-knob (the door being held closed by a magnet), a spring-return latch of the kind found on ordinary doors, a rotary lever latch, a lift latch, a hook and eye, and a sliding bolt. Provisionally, this arrangement of tasks corresponds to a developmental sequence between the ages of 9 months and 2 years. The same panel also contained a narrow slot and a small circular hole (about 1 cm), to elicit the exploratory probing with the forefinger that one so often sees in the everyday behaviour of older infants. A few babies obliged, but for most these stimuli seemed not to be very compelling in their complicated surroundings. Also mounted on this panel was a socket containing a 15-watt light bulb turned on and off by a pull-chain switch with a length of string attached. To attract the baby's attention, I would turn the light on and off a few times and then wait to see what happened. Babies between the ages of 9 and 15 months characteristically touched, pushed, pulled, or twisted the bulb itself, as though direct action would make it work; a few babies in this range tried to use the string, but without success. When the subject could not work the switch, I proceeded to two levels of training: first, I demonstrated again the correct procedure, moving my hand slowly and exaggeratedly, a procedure which worked with a number of babies in the 1–2-year range. If it did not work, I folded the baby's hand around the string, clasped his hand in mine, and worked the switch in this way. This technique was successful with all babies aged 1 year or over, although some continued to have trouble controlling the direction of their pull, and some needed further instruction to teach them that they had to release the tension at the end of the pull to reset the switch.

Some other aspects of spatial perception are indicated by the baby's ability to remove and, at a later age, to replace a screw-on bottle cap, his awareness of the "correct" up-down orientation of objects (tested by placing an object on its side in front of him to see if he sets it upright); pouring from container to container (which he is asked to learn imitatively from the examiner's demonstration); using a stick to reach a distant lure; piling graduated discs on a spindle and assembling a nest of boxes. I tried, with my 4-year-old samples, a test of spatial vocabulary (near, far, in between, on, under, etc.), but it turned out to be too easy for both middle-class and disadvantaged children. By contrast, to my surprise, a test of time words turned out to be much too hard.

PERCEPTION OF OBJECTS AND OBJECT ATTRIBUTES

An index of early learning is the baby's visual recognition of the nursing bottle, shown by his opening his mouth and straining towards the bottle. Cattell places this behaviour in the third month, but I find it by the age of 1 month in bottle-fed babies, obviously. A complication, however, is that the 1-month-old does not discriminate between a nursing bottle and a host of other objects, and it remains to be seen how wide a range of equivalent stimuli he will react to, and at what age he reacts only to the bottle.

Visually guided reaching and grasping can also be understood as an aspect of object perception in that it implies that the object exists for the baby as a graspable solid. Both Little and I have been interested in the baby's systematic visual inspection of novel objects, although I am still in search of the ideal stimulus. Piaget, Cattell and Little have studied object conservation; most successfully, I believe, by the technique of slowly lowering an object behind an opaque screen, the index of conservation being whether the baby tries to rise upward to follow the vanishing object.

It has to be learned that wheeled vehicles roll; and one can see the contrast between younger babies, who move a toy car without regard to the wheels, and older ones, who consistently move the car only forwards or backwards. I have long intended to study the baby's tactual exploration of textured surfaces (e.g., window screening, fur, sandpaper, etc.) but have not yet done so, although one can observe such exploration in everyday life.

Standard playthings of middle-class babies are the kitchen pots and pans, which he learns to disassemble and eventually to reassemble. There seem to be marked social-class differences in the sophistication with which babies deal for instance with a double-boiler, which is apparently related to the restricted access poor children have to such playthings. To a middle-class family such utensils are not expensive, to a poor family they are.

We move here into the linguistic sphere, testing the baby's passive and active knowledge of object names, colour names, and size terms. It still comes as a surprise to many people to learn that disadvantaged 4-year-olds are likely not to know colour names, which many middle-class 2-year-olds have mastered.

With 3- and 4-year-olds we have used various tests of sameness and difference (a key concept in the Coller and Victor tasks), with middle-class 3-year-olds surpassing disadvantaged 4-year-olds in their ability both to say correctly whether two objects are the same or different and, when the objects are different, to put into words the nature of the difference. We have also used a five-object oddity task, using five blocks of five colours, five sizes, and two shapes (four of the blocks triangular and the fifth a cube). The same social-class differences are observable in the ability to point out the odd block and to verbalize the difference. (It is enough for our purposes that the child be able to say something to the effect that these blocks look like tents and this one does not, or even "they're sort of different here", pointing to the corners.)

PERCEPTION OF TWO-DIMENSIONAL ARRAYS

Although I find the study of the perception of two-dimensional patterns a fascinating pursuit, I have found and developed only a few tasks in this area. Western adults take picture perception so much for granted, and for educated adults this extends to the perception of maps, diagrams, charts, graphs, and all the rest, that they may fail to notice that skills in this area have to develop, and may have to be cultivated. Studies of neonatal and infantile perception, usually by the preference method but also by tracing eye movements, indicate that babies can find some kind of meaning in two-dimensional patterns right from the beginning. The problem is to know what kind. A controversy, reminiscent of that between the atomists and Gestaltists during the 1930s and '40s, seems to be boiling up between elementalists, inspired by Hebb's cell-assembly view of development, and globalists, marching under the banner of Werner's differentiation-integration view (1948). For the moment I see no ready empirical answer to the problem. I will say only that one cannot safely infer that the baby sees only the point he is fixating at a given moment. That is, there is no reason to assume that the baby's visual experience is punctiform, but there is every reason to assume that there is some kind of temporal integration involved in coming to terms with any new perceptual object, whether it be a picture, a piece of music, or a roomful of people. I keep trying to ally myself with the Gibsons (1966) to say that three-dimensional perception is the basic kind, with perception of two-dimensional patterns a more difficult and intricate process, and the Gibsons consistently keep repudiating me. I think part of the difficulty lies in their adherence to stimulus properties, as shown for instance in their study of the kinds of deformations of letter-like forms which can be accepted as equivalent to a standard, whereas I am more concerned with subject variables, for instance, those which will permit equivalence between forms having little in common morphologically, such as printed and cursive, capital and small forms of many actual letters of the alphabet, which are none the less treated by the child as equivalent.

One can sometimes get evidence of picture recognition even from preverbal babies—indeed, the Hayes (Hayes, 1951) observed picture recognition in their chimpanzee, Viki. The baby usually demonstrates his recognition by some appropriate action: rocking to a picture of a rocking-horse, making the sound of a motor to a picture of a car, petting a pictured animal, smelling the picture of a flower, or, like Viki, trying to hear the ticking of a pictured watch. My attempts to duplicate such responding in test situations have been a failure, partly perhaps because I could not find culturally relevant pictures for my Hawaiian sample. My pictures included an apple and a banana, both of which are common in Hawaii, but neither of which can be considered a really gripping stimulus. For what it is worth, none of my Hawaiian 1–2-year-olds reacted to a picture card as a picture: they chewed, bent, pounded, and threw the cards, but they seemed impervious to the fact that the cards bore meaningful representations of objects.

There are several tasks which test perceptual organization in 3-, 4-, and 5-year-olds. For instance, asking the child simply to trace a looping line indicates that younger children do not see the good continuation of the line, as shown by the way they detour around the loops. A similar effect is seen in asking the child to colour two crossed oblongs, the "nearer" of which masks the centre section of the "more distant" one. The youngest children ignore the lines separating the two oblongs and simply colour the cross as a whole. Somewhat older subjects are likely to colour the two exposed ends of the partly masked oblong different colours, suggesting that they appear disconnected. It is only at about the age of 4 or 5 that children consistently begin to assign the same colour to the exposed ends of the rearward oblong.

A number of people have studied the development of ability to copy geometric forms. I have data indicating reliably superior performance of a group of 16 middle-class 4-year-olds over 23 disadvantaged 4-year-olds in the task of copying the block capital letters A, E, M, and P. The examiner first printed the letter on a blank sheet of paper and then handed the pencil to the child with an invitation to make the letter, which was named. It is important to sit behind or beside the child when making the standard for him to copy. If one sits across a table from the child and forms the letter upside down so that it is properly oriented for the child, he may try to reciprocate. A number of children have transcended their egocentrism to the extent of making the letter upside down, for the examiner's benefit, but none has transcended egocentrism so far as to do it correctly. Performance on each letter is scored zero for no response (although every effort is made to teach the child the operation, to the point of moving his hand through the necessary strokes), one point for any effort resulting in a mark or scribble, two points for a form obviously derived from the model (such as a zigzag in response to M) but not recognizable as the particular letter, and three points for a recognizable copy, no matter how poor (e.g., any perceptible bit of stem below and to the left of the loop in the P, differentiating it from an O or a D or a Q). With the maximum individual score being 12, middle-class 4-year-olds had a mean of 10·56 and deprived 4-year-olds a mean of 7·6.

Drawing a person is a task ambiguously both two-dimensional and three-dimensional, but in any case middle-class 4-year-olds do somewhat better at it than their disadvantaged age-mates. In fact, the performance of deprived 4-year-olds is at about the same level as that of middle-class 3-year-olds.

Paper-and-pencil mazes, as Porteous has always proclaimed, are a sensitive measure of age differences, although the age norms embodied in the different mazes are probably too low. In our comparison of middle-class and disadvantaged 4-year-olds, we used the age-4 mazes to demonstrate the task, and the age-5 mazes as a test. We ignored Porteous's scoring, which penalizes the child for bumping into the walls, on the ground that our interest in fine motor control was minimal. The middle-class group did significantly better than the disadvantaged group, who again performed at about the same level as middle-class 3-year-olds. Two interesting kinds of response showed up in deprived children. One I call "short-cut": after following the maze for a while, the child travels in a straight line to the exit, disregarding the barrier; 6 out of 28 disadvantaged children responded in this way. The other, which appeared in 2 other deprived children, I call "roundabout": instead of tracing a line through the maze, the children detoured around the outside of the maze from entrance to exit.

We attempted to use the jigsaw puzzles from the Merrill-Palmer scale with our groups, but they proved too easy for all our subjects.

Ann Berens and I (Church, 1969) have done a study comparing deprived (in this case part-Hawaiian) and middle-class Americans (of mixed origin with a large Japanese component). 3–5-year-olds on a task of completing various geometric forms (and some real-life equivalents) with a corner left off. The demands of Prägnanz, or good form, became apparent to our middle-class subjects at the age of 4 or 5, whereas younger middle-class subjects and all our disadvantaged subjects completed the break simply by drawing a line directly between the two ends. It made no detectable difference whether abstract or concrete forms were used.

Let me end on a note of even more unfinished business. I have worked out an *a priori* scheme for the analysis of picture descriptions. This scheme has something in common with the Hemmendinger–Seigel–

Philips (Hemmendinger, 1951) developmental scoring system for Rorschach responses. Picture descriptions can be scored in terms of (a) whether they begin with an integral statement of what the picture is about, and whether this statement is further elaborated, or whether the response consists of the enumeration of isolated objects or features; (b) specification of object attributes; (c) specification of concrete relations between people or objects (e.g., "she's washing the dishes" or "the wagon is bumping into the tree"); (d) specification of social roles (e.g., "daddy", "policeman") or of formal relationships; (e) reference to psychological states such as motives or feelings; (f) mention of antecedent or subsequent events that put the picture in temporal, historical, or evolutionary perspective; and (g) gross misperceptions of content. Notice that the emphasis here is on cognitive powers of analysis and integration, and not on projective themes. The reason that this technique remains untested is that I have never managed to find the right pictures. For my purposes, if I am going to keep my stimuli constant, I need interracial pictures, and good, interesting, interracial pictures suitable for the pre-school years are far from abundant. However, a graduate student at the City University has found some materials for use with school-age children, and is now making a comparison of the responses of normal and disturbed middle-years children, which may provide a test of the method.

In closing, then, I wish to stress the wealth of techniques available to us. Furthermore, these techniques are not merely techniques: they reveal important facts of cognitive development. These facts do not yet exist in any organized pattern, but even in their present incoherent state they carry some implications. It seems to me, for instance, that there can no longer be any serious question about discontinuities in cognitive development. We are now in a position to move on to the more interesting problems of differential cognitive development and its occasions. And we are in a favourable position to reintegrate the study of linguistic and cognitive developments, which have tended recently to go their separate ways. Instead of debating the Whorfian hypothesis, we can begin in earnest to investigate it.

Discussion

Foss: You say that you are intending to test the Whorfian hypothesis; but presumably this would be some re-formulation of it. You would be looking at the function of language, rather than anything else.

Church: Part of my point, at least, is that we have to find some way of relating development in the linguistic sphere to development in the more basic perceptual sphere. I think we can make a case for perception being phylogenetically and ontogenetically prior to language and it might be helpful to postulate a few of the basics of perception which, whether they are innate or not, seem to be reasonably universal. It seems to be clear that there is a basic figure-ground organization in all perception. I've never yet seen an organism, of any species that I know of, trying to walk through an object rather than through the space between objects. There seem to be a few basic things that one finds in virtually all human beings, and virtually all reasonably related species, that point to some basics of experience. I was talking about the visual cliff, and there is the looming effect that William Schiff has reported, which is probably another similar universal: you enlarge a shadow very rapidly on a wall, creating the apparent impression of something approaching very fast, and this is a terrifying experience for baby monkeys, and human babies too.

SINCLAIR: In the case of perception, I think it is necessary to distinguish between a *structure* that is given, or simply a *function* that is given. The fact that certain perceptions will have a discharge of neurones, in a certain line, as an effect, is one thing; the way the species reacts is another thing. Exactly the same constellation of stimuli will not have exactly the same effect for another species. If you are talking about basics in perception, are you talking about the mechanism that is released by the perception, or are you talking about the behaviour that is the result of a certain release mechanism in the brain being set in motion? There are at least three stages.

CHURCH: All I am interested in is the world, and the behaviour consequent upon it. If you want to talk about mediating mechanisms, whether they be in the retina, or in the brain, or wherever, I am not prepared to do so. At this point, all I know about is stimulus and response, and establishing some range of equivalence among stimuli and some range of equivalence among responses. It is very interesting to ask what intervenes, in terms of the pattern of firing of the cones, but I don't know the answer. I am saying that there are some aspects of what perception is, which we can take as pretty much given, without any necessary component of learning. How they determine the structure of language I'm not sure—whether language grows up autonomously from these perceptual things; but I think we are going to have to relate language to perceiving, to thinking, to feeling, to reasoning, and obviously we cannot take it at face value. There has to be some version of the Whorfian hypothesis eventually, if we are going to come to some kind of unitary cognitive psychology.

BEVER: You have indicated that the general goal is to explore the relationship between thought and language; but it isn't clear to me that the tasks that you use bring out anything except the child's capacity to understand instructions. I think this is why you find social class differences and why you don't find figure completion phenomena. In other words, it takes a certain amount of understanding for the child to complete a figure with a square when you present him with an incomplete figure and ask him to complete it. Actually, he is contributing something to your instructions when he decides that you really meant him to make a sensible figure out of it, as opposed to simply closing the gap.

CHURCH: Now we are up against another problem, which is very much reminiscent of the atomist-gestaltist dispute of the 1930's and 1940's—in a slightly different form. Let me tell you the kind of things that the present-day elementalists are talking about, the kind of things that Kessen (1966) sees in studies of new-born perception. He seems to get two different kinds of response: babies who fixate on the angles of a triangle and babies who fixate on the sides, and disregard the angles. The people who, like Kessen, view this in the light of Hebb's assembly theory (Hebb, 1949) see perceptual development as a piecing together of these elements. This is not my view at all: I think there is a global characteristic of triangularity which appears to the child very early in life, that he can recognize without knowing how it is constituted. You can teach 2-year-olds, I have done it myself, to recognize triangularity so that they recognize triangles, of whatever configuration or orientation, very readily. But when you ask them how many sides a triangle has, they have no idea; they cannot draw a triangle, they cannot tell you how many sides it has. By the same token, you can teach them the alphabet and they can recognize all the letters of the alphabet, without having any notion of how these letters were constituted.

MEHLER: We have been testing children of 2 to $2\frac{1}{2}$ years, who had to trace different geometrical figures which were under transparent paper. They had to trace the figures over the transparent paper. One noticeable thing was that these children will fixate the angles and draw the angles first and then they do almost anything else with the lines. This was true for squares and hexagons as well as triangles; so I don't think one can conclude, from the fact that they sometimes draw the shortest line, or the smallest segment between two points that they do, or they don't, have any sort of gestalt disposition at the age of 3, 4 or 5.

CHURCH: Obviously, you have to regard a kind of figure-ground organization as basic in perception. That is, things in the environment look like things. What you cannot assume is either that things are grouped the way adults would group them, according to proximity, similarity or whatever it may be; or that the internal figure-ground organization of the thing is the same for the child as it is for the adult. It is a way of thinking, perhaps peculiar to developmental psychologists, that we assume that what tends to be universal at early ages, such as the tendency to complete a figure in the most direct way possible, represents the spontaneous way of seeing things.

BEVER: That seems to me to be a very questionable assumption. Ontogenetic priority is not necessarily reflected by priority in the organization of adult behaviour.

HYMES: What did you have in mind when you said that according to this view of language, linguistic differences would imply racial differences?

CHURCH: This goes back to the inherent, innate structural view of language, versus language structure built upon what one is exposed to.

HYMES: My understanding is that the view which stressed innateness also stressed the universality of that which is innate.

CHURCH: Universality in principle, but in fact acknowledging that there are group differences in linguistic structure.

BEVER: Some linguists do claim that certain aspects of linguistic structure are genetic in the strong sense, not due just to a general cognitive system but to species-specific linguistic structures. They are claiming that such structures are universal just in the sense that arms are universal. The fact that we claim it universal that a man has two arms leaves open the possibility that there can be genetic differences from one group of men to another in, say, the relative length of the forearm versus the upper arm. Nevertheless, they all have two arms. Whenever one claims that something is genetic, one leaves open the possibility of genetic variation. But a claim that a structure is universal does not admit any, absence of that structure. As soon as somebody claims a skill to be partly innate, other people, seeing differences in the apparent expression of the skill in different social classes or racial groups, draw the conclusion that it must be because there is a different innate structure involved, but that is an entirely unwarranted conclusion.

CHURCH: But, I would like to know where, in the Chomskyan thesis, there is room for environmentally produced differences in structure.

BEVER: Well, the fact that a Chinese child will learn Chinese and an English child will learn English.

CHURCH: But Chinese deep structure is supposed to be the same as English deep structure.

BEVER: No; it is only certain structural properties which are identical

across languages. That is what one means, when one says there are universals. This is independent of the question whether they are innate.
Foss: Is the difference between male and female relevant here? They are pretty consistent. In many languages females tend to be rather more advanced than males in acquisition and they don't have so many kinds of language disorders.

Is this going to be explained genetically? If so, is there a genetic difference in learning ability? Now, supposing there are these observational differences, how are you going to decide whether they are genetic in origin, or whether they depend on factors of motivation and experience? You could perhaps say that the difference in the rate of acquisition would be explained in terms of social role characteristics, but this wouldn't explain differences in language disorders between classes.

Bever: Experience, of course, has an effect on language development. The children we studied in New York came from a much higher social class than the children we studied in Boston. The New York children were 3 to 4 months ahead of the Boston children in their perceptual strategies, and in their syntactic development too. There is a stage of development when older children make mistakes in passives which younger children do not do. Now, the New York children made these advanced kinds of mistakes 4 or 5 months *earlier* than the Boston children. The developmental pattern is the same, the time factor is displaced, which suggests that experience is a vital factor. In an environment where people talk to you and stimulate you, you get pushed into making mistakes earlier. But there is no way, it seems to me, to disconfirm the hypothesis of language universals.

Klima: Let's just assume for the moment that all children are born with the same universal innate linguistic principles; that they are all there, right at the beginning. No Chomskyan linguist would ever say that a certain amount of experience, both real world experience and language experience, isn't absolutely necessary so that certain of these principles can be realized in the language form; and that would vary obviously with differences in the social background.

Cazden: It seems to me that in addition to obvious differences in the child's linguistic environment, there are probably biological differences, which are not genetic. I am thinking of nutrition, not only in the child. There is some recent evidence that protein deficiencies in the mother, before the child is born, affect the child's intellectual function; and this would certainly affect his ability to take advantage of what there is in the linguistic environment for language learning.

T. Ingram: There is also some evidence that the social status of the maternal grandfather may be even more important than the social status of the father. This might indicate something about the nutrition of the mother. This was brought out in a study by Drillien (1957). She measured physical and behavioural development of children of various social classes in Edinburgh and found that the only two children in social class 1 who hadn't done well both had refugee mothers, born in concentration camps.

Foss: Isn't there a correlation between social class and the possibility of minimal brain damage at birth?

T. INGRAM: Yes, and there is also a correlation with brain weight, brain mass, which is probably even more significant.

CHURCH: There are probably inter-correlations between brain weight and brain differentiation as well. Also, there is a strong social-class correlation with prematurity at birth, so that the lower the social class, the greater the chance of premature birth, and all the complications that go with that.

E. INGRAM: It seems that there is, in fact, a consensus that there is an interaction between the environmental factors and the biological factors —I won't call them innate. Perhaps it would be more useful for us to discuss the details of this interaction than to go on demonstrating that both are important.

BERNSTEIN: I want to get back to the point about universals. Now I think there is a conflict between theories of universals and the kinds of findings that you get from that. A theory of universals will tend to study the child as an isolate. The postulated regulative mechanisms will be located within the isolate. Theories of variation tend to seek out regulative mechanisms and processes that arise mainly out of interactions with relationships; which means individuals in a group. In psychology, for instance, there are theories that are concerned with universals; in sociology, one is often concerned with the variations. When one tries to relate sociology to psychology one is apparently dealing with the same phenomenon. It's very difficult because it is not the same phenomenon at all, but rather the same set of phenomena seen in a completely different focus with a completely different theoretical apparatus.

MEHLER: I think perhaps you are making an indictment against what you call the more universal theories. In a sense, I think you are right. Take learning theories in psychology. We could have an adequate theory of learning in the rat and an adequate theory of learning in the man. Now this would look like a theory of variation, but if we had a really adequate universal theory of learning, then perhaps we could view the two separate theories—rat learning and man learning as special cases of the more universal or more general theory, where change is specified as limitations in hardware.

ROBINSON: Yes, this is what I hoped. I thought by now the universalists had done such a good job that we might very well be able to marry up; but it seems that that is not so, at least yet.

HYMES: The trouble is, we are using the term "language" too loosely here, and also we are using the term "universals" too loosely. When we speak about linguistic universals, we mean the underlying general formal properties of the phonology, and the underlying general formal properties of the structural relationships among syntactic categories. These are all of the structural relationships within linguistic theories. These are rather far away from any observable differences of language behaviour of different individuals from different groups. This language behaviour is obviously also partly an outcome of the difference in the ability of different individuals who are confined to playing one role or another, in utilizing whatever linguistic structures they have, in a given communicative situation.

Studies in Language and Thought Development[1]

Centre Nationale de la Recherche Scientifique, France

FOR SOME TIME now I have been engaged in research on the development of cognition, language, and memory. From these studies, a very simple statement ensues: different higher mental processes seem closely interrelated. None the less, some experimental results (those of Piaget, for example, 1956) seem to indicate a much slower development for cognitive functions than for language acquisition as indicated by more recent findings in the latter field. Two years ago we began questioning the feasibility of postulating two independent generators—one that computes logical propositions and the other that outputs well-formed sentences. I was reluctant to accept this possibility since I do not think that nature duplicates uselessly. I suspected that some facts needed verification and that certain interpretations called for serious reformulation.

Psycholinguists generally distinguish two abstract levels, *competence* and *performance*, about which I shall comment in greater detail in the concluding sections of this paper. While the distinction itself is one of Chomsky's major contributions to psychology, there was confusion when these terms became widely adopted. Some psychologists took competence to be merely a synonym for the mechanism underlying behaviour; others accepted competence as whatever we could account for in simple terms, and performance as whatever was difficult to describe. In view of these different assumptions, a definition of these terms might be useful to avoid confusion. Competence is a relational term referring to the theoretical accounts and boundaries of certain capacities; in other words competence concerns the rules limiting the class of possible theories. In the case of language, competence is merely a statement of the power and structure of a theory to arrive at an adequate grammar. It must define the sentences that make up a language *L* as well as attach structural descriptions to sentences accepted in the range of L. Competence remains totally neutral in relation to the equivalent grammars for L. Thus competence cannot be equated to a mechanism since a mechanism cannot be neutral in relation to different grammars which really are mechanisms themselves. Moreover, a mechanism is not a relational term, whereas competence is. Performance does not refer to actual behaviour but to behaviour in an ideal situation, and in reality resembles more closely the interpretation others have given to the term "competence" (an error of which I have also been guilty). Before I discuss these theoretical and methodological questions in greater detail, I shall present some experiments and the underlying hypotheses relevant to these questions.

For some time I have explored the changes that characterize the development of memory processes. Memory is one of the ancillary processes that has been used in a general way to account for the differences between competence and performance (or as we would now say, between performance and behaviour). That the intervention of memory provides quantitative but never qualitative filtering has been widely held in psychology. However, it can be shown that the memory changes in development are not purely quantitative. This fact among others makes most views on language acquisition seem rather simplistic. We are going to deal with *three* experimental situations, all of which demonstrate that current conceptions are confusing because they are far too simple.

In the course of memory experimentation, I made the following hypothesis concerning the development of the mnemonic capacity: memory develops in a manner that can be characterized by schemata that are fairly stable throughout development *plus* some corrections (tags) that increase regularly with age. The hypothesis states that certain features in the traces of adults and children are shared and others are not. Among the former, I included characteristics of the stimuli (Gestalt properties for visual stimuli, etc.) and among the latter, features such as orientation, size, colour, texture, etc., which designate members of a generic class and not the set as a whole.

Let me describe a pilot experiment that I have carried out partly with Bostonian subjects and partly with Parisian subjects to test this hypothesis. Two hundred and eighty children between 2:4 and 3:11 years were shown one of five possible stimulus figures. Figure 1 shows the five stimuli that were used in the course of the experiment. Each child saw one and only one of the five patterns.[1] Then the pattern was removed, and

[1] We want to call the attention of the reader to the fact that four of the five stimuli (a, b, d, e,) of this memory experiment were taken from Piaget and Inhelde (1968).

he was requested to draw on a blank sheet of paper the pattern he had just seen. We expected the child's first reproduction to give us some insight into the nature of the input that he had coded. This hypothesis proved to be too optimistic, since our subjects were rarely, if at all,

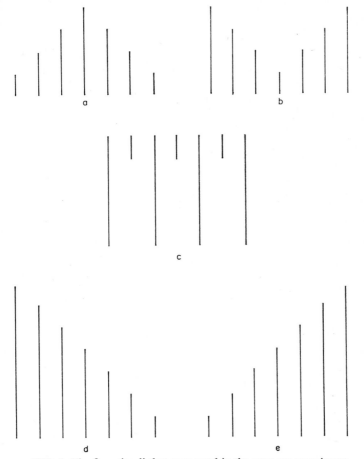

FIG. 1. The five stimuli that were used in the memory experiment.

capable of even copying the pattern presented to them, although they could recognize these patterns at a later time. Therefore, the immediate drawing reveals more about their motor limitations than about their memory or encoding capabilities.

After an interval of 1 hour or 1 day, according to the experimental group, a recognition test was given. The child was presented with a sheet on which there were three drawings. These drawings were: the original pattern, the child's own drawing, and a transformed version of the pattern. Pattern *b* was presented as the transformation of pattern *a* and vice versa. These patterns are complementary to each other, in that

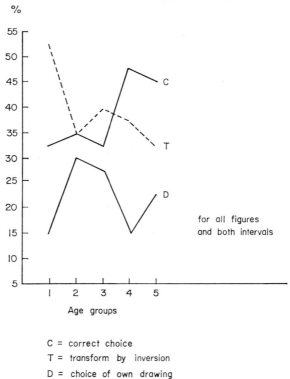

%

C = correct choice
T = transform by inversion
D = choice of own drawing

The age groups represent children between 2:4 and 2:7 years for Group I and subsequent groups are subdivided into three–month periods

FIG. 2.

together they form a square. The transforms presented for patterns *d* and *e* were inversions of the original patterns, obtained by rotation: *e* was presented as the transform for *d* and vice versa, the transform of *c* was the same pattern rotated 180°.

Figure 2 shows the pooled results for all the five patterns and both time intervals. The three different lines represent the children's choices in the recognition test. The line *T* refers to the choice of the transformation, the line *D*, to the choice of his own drawing, while line *C* reflects the correct choice. Few, if any, of the drawings were faithful reproductions of the stimulus presented to the children. From Fig. 2 we can observe that with an increase in age, there is a fairly constant decrease in the

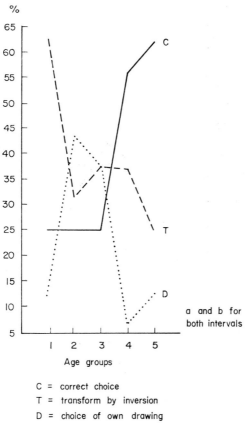

C = correct choice
T = transform by inversion
D = choice of own drawing

FIG. 3.

choice of transformation during recognition. The line of correct choices is a little more uneven, but we can observe a distinct increase in the number of times this pattern is chosen. Finally, the number of times the subjects choose their own drawings is described by a sort of inverted U-shaped line. Most of the time the choice of the child's own drawing falls below the expectation for a subject operating randomly. The most interesting finding here is the dip in the curve *C* representing the correct choice. Examining this further, I separated out the results for patterns *a* and *b* from the results for *c*, *d*, and *e*. The transforms for *c*, *d* and *e* were inversions of the original figure, those for *a* and *b* were not. Figure 3 shows the results for patterns *a* and *b* for both time intervals. We see

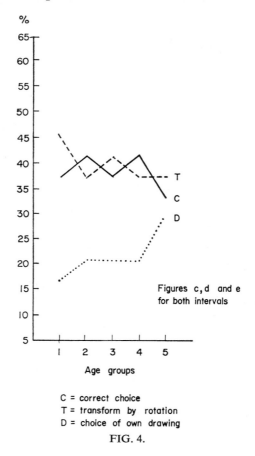

C = correct choice
T = transform by rotation
D = choice of own drawing

FIG. 4.

that there is a massive learning effect similar to that which takes place when children pass from one cognitive stage to the next. In fact the correct performance between the ages of 3:3 years and 3:7 years rises from 25 per cent to about 60 per cent in the selection of the correct stimulus during recognition. The selection of the transform decreases from about 65 per cent for the youngest children to about chance level for all other age groups. Curiously enough the line representing the selection of their own drawings still remains an inverted U-shape. In considering all these facts together, we can only conclude that the children attain good memory performance for the shape of patterns from the age of about 3:3 years. This does not mean that this memory is not present earlier, but that before this age, the encoding is not sufficiently well-preserved after intervals of 1 hour or 1 day to

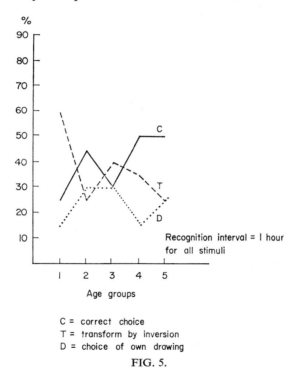

C = correct choice
T = transform by inversion
D = choice of own drawing

FIG. 5.

allow the child to perform adequately in the conditions of the present experiment.

If we now look at the results for the other patterns shown in Fig. 4, the picture that emerges appears quite different. Here all the lines are rather flat and they show no sign of any improved memory performance. For one thing, there is a strong tendency to confuse any pattern with its rotated transform. This confusion indicates that for children younger than 4 years, *directionality* (the orientation of patterns in space) is not encoded in memory. Figure 5 shows the results for all stimuli for the 1-

hour interval, Fig. 6 the results of the 1-day interval. There is little, if any, systematic difference in the efficiency of the children's performance.

From the results just presented and from two other ancillary experiments (Mehler, 1969), we concluded that the change in the development of memory is in part due to the increasing number of corrections that operate on the primary schemata. That is to say, the memory of the very young has a common base with the primary schemata of adults. In the

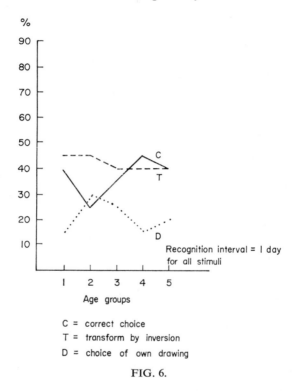

C = correct choice
T = transform by inversion
D = choice of own drawing

FIG. 6.

visual domain, I would call these schemata the Gestalt aspects of the stimulus. The child seems to add some corrections to that, which would modify the innate trace to mirror the actual stimulus that he must copy. These corrections seem to consist of features such as colour, orientation, size, etc. of the stimuli. I suspect that a careful search of the memory processes in the very young will reveal many more corrections than those which I have just mentioned. The interesting point is that all of the corrections that we have studied so far appear to be acquired between the ages of 3 and 5 years. Often the acquisition of the feature precedes the ability to name it. As far as patterns *a* and *b* are concerned, the correct performance is first present at the same age at which some interesting cognitive features emerge. But before talking about these aspects, I would like to point out that the study of memory development in young children has been largely neglected; and when it has been investigated, it has been solely from the angle of the quantitative evolution of the memory store. What our experiment shows is that the changes are not only to be considered as reflecting the expansion of the memory span but as reflecting a qualitative alteration in the memory trace itself. Of course, for those of us who are interested in the acquisition of language, this is very important, but we shall return to that shortly.

Before going on to discuss the more theoretical aspects that interest me, I would like to present a series of experiments that may, at first glance, appear unrelated, but which actually do fall into some sort of order once some basic premises are accepted. I collaborated with Bever, and Valian (Bever *et al.*, in press) in an experiment which tested some language performance abilities of very young children. For instance, we were able to show that 2-year-old children had no trouble in understanding transitive, active sentences. We distinguished sentences like (*a*) the man drank the beer; (*b*) the car hit the truck. In sentence (*a*), if we inverted N_1 by N_2 and vice versa, we would not have an acceptable sentence, while for (*b*) such a change would still produce an acceptable sentence. We call (*a*)-type sentences irreversible and (*b*)-type sentences reversible. Three-year-old children can understand many passive sentences. Figure 7 illustrates that comprehension for the passive voice is better than 50 per cent for the boys and girls of about 3:0 years, but that at a later age, there is a decrease in comprehension which seems to occur during the last third of the third year of life. We concluded that temporary over-generalization of perceptual strategies is responsible for this decrease in the children's performance. Such a perceptual strategy might be: *noun-verb-noun corresponds to actor-action-object, and in that order*. Of course once this strategy is adopted, the child's understanding of passives will suffer greatly.

In any case, understanding sentences is quite an achievement since it implies extracting the relations that are expressed by the underlying phrase structure of the sentence. Moreover, from the experiments we have been carrying out on adults, we are convinced that there is no processing of sentences leading to long-term memory or to comprehension which does not tap the sentence base structure. In this sense, the child that can assign the same meaning to an active and to a passive sentence must in some way or another perform some highly complex tasks which encompass the recognition of invariants under certain transformations. In the solution of logical problems, this type of behaviour is not observed until children are much older. We can recall the many and ingenious experiments that Piaget presented to illustrate this point. For instance, we are reminded of a conservation experiment in which a child sees two

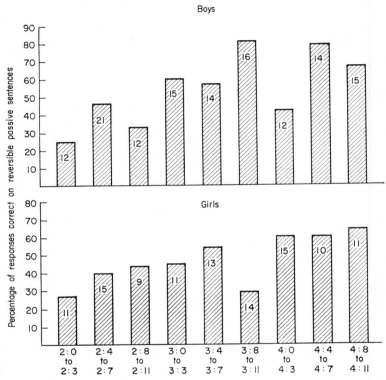

FIG. 7. Comprehension of passives in boys and girls from 2 to 5 years of age. Numbers inside bars indicate total numbers of subjects of that age.

identical arrays of marbles and is asked if he thinks they are the same. In general, if the marbles in the bottom array are spaced out to correspond one-to-one with the marbles in the top array, a child of about 4 will judge that both arrays are "the same". If then the experimenter decreases the distance between the marbles in one row, without removing any, the child will judge that the longer array contains more marbles. Although this experiment has often been criticized for lack of linguistic control of the manner in which the question is presented, I believe that the critics use a circular argument. For one thing, how can they explain the regular change in the meaning of the word *more* for children? In fact, to claim that the response is due to some interpretation of the word *more*— not the same for children as for adults—is in one sense saying exactly what Piaget claims. He feels that this experiment reflects the fact that the child has not attained the invariance of numerosity under spatial trans-formations. This might be due to the absence of operations that are needed in order to perform properly: for instance, the ability to recognize that a new layout has been arranged by spatial transformation of the original arrays, without adding or subtracting any element. This in fact would require the child to be able to reverse the situation to the "ante quo" which he is apparently incapable of doing.

In view of some of the results (preliminary at the time) of language aquisition, we were somewhat sceptical about this interpretation. Further-more, espousing rather strong nativist leanings shared by those of us who formed part of the group Goodman called the *Nomads of Outer Canta-brigia* (Goodman, 1967), we disliked the notion that very simple opera-tions are attained as late as 4 or 5 years of age. I viewed development as the co-ordination of some simple rules and operations into very complex heuristics. But then how would it be possible for the children to discover identity, reversibility and the rest?

Before discussing our doubts further I would like to describe the experiment that we performed with Bever last year (Mehler and Bever, 1967). Using Piagetian-type arrays, as is shown in Fig. 8a, we biased the choice of one of the arrays in relation to the other by adding two pellets to the shortened row (Fig. 8b). For one set of trials we used clay pellets, for the rest candy pellets.[1] The children were divided into two groups, one group was asked to judge which array contained the greater number of pellets; the other group was asked to decide which array they wanted to keep for eating. The results of this experiment are presented in Fig. 9. It becomes immediately evident that younger children do perform much more efficiently than the older ones—at least with the clay pellets. Chil-dren attain a minimum at the ages of 3:9–3:11. With the M & M's, however, no such dramatic drop is observed. This we interpret as mean-ing that the performance of the children changes with age and that the rules that allow them to be successful at a younger age can be again tapped if motivation is sufficiently strong. Our results indicate that children's ability to select the larger of two discontinuous quantity arrays does not appear gradually during the course of development. It

[1] Small coloured sugar-coated chocolate sweets, later referred to as M & M's.

H

seems in some respects to be a cyclical process, in which a choice that is correctly performed at an early age is wrongly performed at a later age and is then correctly performed at an even later age. We do not intend to claim that the underlying processes leading to a successful performance at 2:4 years are the same that lead to such performances in adulthood or even at 5:6 years. In fact, we know that the child solves the problem at an early age by a routine that is not based on counting, which is how any adult would solve the problem. At the time we published our paper, we

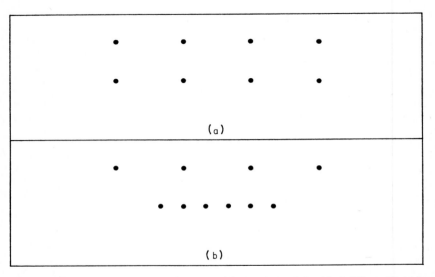

FIG. 8. The length of the rows in (a) was 7 inches (18 cm) for M & M's and 8 inches (20 cm) for clay pellets; in (b) 7 and 3 inches (18 and 8 cm) for M & M's and 8 and 5 inches (20 and 13 cm) for clay pellets. There was a $1\frac{1}{4}$ inch (3 cm) space between each of the four clay pellets and a 2 inch (5 cm) space between each of the four M & M's. The clay pellets were $\frac{1}{2}$ inch (1·3 cm) in diameter. The M & M candies were all of the same colour.

thought that the decrease in conservation was due to an over-dependence on perceptual strategies in which some parameters like length and density, etc. would have weights that could result in one of the parameters being used almost exclusively in a judgement. We had a procedure in mind similar to that presented by E. Brunswick (1956) in his accounts of perceptual constancies. The M & M's, however, indicate that the perceptual strategies can be overcome—given enough motivation.

In order to verify the generality of these findings, we continued to study other similar tasks. We studied very young children by testing

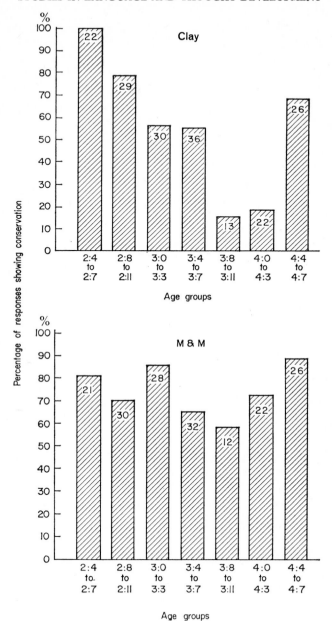

FIG. 9. The proportion of age by responses choosing the row with more members in the situation shown in Fig. 8(b). Numbers inside bars indicate total number of subjects of that age.

them with a task of volume conservation. We used containers like the ones shown in Fig. 10. In an experiment with Parisian children, we tried out two different procedures: (1) we put ten M & M's into each of two identical beakers (Fig. 10a) and established identity in the usual way. Then we asked the child to put one M & M into *one* of the unequal containers; i.e. either into the "test-tube" (Fig. 10b) or into the "dish" (Fig. 10c). Thereafter, the contents of one beaker was poured into the test-tube and the contents of the other into the dish. The child was tested

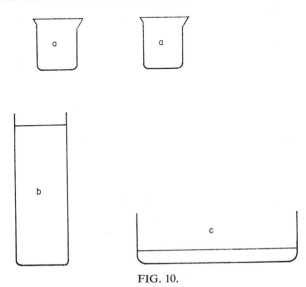

FIG. 10.

in two ways: he was first asked which container had more M & M's in it; and he was then asked to choose which one he wanted to keep for eating. Results are presented in Fig. 11. They indicate that up to about 3:4 years, the child chooses the container that has more candy in it, while the older children seem to base their choice on the shape of the container—they prefer the test-tube. (2) The second procedure follows the classical Piaget method more closely. Ten M & M's are put into two identical beakers, and identity is established by the child. Then the contents of each beaker is poured into the test-tube and the dish respectively, without adding or subtracting any M & M's. Children between 2 : 6 and 3 : 0 chose to keep either container with equal probability. When they were asked whether the two containers had the same number of M & M's, or whether the one they had just chosen had more, 10 out of 22 children replied that they were equal. Ten children between the ages of 3:6 and 4:5 were tested, and eight out of these ten chose the test-tube and claimed that it contained more M & M's. These results are of course preliminary; we need to test many more children, particularly for procedure (2), where no extra M & M's are added. The results that we were able to gather concerning the development of thought processes in young children seem to indicate that they are capable of solving problems at an early age, by using rudimentary logic—probably the core from which they attain the sort of logical functioning characteristic of adults. But before discussing the relational hypothesis underlying our work, I shall present the third area on which we based our theories.

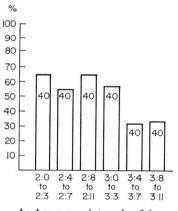

A: Age-group intervals of 4 months

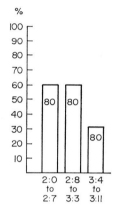

B: Age-group intervals of 8 months

FIG. 11. Results on conservation-type behaviour by age-groups. Numbers inside bars indicate total number of subjects of that age.

In our laboratory in Paris, Madame de Bardies (1969) has been studying the development of negation in French. In general her findings are compatible with those of Bellugi (this volume) and others. In addition, by means of a rather simple experimental procedure she has recently been able to study the immediate memory for negative sentences in very young children. She investigated the ability to repeat certain negations in sentences containing verbs regarded as being semantically positive or negative. For instance, if we compare the French verbs *oter* (to remove), *perdre* (to lose), *enlever* (to take away or remove), *oublier* (to forget) with verbs like *mettre* (to put), *prendre* (to take), *laver* (to wash), and *manger* (to eat), it is clear that the first four verbs indicate a concept that is semantically considered as negative or indicating an absence. It is difficult to define exactly why the first four verbs are considered negative although we have little trouble in recognizing the fact. That intuition is available to all native speakers of French.

Mme. de Bardies presented sets of four sentences to children between the ages of 3:6 and 5:6, two sets for each child. Their task was to recall all four sentences of a set, after the set had been presented. In each set there was:

(i) one affirmative sentence with a semantically positive verb: *la dame a lavé le tablier* (the lady washed the apron)

(ii) one affirmative sentence with a semantically negative verb: *le garçon a perdu son bonnet* (the boy lost his cap)

(iii) one negative sentence with a semantically positive verb: *la dame n'a pas lavé la serviette* (the lady did not wash the towel)

(iv) one negative sentence with a semantically negative verb: *le garçon n'a pas perdu son gant* (the boy did not lose his glove)

The order of presentation was systematically varied over the sets, and the number of syllables was equal in French for all sentences. Figure 12 shows the ease of recall for the various sentence types. Affirmative sentences with positive verbs were by far the easiest to recall; negative sentences with negative verbs were the most difficult. Sentences containing both positive and negative features (that is, affirmative sentences with negative verbs and negative sentences with positive verbs) were intermediate in difficulty level, and not significantly different from each other. Negative sentences (whatever the verb) were significantly more difficult than affirmative sentences (whatever the verb), and sentences with negative verbs (whether the sentence was negative or not) were significantly more difficult than sentences with positive verbs; in both cases $p < 0001$.

The results indicate that, in accounting for the complexity of sentences, their semantic properties must be considered as well as their syntactic structure. The difficulty of sentences for children is due simultaneously to lexical aspects of sentences as well as to their syntactic complexity. In another experiment Mme. de Bardies studied children's usage of *être* (to be) and *avoir* (to have) in an experimental situation. The children were presented with sentences that could take either verb or only one of the verbs. For instance, the sentences, *La petite fille est tombée* and *La petite fille a tombé* were presented to the child. After the child recalled both sentences correctly, the experimenter asked him to say which sentence he preferred. There were some problems in this experiment that could have biased the results, but one factor became apparent. Figure 13 shows the children's choice of the auxiliary *to be* for the different type of verbs that were used during the course of the experiment. *Perdre* can take *avoir* with animate or inanimate subjects, while it can take *être* with an animate or inanimate subject depending upon the construction. The same holds true for *pousser* and *recevoir*. *Fumer* is conjugated with *avoir* with either animate or inanimate subjects but with *être* for inanimate

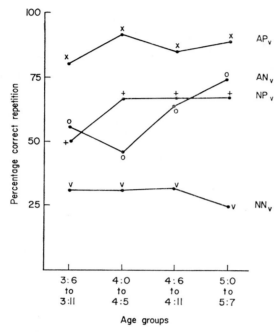

AP$_v$ = affirmative sentence , positive verbs
AN$_v$ = affirmative sentence , negative verbs
NP$_v$ = negative sentence , positive verbs
NN$_v$ = negative sentence , negative verbs

FIG. 12.

subjects only. *Dormir* can take *avoir* with an animate subject only. *Tomber* takes only *être*, with either animate or inanimate objects (unless of course one speaks argot and says *La fille a tombé le garçon* or some similar expression). *Perdre*, which is the only semantically negative verb, is most commonly used with *être*. On the other hand, the verb *tomber*, which can only take *être*, is seldom used with that construction at an early age but is chosen quite frequently later on. *Dormir* constructed only with *avoir* is correctly used by all ages most of the time. Most of the points on the curve fall within a random choice. Nevertheless, there are some extreme cases that merit greater interest: those verbs which employ both auxiliaries seem to be constructed preferentially with *être* at an

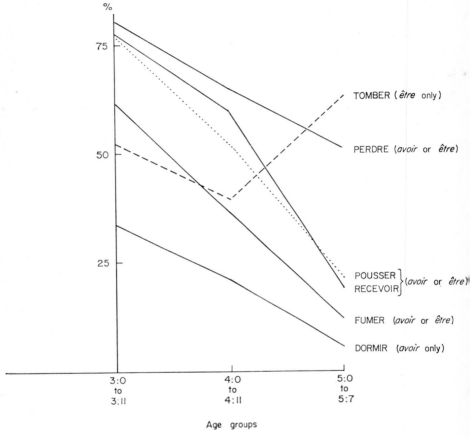

FIG. 13. Percentage of sentences chosen possessing the *to be* construction at different ages.

earlier age (3:0), while *avoir* is used by the older group (5:7 years). This could, in a sense, reveal some rather surprising, although not particularly counter-intuitive facts concerning the structure of the language acquisition process. In fact, it would seem that Existence, implied by the verb *être*, in one of its forms is a determining factor in the acquisition process, and Inclusion entailed by the verb *avoir* becomes a derivative acquisition. Let me elaborate for a moment upon this last statement.

In French the corpus studies frequently indicate that the first appearance of a verb is through the sound *a*. However, this sound seems to a great extent ambiguous when in the case of a child (speaking of her doll that has just fallen) says *a tombé* or *la tombé, a la* or *á pas la*; it is very difficult to specify just exactly what the *a* stands for. It certainly seems that to conclude that the *a* functions as an instance of the verb *avoir* is somewhat prejudged. The lines suggest that the younger child prefers the verb *être*. This statement can only be accepted with extreme caution since the relation of Existence and Identity might be primary factors while the other relations that are expressed by the verb *être* might be in fact late in appearing. In one sense it is the relationship *X is Y* and *X is X* that seems to function from a very early age. On the other hand, the properties of the verb *avoir* allow definition by extension of a class and not by intension. It is the relationship in the form of *X has Y* that is the basis for class inclusion. A class as well as its corresponding relationships is defined by the type of predicate that I have just indicated. All the experimental literature I have studied seems to indicate that the relationship *X is X* appears rather late. This statement presents some intricate implications. For one thing, when one says *it is a cow*, the relationship *X is X* is already present in the sentence base structure. If one said that *the cow is a cow* or *it is a cow that is a cow*, we face the problems of recursion—those that generally give the most trouble to children and adults. This particular factor might also account for the late usage of the copula form for the verb *être* (as opposed to the auxiliary).

Results have been presented dealing with memory, thought and language development. These experiments were carried out with some hypotheses in mind that we can now try to evaluate in the light of the results obtained and current views. Some general indications from our research show that age cannot be considered as the perfect correlate of success of performance in any area of development. In fact, the relationship between the success in performance and the subject's age seems to resemble a U-shaped curve rather than a simple linear one. This is true at least for some stages of development. On the other hand, some of the processes that have been considered as merely filters between knowledge and performance are really much more complex, since they change qualitatively as well as quantitatively. Finally some of our results have convinced us that our research may have been somewhat oversimplified. For instance, in the case of language, concentration on the abstract syntactical features of sentences without taking into account lexical insertions within these features might have made it more difficult to find the relevant invariants in terms of which development can be understood. Also, the separation of language acquisition studies from studies of thought development might have something to do with the production of inadequate models. But all these aspects fall within a theoretical and methodological context that is important to analyse.

For too long the history of psychology has been directed towards discovering simple laws of learning without taking into consideration the contribution that the organism brings to the learning situation. More recently, psychology has started to formulate some generative models of behaviour. These models require an exhaustive definition of the elements composing the system; this explains the renewed interest in the possible units of description. Further, to postulate generative systems for the natural philosophy of cognition is equivalent to stating that the explication of behaviour is best achieved through the postulation of an axiomatic system. An axiomatic system possesses:

(a) a *vocabulary* which exhaustively enumerates all the symbols belonging to the system;
(b) a set of *formation rules* that permit the determination of all derivations permissible within the system;
(c) a set of *axioms* comprising the terminal strings and the intermediate irreducible parameters that need no further proof;
(d) and finally a set of *inference rules* that determine the set of theorems with respect to the set of axioms.

The question that needs to be raised is whether an axiomatic system can be envisaged, such that the cognitive abilities of which humans are capable could be accounted for. If that were conceivable, the structure of all cognitive psychology would be very similar to that of linguistics today.

In any axiomatic system, the vocabulary is not arbitrary with respect to the set of axioms, inference and formation rules. In the case of language the great advantage is that native speakers can get at the formation rules through their intuitions. That is not true for some other domains, at least up to now. It would be interesting to be able to determine the nature of the axioms for language. Although progress has been made recently in this respect, we cannot say that any goal has been reached. In some ways one could consider that axioms are equivalent to the formulation of the language user's initial state under the most abstract conditions. In fact many have postulated that it is necessary to consider that the axioms are innately given and that they will become operative once the vocabulary appears. Nevertheless, this still leaves the question unanswered as to how the vocabulary is established. The main problem here is to understand the manner in which the child segments his universe so that labels can be assigned. Although one could argue that segmentation is learned, it must be made clear how it is learned. Doubtless it would seem necessary to state that the vocabulary is learned much in the same manner as we described for the first axiomatic system. But it is obvious that such a formulation would trigger an infinite regression which could only be checked by a clear statement as to the nature of the learning organism's innate components. In other words we can dispute the correctness of postulating an axiomatic system as being basic for the learning formalization.

But once we accept that an axiomatic system is the best formalization of the learning processes, we cannot account for the learning of the vocabulary at the base of the axiomatic system by still another axiomatic system. The same reasoning can be utilized for all the levels of the axiomatic system. Therefore, the only way to halt this regression is to define the initial state and structure of the system. Although many psycholinguists have tried to resolve this very problem, most of them have concluded without any relevant data that grammar itself, or the base structure component, is innate. Fodor has argued that the nature of the learning strategies could be innate and of such a nature that they would necessarily lead to the establishment of the base structure. The proposals that we are presenting lie much closer to those of Fodor (1966) than to those of Katz (1966) and McNeill (1966a).

Once an axiomatic system is proposed, the inevitable question concerning the distinction between competence and performance is raised. In general the distinction between *competence* and *performance* is stated in a manner such that competence refers to the general knowledge of the language, while performance indicates the manner of translating such knowledge into potential behaviour. Competence will account for the fact that the number of sentences that we can either produce or understand is infinitely large. Furthermore, competence permits us to postulate that a sentence can also be arbitrarily long.

Although at the beginning of this paper I suggested that a change in terminology might be warranted, I shall use the current terminology to avoid confusion. How is competence established? It is the linguist's intuition that permits us to establish the sentences that make up the set of well-formed strings in language. There is nothing wrong with accepting the linguist's intuition as the source data to delimit and establish the set L. Nevertheless, there are some problems that require further discussion.

Most of the sentences that we analyse are usually considered grammatical and acceptable. Some sentences, like those we encounter in telegrams, conversation, etc. are non-grammatical but acceptable (perhaps because we can easily transpose these sentences into equivalent well-formed strings); and one also encounters a great number of sentences that are neither grammatical nor acceptable. But the problems arise when the linguist defines as grammatical some of the sentences that are unacceptable. The linguist's intuition is no different from ours; but formal demands of the putative grammars on which he works require that those sentences be accepted. Alternatively, some acceptable sentences would have to be eliminated from the set that defines the domain of L for a certain generator G. Thus there is something more than the linguist's intuition involved in the establishment of L.

If the definition of L were only the reflection of intuitions, one could presumably expect the psychologist to operate on the data as if it were any other psychological domain. But this is not the case. We have a proposal of L and a set of grammars $G_1 \ldots G_n$ which are tried out as generators of L. There are some properties of L that are rendered necessary by the consideration of $G_1 \ldots G_n$. These properties are thereafter incorporated in L and thus perhaps require further modification in G. Of course, it is not necessary that the linguist select one mechanism, i.e. G_i out of $G_1 \ldots G_n$ instead of G_j. Rather he characterizes the general properties required of many of the generators compatible with L. Furthermore, the definition of the set of well-formed strings in L interacts by successive approximations with the nature of the generators $G_1 \ldots G_n$ that are being proposed, until finally the general properties of L and G are established. This manner of considering the problem avoids the contradictions in some of the former linguistic propositions. For one thing, once the nature of $G_1 \ldots G_n$ is established, the only relevant problem that remains for the psychologists is to select a G_x model which shares all the properties of $G_1 \ldots G_n$ and which has psychological reality as well. If there is sufficient reason to think that G_x has psychological reality, it would certainly be desirable to incorporate it in the performance model, although it may be still too early to achieve such a feat. On the basis of the claim that ancillary capacities (attention, memory, etc.) filter competence into performance, we arrive at a rather ambivalent position. For instance, it is frequently argued that the difference between the language performance of the child and the adult is that children have a much more limited memory store which hinders them from handling certain sentences. Nevertheless, our experimental evidence is not compatible with the idea that children and adults are more or less equivalent except for the size of their memories. On the contrary, the view that seems more justified is that the nature of the encoding itself changes with age and that, therefore, not only the quantity but also the quality of the trace differs in children and in adults. Since the methods of trace retrieval must necessarily suit the particular trace system on which they operate, it is inconceivable to consider the memory differences in children and adults as simply a filter between competence and performance.

The first experiment that we considered was one in which we showed in a rather preliminary fashion that memory develops in a manner compatible with the above hypothesis. That is, memory development can be conceived as the increase in the number of corrections that are made on an invariant core or schemata. This implies that the memory changes related to age are qualitative as well as quantitative.

In my former psycholinguistics research, I suggested that sentences are encoded as a function of a schema (sentence content or underlying base structure) *plus* some tags or corrections to alter or complete this schema. For further details concerning the nature of these corrections, I suggest the work of Mehler and Savin (in press). For children processing non-linguistic material, there are indications that there is a similar manner of encoding. It appears that children encode some figural aspects of the stimuli that are given to them. In addition, they seem to employ corrections to handle such features as, for instance, size, colour, orientation, etc. In fact, these tags are sequentially added through ontogenesis in an orderly fashion that we have just begun to map out. These changes in the memory correction's size will create a different memory structure at different ages. A greater number of tags will make the memory trace develop ontogenetically. This course of development demonstrates that the mechanisms themselves might be rather complex, and it further points out that a simplistic view claiming that memory is qualitatively invariant is untenable.

The second set of experiments that influences our caution towards overly simplistic performance accounts is derived from the solution children give to logical problems. It would be tempting to formulate all-encompassing theories for the development of cognitive capacities. Nevertheless, we must be very careful for both experimental and formal reasons. In a sense we have no idea as to the limitations imposed upon the mode and the possibility of thought; therefore, we cannot claim that the notion even exists as to what a competence theory means for cognition in general. In terms of Chomsky (1968) and Pierce (1957), there has been no successful investigation yet concerning the principles of *Abduction*. In so far as the experimental results are concerned, we feel that children possess a certain strategy that allows them to solve certain problems at a very early age. This strategy is based upon the application of very simple rules. However, children eventually discover that there are alternative ways of interacting with their environment which perhaps prove more efficient in the long run. This leads to the construction of specific heuristics based partly on the same rules that made up their first behaviour *plus* some general notions about what their environment is like (together with the organization of simple rules into larger programmes or routines). Therefore, we claim that children change drastically in their behaviour from ages 2:4 to 4:4 years, solving the same type of problems at these two ages, though not during the years in between. Again, we want to make it clear that we do not think that the way in which the problem itself is solved is the same for the early and late years. Nevertheless, the importance of the fact is the same even if the underlying means of solution change; provided that the change leads from correct to incorrect and back to correct solutions.

The third set of experiments demonstrates that further research must be carried out in the field of language acquisition before we can fully understand this process. The fact that during development the semantic status of verbs seems to interact with optional sentence transformations demonstrates further the impracticability of trying to understand the development of syntax without including other linguistic aspects. At least the semantic aspects of the words comprising the sentences should be taken into consideration.

Since our primary interest is to characterize the development of cognitive abilities, it would seem that the best step to take would be to try to establish what the initial state of the organism is or what its dispositions are. Previously we believed that the simplest environmental parameters were related to the invariants of behaviour. This hypothesis finds no support in results from the experiments that we have presented. Most of these results seem to favour the view that the simpler parameters of the stabilized performer are not at all the basic parameters of the learner. In fact, Bower's (1966) results might be interpreted as showing that the more complex parameters (the perceptual constancies, for example) are the basis of the extraction of the simpler parameters, like the real distance or the retinal image. The apparently simpler parameters seem to be derived from richer initial programmes. This indicates that one must proceed with extreme caution when incorporating common-sense assumptions into the theories of development.

For cognition in general it is still too early to suggest how the system might work; however, some general remarks can be made about useful ways of carrying out research. First there seems to be no reason to postulate a performance of linguistic capacities that is totally separate from the performance of solving logical problems or for that matter in performing any other cognitive task. Therefore, it seems necessary to carry out studies in all the cognitive domains simultaneously. Ideally, these studies should concentrate on the initial state or capacities characteristic of the newborn human. In parallel, we must establish the nature of stable performance in the adult so that the form and the structure of the learning function can then be determined. The learning function could then be conceived as the mapping of the initial state on to the terminal stable state. It is clear that the determination of the initial state is important since it is the only way in which one can be certain that the terminal state is described in terms of a non-arbitrary structure and mechanism.

Discussion

SCHLESINGER: What do you consider is the input to your generator, or are you not worried about that?

MEHLER: Eventually, whatever model of the language user one adopts, it has to be given a starting point. You have to put it in motion. Eventually it would be nice if what put it in motion also restricted its output. That would be very elegant, but I don't see how it could be done and I don't even necessarily think we have anything to tell each other yet about this. In any given output, on the other hand, we look at several things. From the linguistic point of view, we want to know the structure of the sentence, if possible a derivational history of the sentence and how the derivational history of the sentence relates to the psychological phenomenon of production as the subject says it.

KLIMA: If the sentence is perceived to be difficult to keep together and produce, you want some systematic reason for this.

BEVER: It is all very well to view whatever problem you have an interest in as the problem of building a model with an "input" and an "output". But, in itself, every such model is wrong and is clearly artifactual to an even greater degree than just a general statement. We have a model as a goal because it forces us to gather insight into some of the more general issues about perception or memory or cognition or social processes. We can't believe in a model to such an extent that we then go on to talk about the relations between two aspects of the study of the same organism in terms of the problem of matching up two different models. The organism is one even if the models are different. The motive for the models is to discover the general principles and the general principles ought to be the same. My point is merely that the enterprise of model-building is heuristic, not anything else; and that is not a very novel point.

MEHLER: The model is one thing, and the form of the model or the form of the syntactic or semantic theory is another. I have not been discussing one particular model, I have been arguing about their general form.

BEVER: But you did; you referred to such specific things as the difference between animate and inanimate structures in the role of surface structure.

MEHLER: This was merely to exemplify things that *might* come in, and eventually the model would have to justify the phenomenological reality between such differences as animate and inanimate or transitive and intransitive constructs. I know *a priori* that I want my theory to have psychological reality, but I have still been arguing mostly about forms.

BEVER: Well, I agree, if you mean that you start with something with certain basic elementary capacities, which interact with experience and with emergent autonomous functions and so on, to elaborate a system which eventually ends up with adult linguistic constants. But just in that sense, the fact that the child changes these strategies, and develops heuristics, explicitly makes him dependent at certain critical points in his development on input and on the nature of the input and on the environment. I can see no reason to believe *a priori* that one cannot expect to be able to use some of the systematizations and insights from sociological studies.

MEHLER: It is obvious that certain events restrict certain output. If this could be formalized it would be very nice, and that certainly is the job of the psycho-linguists and the socio-linguists. Whether it can be put in such a form that you can feed it directly into this language machine I don't know.

HUXLEY: I would like to ask Dr. Mehler what his theory suggests the child starts off with as given?

MEHLER: I think that a child has certain logical operators, which pre-exist all along. I don't know if I have got the right ones, but I would like to put into my model identity relations, inclusion relations, partition and something like comparator. The child might not use all these from the outset, but if he has these as "given" possibilities, then he has the opportunity to process a problem. Why should I postulate the use of comparators as a given? I'm not a linguist, but if I look at sentences like "J is the father of M" I don't think we would have any trouble in finding its base structure. If on the other hand we take "J is older than M" and look for its base structure, you find a kind of hierarchy of sentences. But I cannot see a way of limiting the number of simple sentences in the base, without a comparator. That is the way Chomsky in *Aspects* would have dealt with that sentence. You have a basic logical concept, which apparently cannot be treated as anything other than hierarchical from a linguistic point of view. You are stuck with this. The question now is whether linguistically this could be approached from a totally different point of view. For instance, could you approach it through logical operators? It seems to me that even if you look at these sentences from a purely linguistic point of view, you still have to bring in some logical operators.

KLIMA: With your first example of the M & M's, aren't you really saying that you preserve the original strategy of pairing and then add some short cuts to that?

MEHLER: Yes. Do you know any way of treating comparatives that would avoid the succession of underlying sentences?

KLIMA: Well, you could consider it as a type of conjunction.

MEHLER: By introducing negation? Well, Maurice Grosse, a French linguist, is working along this type of line.

KLIMA: Many languages express it in this way.

MEHLER: That's right. In French for instance, "il est plus âgé", you have this type of thing. "Jean est plus âgé que . . ." but you have to answer "non, il n'est plus âgé" which indicates that *plus* might have some negative feature.

KLIMA: Many languages don't have a proper comparative at all. All they have is a special use of conjunction-positive and conjunction-negative to express the idea of comparisons. That is common. European languages are rather highly developed in comparatives, but you get many others that don't have strict comparatives.

MEHLER: But in those languages that don't have strict comparatives, could you do the analysis of the base structure of the sentence without having to postulate something like comparators in order for the semantic sense to work out?

KLIMA: No. The interpretation of a comparative is precisely that you have a certain degree of a quality and then not a degree of a quality. That is to say, you have a special interpretation of *not* meaning *less than* without any special semantic marker.

SINCLAIR: In some languages you find exactly what our younger children do. You can only say: "He is big", "He is small". You can't even say "He is as big as . . ."; you have to say "He is big and the other one is also big". This is exactly what we find in French. As at the beginning, they only have *beaucoup* and *pas beaucoup*. They do not even have *le même* (the same).

Foss: But, for your model to work, is it essential that the comparator should be a verbal one? Animals can react, in fact they tend to react to comparative properties of stimuli rather than to absolute properties. So one would expect man to be able to do the same without the mediation of language.

Mehler: That is so. I'm not trying to enter into details of whether these rules like partition or identity or comparator are linguistic or not; I hope that they serve the purpose for solving logical problems as well as serve in the computation of the semantics of sentences. I describe here the very formal, abstract domain. Of course there might be filters of application for different domains. They might apply totally differently when they are included in a sentence than when they are included in, say, inter-perceptual comparison. They might apply differently, but they are the same operators.

Sinclair: You said that these children come to incorrect solutions, so they change their strategy. I don't understand this, because they do not know their solution is incorrect at all. This goes back to your explanation of development. But I was really struck by your formulation; maybe you didn't mean that.

Mehler: I don't mean that exactly.

Sinclair: But how do they know? They choose one thing rather than another. How do they know they have got the wrong solution? It seems to me that they don't. Far be it from me to accuse you of being an empiricist, but it sounded nevertheless almost as if you said that these children could somehow discover what was incorrect, and that this was what would push them towards a change of strategy. But they can't see or perceive it, they can only construct it. They have no way of *seeing* that they are wrong.

Mehler: I think there is a great danger in considering that a problem has disappeared when a child makes a choice. The child can operate on the problem and if you question him about it, even a week later, the children who are about 3 can reconstruct the problem perfectly, which means that they can at some low level continue to process this problem and find further solutions. There is also the problem of inter-action of memory, and that is why we ask the child to reconstruct the set we have given him. They are away from the task so they have got to have a very good discovery procedure to remember what the problem was. They have to reconstruct either the volume conservation or the discon-tinuous quantity conservation, and you get more than 60 per cent of the children who can do it, up to the precise number of pellets. I don't think that we should say that because the child is not concentrating on the problem any more, he has erased it from his cognitive apparatus.

FOSS: That still doesn't explain why he is trying different solutions when he has no basis for choice between them.

MEHLER: No it doesn't explain that, but it shows that he can compute solutions on the problem even after a time interval.

FOSS: But for learning to occur he must have knowledge of results, like any other kind of learning.

MEHLER: Well, it depends a little bit on what we understand by "knowledge of results". If he says, for instance, that one of the lines is longer, that the longer line has more, he might be proceeding like this —though I'm sure he doesn't—he might be carrying out a logical operation of this sort. He can say: "let's see whether in fact in nature everything which is longer is correlated with greater numbers of examples"; then he suddenly finds counter examples, so when he is faced with the same problem again, he doesn't use this heuristic with the same confidence he did before, and so he might find the correct solution. It is interesting that for almost all the problems we worked with, changes in strategies followed after the child had attained almost errorless performance. Even though we have no very good way of accounting for this fact, yet it would not be reasonable to ignore it or to ascribe it to chance.

The Nature of Cerebral Dominance in Speech Behaviour of the Child and Adult[1]

T. G. BEVER

Columbia University, New York

INTRODUCTION AND SUMMARY

A CORRECT understanding of the relation between human behaviour and brain function requires a theory of human brain function and a theory of human behaviour. Since neither theory is available today, it is futile to attempt a strict account of even a limited area of the problem, such as the relation between speech behaviour and anatomical specificity of neurological functioning. Consequently such terms as "speech perception" or "neurological locus of function" are only conceptual representations of behavioural and neuro-physiological structures which await real analysis and explanation.

Given these limitations, this paper presents a taxonomy of human cognition, as exemplified in language, which separates actual language behaviour (or language "performance") from primitive characteristics of language and from sensitivity to language structure. On the basis of evidence from functional ear asymmetries in adult speech behaviour and their development in children, I suggest that cerebral dominance for speech is specifically related to the behavioural strategies we use in actually listening to sentences. Since the development of these behavioural strategies appears to be responsive to actual experience, their close relation to dominance suggests that cerebral dominance develops (at least in part) in response to external experiences.

[1] Research supported by ARPA. No. DAHC 1567G-5 to the Rockefeller University. I am indebted to P. Carey, J. Epstein, A. Fenvessey, N. Stein, and V. Valian for assistance in the preparation of this paper.

THREE ASPECTS OF HUMAN THOUGHT

In our research we have distinguished three aspects of cognition for separate study: basic capacities, behavioural strategies and epistemological structures (see Mehler and Bever, 1968b; Bever, 1970). First, we investigate the *basic capacities* which appear in young children without obvious specific environmental training. Consider, for example, the 2-year-old's capacity to judge numerical inequalities (Mehler and Bever, 1968a; Bever *et al.*, 1968; Mehler, this volume), or his ability to predicate actions in speech. Second, in both perceptual and productive behaviour, children and adults utilize many systems of *behavioural strategies* to shortcut the internal structure implied by the regularities in their behaviour. For example, to make relative judgements of large numbers, we may suspend our knowledge in integers and counting, and simply use the perceptual rule that an array that "looks" larger has more components; or if we hear a series of words with only one reasonable semantic connection (e.g., "dog bite cracker"), then we may suspend any further perceptual analysis of the speech signal and assume that the sentence follows the usual semantic constraints on "dog", "bite", "cracker". Finally, as adults, we have a set of *epistemological structures* —systematic generalizations of our intuitions about the regularities in our own behaviour. Consider, for example, the concept of an integer and counting which we use in justifying our judgements of quantities; or the intuition of relative "grammaticality" that a parent uses to guide a child's speech and a linguist depends on for the isolation of linguistically relevant data.

PREVIOUS STUDIES

In this paper I follow a century of research in making certain assumptions about the nature of cerebral dominance in speech function. While each ear has direct neurological connections with each hemisphere, the contralateral connections (right ear to left hemisphere, left ear to right hemisphere) are taken to be the functionally relevant neurological connections. (It has been shown that almost all right-handed adults have a dominant right-ear/left-hemisphere, as do many left-handed subjects. In general, most investigations of auditory asymmetry are confined to "right-handed" subjects, so the right ear is generally the dominant ear.) One hemisphere of the adult brain is normally primary in speech activity. Much of the evidence for this hemispheric dominance derives from clinical studies of the relative effect of lesions in the right or left hemispheres on language ability (reviewed in Teuber, Battersby and

Bender, 1960; Mountcastle, 1962; Hecaen and Ajuriaguerra, 1964; Geschwind, 1965). These clinical studies indicate that more severe aphasia results from insult to the dominant hemisphere.

Recent work with normal subjects has expanded the basic clinical findings (reviewed by Zangwill, 1960; Milner, 1962; Kimura, 1967). Experiments by Bryden (1965), and by Kimura and Milner and others have shown that the perception of digits and words is superior when the stimuli are presented to the dominant ear. Recently, Shankweiler and Studdert-Kennedy (1967) have shown that consonants presented to the right ear are identified better than those simultaneously presented to the left ear. Using relative ease of perception of different digits presented simultaneously to both ears as a criterion, Kimura (1963) found that auditory cerebral dominance is tentatively established by 6 years of age. Lenneberg (1967) has concluded that cerebral dominance is permanently established by the age of ten, since aphasia caused by brain injury after that age is relatively difficult to overcome.

These clinical and experimental findings are generally quantitative: the dominant hemisphere is *better* than the non-dominant hemisphere at processing speech stimuli. Other findings indicate that there are basic qualitative differences as well. (In all our studies we use monolingual right-handed subjects whose close relatives are all right-handed, in order to be as sure as possible that all subjects are dominant in the right-ear/left-hemisphere.) The amplitude of the GSR in response to mild shocks, administered while Ss are listening to sentences, varied depending on the structure of the sentence. The interaction between linguistic structure and GSR is stronger if the sentences are heard in the right ear than if they are heard in the left (Bever *et al.*, 1968). We also found that if a click is presented to one ear while a sentence is presented to the other ear, the click is reported as occurring earlier in the sentence if the click is heard in the left ear than if it is heard in the right ear (Fodor and Bever, 1965, replicated in Bever *et al.*, 1969a; Bever *et al.*, 1969b). In a small pilot experiment we found that this effect obtains only if the speech is in the form of a sentence; random word sequences of the same length do not show the ear asymmetry. On the basis of this preliminary evidence, I suggested that certain perceptual mechanisms in the dominant ear-hemisphere system are selectively sensitive to more abstract aspects of syntactic organization than the internal structure of words.

This suggestion left unexplained the nature and source of those perceptual processes asymmetrically devoted to syntax. However, several authors suggest that functional cerebral asymmetry may be related to learning strategies. Milner (1962, pp. 177–178) reports: "Perhaps the most clear-cut result to emerge from the study of human temporal lobe function is the disturbance in the recall of verbal material, which regularly accompanies lesions of the left temporal lobe when speech is represented in the left hemisphere. This has been shown both for verbal associative learning (Meyer and Yates, 1955) and for story recall." Teuber (Teuber *et al.*, 1960) reported that brain damage in one hemisphere results in deficits of the contralateral hand in the learning of tactile discriminations (i.e., tactile discrimination does not improve in successive trials). Recently, Liberman *et al.* (1967) have claimed that consonant perception is better in the dominant ear while vowel perception is not, because consonant perception is relatively dependent on learned acoustic patterns. Finally, Kimura (1963, 1967) suggested that the early development of speech lateralization is facilitated by enriched cultural experience. Extrapolating from these observations we can argue that lateralization is, in part, a function of learning, not just an internal physiological development.

I shall explore a possibility suggested by the observations of these authors and by our analysis of cognition as three systems: *the dominant hemisphere is the locus for behavioural strategies of speech comprehension*; these strategies are acquired by the young child as functional lateralization develops and persevere as components of adult perceptual mechanisms. I must emphasize again that these strategies of speech processing are not directly related either to universal properties of speech (e.g., the fact that words have reference) nor to sophisticated adult knowledge of grammar. That is, the processing strategies constitute an inductive, non-grammatical system of speech comprehension, that of immediate apprehension of the internal, "logical" structure of actual verbal sequences. Thus, I am not claiming that either basic linguistic capacities or grammatically defined adult knowledge of linguistic structure is asymmetrically represented in the brain. Rather, I am claiming that the learned processes of *utilization* of language structure in actual comprehension are functionally "located" in the dominant hemisphere.

There are three kinds of recent findings which support this thesis. (1) There are qualitative differences between the ears in simple perceptual and memory tasks and monaural stimulation. (2) There is a particular syntactic strategy of speech-processing which is utilized most strongly in the dominant ear in adults. (3) Young children who have developed auditory asymmetry utilize this perceptual strategy much more than children of the same age who have not developed auditory asymmetry.

QUALITATIVE MONAURAL DIFFERENCES

It has been a canon of the investigation of speech lateralization that perceptual differences between the ears are quantitative and appear only under conditions of dichotic stimulation (different stimuli presented simultaneously to the two ears). For example, more digits are recalled of those presented to the right ear than of those presented simultaneously to the left ear; but subjects perform equally well if digits are presented to the left ear or right ear alone (Kimura, 1963). If this claim were general it would suggest that asymmetries in auditory functioning are due to qualitative differences which appear only if the dominant ear "inhibits" perception in the other ear. Recently, we investigated whether differences can appear without simultaneous stimulation. We used a task that allows both quantitative and qualitative differences to appear, namely the location of a brief tone in a sentence.

Our previous research has shown that if a tone is presented in one ear and a sentence in the other, subjects who hear the tone in the left ear report it as having occurred earlier than subjects who hear the tone in the right ear (Fodor and Bever, 1965). (Note that this effect only obtains if both ears do not receive the same stimuli; a binaural click is not heard as preceding in the left ear.) That is, there is a relative facilitation of the tone in the left ear and/or a relative delay of the tone in the right ear. This finding was perplexing to us, since we had expected the reverse difference (if any) to appear on functional-anatomical neurological grounds. Because the right ear functionally enervates the left hemisphere it should therefore produce a relative temporal facilitation of the tone rather than a relative delay.

To investigate this finding further, we had subjects locate short tones presented during sentences heard in the same ear, with nothing presented to the other ear. After each sentence-tone combination, the subject wrote down the sentence and indicated with a slash where in the sentence he thought the tone had occurred (Bever and Stein, in press). Fifty right-handed college students (25 male and 25 female) heard 25 sentence-tone combinations in the right ear and 50 (25 male and 25 female) heard the stimuli in the left ear. Each sentence was 12 words long and had two major clauses. There was one 35 msec. 1000 Hz sine wave tone located within each sentence, adjusted in intensity to be equal to the most intense vowel sound in the sentences. If a subject thought that his response was highly unreliable he indicated it as a "guess"; such responses were excluded from the overall analysis, as were a few responses in which the sentence was so badly recalled that the tone location

TABLE I. RESULTS OF LOCATING SINGLE TONES IN SENTENCES

	Tone location absolute error (syllables)	Tone location relative error (syllables)	Percentage locations correct	Percentage reported location guesses
Sentences and tones heard in . . .				
Left ear	1·00	−0·63	32	4·8
Right ear	0·95	−0·57	32	6·5

could not be assessed. The results scored to the nearest half syllable for each response are summarized in Table I according to the ear in which the stimuli were heard (Bever *et al.*, 1968; Bever *et al.*, 1969a).

There were no striking differences in the overall pattern of response between the two ears; most subjects preposed the actual location of the tone (i.e., subjects generally located the tone as having occurred at a point in the sentence preceding its objective location). Subjects who heard the stimuli in the left ear responded with a slightly larger magnitude of error. However, the subjects who heard the stimuli in the right ear produced a larger number of "guesses" and more responses in which the sentence was badly recalled.

Subjects who heard the stimuli in the left ear tended to prepose the location of the tone more than subjects who heard the stimuli in the right ear. However, there was a large range of average error magnitudes and of overall relative position of subjective location across subjects: some subjects in both conditions responded with a very small average error magnitude, and some subjects in both conditions responded with a very small average tendency to prepose the location of tones.

There was a positive correlation between a subject's mean accuracy of tone location and his overall tendency to prepose; subjects who responded accurately showed a relatively small tendency to prepose (Fig. 1). However, the correlation between average error size and average tendency to prepose was much higher across subjects who heard the stimuli in the left ear (Pearson $r = 0·71$) than across subjects who heard the stimuli in the right ear (Pearson $r = 0·43$). Most of the difference in the error-magnitude/subjective-preposition correlation between the right and left ears is due to subjects whose mean error was larger than one syllable: a small group of subjects who heard the stimuli in the right ear and who had a large average error systematically *reversed* this correlation. Conversely the correlations between mean error size and tending to prepose tones for the 25 most accurate subjects in each condition are nearly identical (0·56 across the left-ear subjects and 0·52 across the right-ear subjects).

There are various specific perceptual mechanisms which might account for these ear differences. A consistent interpretation of them is the following: there is a tendency subjectively to prepose the position of single tones in sentences; thus, the larger the average location error of a subject the larger is his average tendency to prepose. This correlation is weaker

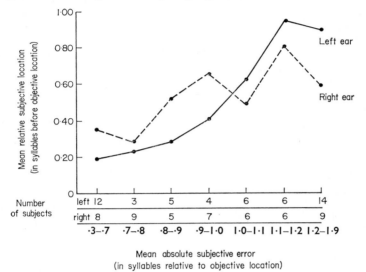

FIG. 1. The relation of absolute error size in the location of clicks and tendency to prepose the clicks.

when the sentence (and tone) is heard in the dominant ear. That is, immediate speech-processing interferes more with other perceptual activities when speech is presented to the right ear (e.g., the locating of a tone) than it does when the speech is heard in the left ear. (The proposal that hearing speech in the dominant ear interacts more with other tasks also accounts for the fact that there were more reported guesses of tone locations and failures to record the sentence correctly among those subjects who heard the stimuli in the right ear.)

We have also found a difference between the ears in immediate processing of sentences which does not appear for lists of random words. The paradigm is outlined in Fig. 2. Subjects heard ten seven-word sequences

Hear	Silent	Hear	Count	Say
Sentence	Interval	Number	Backwards	Sentence

FIG. 2. Paradigm of Experimental Sequence in Studies of Immediate Recall.

in one ear. Each sequence was followed by a two-second silence, which was followed by a two-digit number. Subjects counted backwards by threes from that number for five seconds (to block rehearsal) and then reported the original verbal sequence.

The verbal strings were either randomly ordered words (1a), or those same words ordered into a sentence (1b):

1a. Nice in seem did fact very they.
b. They in fact did seem very nice.

Both the random word strings and the sentences were constructed by splicing together the words read originally in a random list. Thus, there were no acoustic cues (other than the order of the words) which differentiated the sentences from the random strings. Sixteen subjects heard the random strings and 16 subjects heard the sentences (eight in the left ear and eight in the right ear for each type of stimulus material). The results are presented in Table II. More sentences were responded to correctly by subjects who heard them in the right ear ($p < 0.05$ by Wilcoxon matched pairs signed ranks two-tail across the ten sentences). Also, more words in the sentences were correctly recalled for subjects who heard the sentences in the right ear ($p < 0.06$ Wilcoxon, two-tail). No differences between the ears appeared for subjects who heard the random word sequences. Thus, it would appear that the difference in performance associated with the ear in which the sentence is heard is due to the

TABLE II. RESULTS OF IMMEDIATE RECALL OF WORDS IN ARRANGED SENTENCE ORDER (1a) AND RANDOM ORDER (1b)
(see Fig. 2 for experimental paradigm)

	Words in sentence order		Words in random order	
	% sequences totally correct	% words correct	% sequences totally correct	% words correct
Sequence heard in . . .				
Left ear	54	94	4	57
Right ear	65	96	4	57

higher order syntactic organization of a sentence, not to the fact that the stimulus material is composed of words.

We used the same experimental paradigm in Fig. 2 to bring out a qualitative difference in the immediate recall of sentences presented to the right and left ears. (This research is being conducted with J. Mehler as part of a larger investigation of the differences between short- and long-term memory of sentences. The data in Table III are based on 56 subjects for each ear, with varying intervals between the end of the stimulus sentence and the presentation of the number, from 0 to 5 seconds.) In this study, each subject heard (a) one active sentence; (b) one passive; (c) one negative; (d) one question; (e) one passive negative; (f) one passive question; (g) one negative question; and (h) one negative passive question:

2a. The bug bit the dog. (active)
 b. The dog was bitten by the bug. (passive)
 c. The bug didn't bite the dog. (negative)
 d. Did the bug bite the dog? (question)
 e. The dog wasn't bitten by the bug. (negative passive)
 f. Was the dog bitten by the bug? (passive question)
 g. Didn't the bug bite the dog? (negative question)
 h. Wasn't the dog bitten by the bug? (negative passive question)

Quite often subjects reported the correct words but the wrong syntax. For example, a stimulus passive sentence like (2b) was often recalled as the corresponding active (2a). The erroneous responses, which changed syntax but maintained the words and meaning relations between them, (i.e. "the actor and the object of the action"), fall into two types, *meaning-preserving* syntactic errors (e.g., passive to active; question to negative question, etc.) or *meaning-changing* syntactic errors (e.g. passive to negative passive, active to question, etc.). Sentences presented to the right ear were recalled with fewer meaning-changing syntactic errors than sentences presented to the left ear, while the number of meaning-preserving errors was the same (Table III).

TABLE III. MEAN PERCENTAGE OF SYNTACTIC ERRORS/SUBJECT IN IMMEDIATE RECALL OF SYNTACTICALLY VARYING SENTENCES

	Left ear	*Right ear*
Meaning-preserving syntactic errors	16	19
Meaning-changing syntactic errors	16	5
Total	32	24

These studies indicate that the dominant ear is more directly involved in the processing of the syntactic and semantic aspects of speech and that its involvement qualitatively affects perceptual judgements and immediate recall. While this phenomenon requires further study, it indicates that listening to speech affects the dominant ear differently from the non-dominant ear, *even with monaural stimulation*. The next sections argue that this difference is in part due to the relative availability to the dominant ear-hemisphere system of immediate processing strategies which organize the incoming speech signal.

STRATEGIES OF SPEECH PERCEPTION

The three aspects of cognition (basic capacities, behavioural strategies and epistemological structures) are simultaneously present in adult functioning. For example, in their use of language, adults predicate actions and (at least in the case of parents and linguists) can produce conscious intuitions about the acceptability in their dialect of particular speech sequences. But while we can observe these two aspects of adult capacity in actual direct behavioural expressions, we depend on experiments to demonstrate the presence of the behavioural strategies of speech perception. For example, recent experimental evidence demonstrates that there is a sequential, functional labelling strategy which applies to the apparent order of words in a sentence (in the absence of specific semantic information):

> Strategy (A). Any *Noun-Verb-Noun* (NVN) sequence in the actual sequence within a potential underlying syntactic structure unit corresponds to *actor-action-object*.

Notice that strategy (A) is probably valid for most utterances, since the passive order is relatively infrequent in speech. Thus, as a processing *strategy* it allows listeners to shortcut the use of full linguistic rules and structure in comprehension. Of course, on this view, utterances which do not conform to (A) are relatively complex psychologically.

The primary finding which verifies the existence of this strategy is that the passive construction is harder to understand than the active (in the absence of semantic constraints). The following seven experiments have shown this.

(i) McMahon (1963; replicated by Gough, 1966) found that generically true (3b) or false (3d) passives are harder to verify than the corresponding actives (3a, 3c):

3a. 5 precedes 13	c. 13 precedes 5
b. 13 is preceded by 5	d. 5 is preceded by 13

Notice that the functional relations among the major segments in passive sentences are the reverse of the assumptions of strategy (A), that the first noun is the logical subject (actor) and the last noun is the logical object.

(ii) Slobin (1966) found that children verify pictures which correspond to active sentences more quickly than pictures corresponding to passive sentences.

(iii) Savin and Perchonock (1965; replicated by Wright, 1968, and by Epstein, 1969) showed that the number of unrelated words which can be recalled immediately following a passive sentence is smaller than the number recalled following an active sentence.

The fact that the passive is relatively complex perceptually and in immediate memory might be due to its increased length, to its increased transformational complexity, or to its failure to preserve the "$NVN = actor$-$action$-$object$" property in the surface structure. Only the last explanation is consistent with all the following experiments.

(iv) Mehler and Carey (1968) found that the time needed to verify pictures accompanying sentences with the progressive tense construction (4a) is shorter than superficially identical sentences with a participial construction (4b). This would be predicted by the fact that progressive tense constructions preserve the "actor-action-object" order in the surface sequence.

4a. they are fixing benches.
  b. they are performing monkeys.

(v) Blumenthal (1967) analysed the errors subjects make in attempting immediate recall of centre-embedded sentences (5a). His conclusion was that the main strategy which subjects use is to assume that the first three nouns are a compound subject and that the three verbs are a compound action (as in 5b). That is, they impose a general "actor-action" schema on to what they hear.

5a. the man the girl the boy met believed laughed.
  b. the man the girl and the boy met believed and laughed.

(vi) In immediate comprehension I found that subjects cannot avoid assuming that an apparent NVN sequence corresponds to "actor-action-object" even after training on these sequences (Bever, 1967). Subjects gave immediate paraphrases of centre-embedded sentences with apparent NVN sequences, e.g., underlined in (6a). Even after eight trials (with different sentences) the subjects understood the sentences with this property less well than the sentences without it, e.g. (6b).

6a. *the editor authors the newspaper* hired liked laughed.
   b. the editor the authors newspapers hired liked laughed.

That is, the "NVN" sequence in (a) is so compelling, that it can take on the status of a "linguistic illusion" which training cannot overcome.

(vii) J. Mehler and I studied the immediate recall of simple sentences and found that subjects have a strong tendency to reconstruct a sentence to conform maximally to an "NVN" sequence. For example, in (7a) the *NVN* sequence is maintained while in (7b) it is interrupted. Subjects heard an equal number of sentences like (7a) and (7b) for immediate recall in the paradigm presented in Fig. 2.

7a. quickly *the waiter sent the order* back.
   b. *the waiter* quickly *sent* back *the order*.

In immediate recall, 87 per cent of the syntactic order errors were from stimulus sentences like (7b) to response sentences like (7a), rather than the reverse.

NVN STRATEGY AND AUDITORY DOMINANCE IN ADULTS

The "NVN" processing strategy is clearly not part either of basic linguistic capacity or of adult linguistic intuitions. On the one hand, the processing strategy appears to be related specifically to the probabilities in linguistic experience and so may not be a basic capacity of human cognition. On the other hand, such a strategy for the mapping of a lexical sequence on to a functional interpretation is not derived from a linguistic rule or any set of linguistic rules. Therefore, it is not a component of the adult epistemological structure which is implied by our ability to make judgements about grammaticality. Rather, it is part of a system of non-grammatical strategies of immediate speech processing. These strategies guide our comprehension of the functional relations which are internal to each actual utterance.

Elaborations of two of the above experiments give preliminary evidence that this organizing strategy is directly associated with the dominant ear-hemisphere system. First, we investigated the immediate recall of sentences with adverbs and participles (as in experiment (vii) above) with monaural stimulation. When a subject is given 2 seconds to process the sentence, relatively more syntactic errors are made by subjects who hear the sentence in the right ear than by subjects who hear the sentence

TABLE IV. PERCENTAGE OF ERRORS WHICH ARE SYNTACTIC IN IM-
MEDIATE RECALL OF SENTENCES WITH ADVERBS AND PARTICIPLES
(See Fig. 2 for Experimental Paradigm. Each subject heard 16 sentences)

Empty interval after sentence (seconds)	No. of seconds counting backwards	Left ear		Right ear	
		Absolute no. error/subject	% Syntactic errors	Absolute no. error/subject	% Syntactic errors
2	5	2·6	52	2·9	77
0	7	3·8	71	4·4	69
0	5	3·4	70	3·3	55

in the left ear (Table IV). Recall that the tendency of syntactic errors is to segregate the *NVN* cluster, as in (7a). Thus, more sentences presented to the right ear tended to be recalled, as in (7a), even when the original stimulus was (7b); this effect was less strong for subjects who heard the sentences in the left ear. However, the ear differences in this immediate recall experiment appear only for those subjects who are given a 2-second interval following the sentence. Thus, this experiment is not a direct test of *immediate* perceptual processing; rather it demonstrates an ear asymmetry in the organization of a sentence in immediate memory.

In an attempt to test perceptual differences between the ear-hemisphere systems, Carey *et al.* (1970) have studied picture verification time (as in study (iv) above) in which 20 subjects heard five sentences of each construction type monaurally. They found that, without experience, the progressive form (4a) is responded to faster than the participial construction (4b) by subjects who heard the sentences in the right ear ($p < 0.005$ by *t*-test); there is no difference in latency between the two sentence constructions for inexperienced subjects who heard the stimuli in the left ear (see the "without experience" data in Fig. 3). That is, the latency to sentences heard in the right ear is longest for the construction which does not conform to the *NVN* = *actor-action-object* pattern, (4b), and shortest for the construction that does conform to this pattern, (4a). Of course, the fact that adjectival sentences are responded to more slowly when presented to the right ear might only show that the right ear is more sensitive to syntactic complexity, rather than that the right ear utilizes the *NVN* strategy in particular. The adjectival construction is more complex syntactically than the progressive construction, since it has a recursion in the deep syntactic structure (underlying the participial adjectival use of the verb) and it involves at least one more transformation in the linguistic analysis of the derivation from the deep

I

structure to the surface structure (to permute the participle and the noun it modifies in the surface structure). However, the relative complexity of the adjectival construction does not explain why the latency to the progressive construction is *shorter* when presented to the right ear than it is when presented to the left ear, without experience ($p < 0.01$). There is no reason why *absence* of structural complexity should affect the right ear more than the left ear. Rather, the progressive construction must exhibit a construction that *actively* conforms to a perceptual pattern for which the right ear is preset.

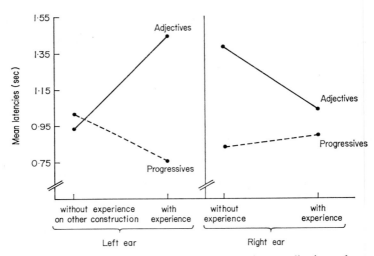

FIG. 3. Latencies to decide that the pictures are appropriate to adjective and progressive constructions.

Subjects heard two groups of five sentences each in the same ear; if a subject heard five progressive sentences in the first group then he heard five adjectival sentences in the second group (in the same ear) and vice versa. Subjects who heard the sentences in the right ear responded faster in the second group; but adjectival constructions still received longer latencies than progressive constructions. (Adjective latencies are longer than progressive, $p < 0.005$ in first group, $p < 0.07$ in the second group for right-ear subjects; see "with experience" data in Fig. 3.) However, subjects who heard the sentences in the left ear reversed the pattern of responses in the second group; adjectival constructions received the shortest latencies in the first group (not significant) and the longest latencies in the second group ($p < 0.005$). Indeed, the pattern and absolute size of response latencies of subjects who heard the second group of sentences in the left ear is nearly identical to that of the responses to the first group of sentences for subjects who heard the sentences in the right ear. That is, *with experience* the non-dominant ear can utilize the same strategies as those indigenous to the dominant ear.

These studies support the view that the dominant ear-hemisphere system in adults involves a strategy of immediate speech-processing which organizes speech-input sequence as actor-action-object if at all possible; this organizing principle is not immediately available to the non-dominant ear-hemisphere, but can be acquired with some experience.

DEVELOPMENT OF THE NVN STRATEGY AND CEREBRAL DOMINANCE

We have some evidence that the perceptual strategy (A) is acquired at about the end of the fourth year. We have been investigating the development of the child's capacity to understand simple passive sentences, which do not have semantic constraints, e.g., (8):

8. The horse is kissed by the cow.

The child's task is to "act out the story" described by the sentence with toy animals. The performance of children from 2 to 5 years on reversible passive sentences like (8) is presented in Fig. 4. (Each child acted out six sentences, one of which was a reversible passive like (8).) The relevant feature of the child's development is the steady improvement until about the age of four; at this age, there is a temporary increase in the tendency to interpret the first noun as the actor and the last noun as the object. This temporary decrease in comprehension was also found in another experiment (run by different research assistants) in which each child acted out 12 sentences, three of which were reversible passives like (8). In other research we have found that at the age of four, children are particularly dependent on superficial perceptual strategies which they have just developed (Bever, in press; and Mehler, this volume). Accordingly, we interpret the temporary decrease in performance on reversible passives as due to development and the *over*-generalization of the perceptual heuristic, *NVN = actor-action-object*. (Further research indicates that this strategy may primarily be the following: "the first noun is the actor".) Note also that from the standpoint of the present paper it is irrelevant whether this strategy is learned entirely by "passive" induction across some characteristics of external linguistic experience, or whether it is developed from internal causes.

We noticed in the first of the experiments on passive comprehension that the perceptual strategy developed earlier in girls than in boys. Since Kimura's research had suggested that auditory dominance develops earlier in girls than in boys, it appeared that the relationship between the acquisition of the perceptual strategy and auditory dominance could be used as a critical test of the hypothesis that there is a general relation

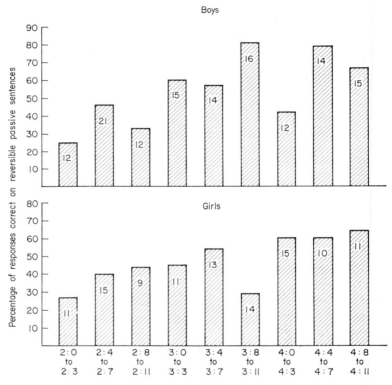

FIG. 4. Comprehension of passives in boys and girls from 2 to 5 years of age.

between cerebral dominance and the utilization of perceptual strategies. Accordingly, in a separate experiment on sentence perception each child (who was willing) was tested for ear-dominance during the same experimental session in which he acted out the 12 sentences. This study showed that those children with a preference for stimuli presented to the right ear have a greater dependence on the linguistic perceptual strategy than children without such an ear preference.

To test the ear dominance of each child I modified Kimura's dichotic-digit technique so that it could be used with young children. Each child was shown a set of inverted paper cups with toy animals glued on to them. Each animal was discussed by the experimenter and the child until the child agreed to its generic name (e.g., "giraffe", "doggie", "bird", etc.). Then the child put on stereophonic earphones and was told that if he picked up the animal(s) which he "heard the lady say on the earphones" he would find an M & M candy (Smartie) under the animal(s). The child heard a pair of animal names, one in each ear; after each trial he was allowed to pick up some animals (but not all) to get the M & M's. In this way we could observe which ear the child attended to most closely, simply by recording which animal he picked up (or which animal he picked up first if he picked up both).

	Trial	Left ear	Right ear
Phase (1)	1	horsie	horsie
	2	bird	bird
	3	cow	cow
	4	bear	bear
	5	doggie	doggie
Phase (2)	6	giraffe	horsie
	7	cow	bear
	8	lion	giraffe
Phase (3)	9	monkey	doggie
		bear	bird
	10	giraffe	horsie
		bird	cow
	etc.		

FIG. 5. Paradigm of the experimental sequence in auditory dominance studies of children.

The experimental sequence of trials had three phases (see Fig. 5): (1) the child hears the same animal name in both ears; (2) the child hears a single pair of different names in each ear (the stereo pairs being matched for intensity and duration); (3) the child hears two pairs of different animal names in quick succession. The response to the double trials in (3) were scored for the relative attention given to the animal names presented to the right ear. Figure 6 presents the distribution of relative preference for the animal heard in the right ear in phase 3 for the 195 children between $2\frac{1}{2}$ and $5\frac{1}{2}$ we have tested to date (October 1968). We classified the children according to their position in this distribution,

as predominantly left-ear dominant, no-dominance and predominantly
right-ear dominant. (The brackets in Fig. 6 indicate where the category
divisions were made.)

Of the children who were studied for ear dominance, 129 between
3 and 5 years also participated in the separate sentence comprehension
experiment outlined above (in which each child heard three reversible

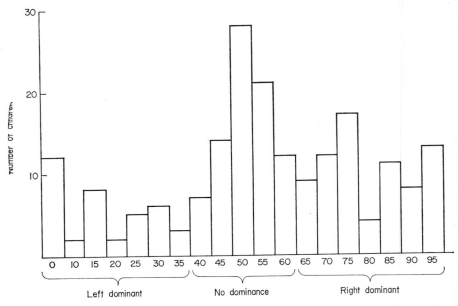

FIG. 6. Histogram of relative tendency to choose animals presented to right ear in
Auditory Dominance Test with children.

actives and three reversible passives). The performance on the reversible
active and passive sentence tasks for those children is given by the graph
in Fig. 7, according to their relative right-ear dominance, shown by the
histogram in the same figure. The size of the active-passive difference
corresponds to the use of strategy (A), since that strategy leads to good
performance on active sentences and bad performance on passive sentences. Inspection of this difference for children with each amount of
right-ear dominance shows that there is a relative increase in the perceptual dependence on strategy (A) correlated with the amount of right
or left dominance shown by each group of children. Conversely, children
with no preference for either ear use strategy (A) very little. To test the
significance of these findings, each child was scored for his relative ten-

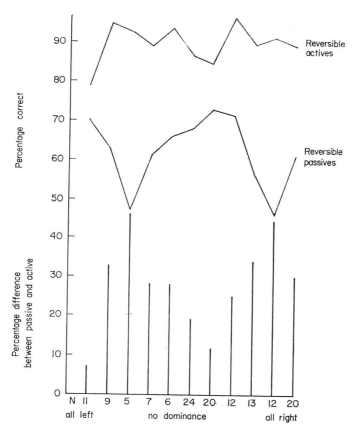

FIG. 7. Performance on acting out sentences presented to the right ear, by children with varying ear preferences.

dency to reverse the interpretation of reversible passive sentences. This was done by taking the number of passive sentences that he reversed and subtracting the number of simple reversible active sentences that he reversed. The latter subtraction was to control for the few subjects who reversed the interpretation of some passives *and* actives. The means in the first row of Table 5 and all of Table 6 exclude subjects who make no reversing errors on reversible actives and passives; since roughly the same proportion of subjects (24 per cent overall) in each ear-dominance

TABLE V. COMPARATIVE ANALYSIS OF SENTENCE COMPREHENSION
AND EAR PREFERENCE IN CHILDREN AGED FROM 3 TO 5

Preferred ear	Left	No dominance	Right
Average relative tendency to reverse passives (see text)	40%	23%	43%
Average percentage of reversible actives and passives correct	75%	78%	75%
Percentage of children without any sentence errors	34%	26%	23%
Average correct animal choices	48·6%	53·5%	49·4%
Median age	3 yr. 11 mo.	4 yr. $\frac{1}{2}$ mo.	4 yr.
Number of children	32	50	47
Percentage of right ear animals chosen	0–37·4	37·5–62·4	62·5–100

category made no errors, the inclusion of these subjects simply decreases the clarity of the data (Fig. 7 includes all children). The mean relative tendency to reverse reversible passives for children in each of the dominance categories is presented in Table V. The tendency is much higher among children who are categorized as having an ear preference. ($\chi^2 = 5.49$, $p < 0.02$ for right-dominant *vs.* no-dominance subjects; $\chi^2 = 2.84$ for left-dominant *vs.* no-dominance subjects.) That is, children with a dominant right ear tend more than non-ear-dominant children to utilize strategy (A) of speech perception, $NVN = actor-action-object$.

There are several difficulties with these data which force me to be cautious in claiming that they demonstrate a direct association between the development of auditory dominance and the development of strategy (A). First, it might be the case that the correlation between ear-preference in the dichotic-listening task and the tendency to reverse passive sentences is simply a function of age: that is, as children get older, they pass through a period in which they reverse reversible passive sentences, and (perhaps independently) they develop auditory asymmetry. However, in our data ear-dominance is not strongly related to age among the children younger than 5. Furthermore, the relative tendency to reverse passive sentences is *higher* for right-ear dominant children at the age of 3 than at the age of four considered separately (see Table VI). Thus, while the development of auditory asymmetry and the linguistic perceptual strategy might still be independent functions of some other aspect of maturation, there is no obvious direct relation between this sort of maturation and age.

An additional problem is raised by the fact that subjects who show no ear asymmetry tend to make fewer errors on the sentence perception tasks. Thus, the fact that more passive reversals are made by children with ear asymmetry than by those without asymmetry could be due to the fact that such children make more errors overall and that reversing

TABLE VI. RELATIVE TENDENCY TO REVERSE PASSIVE SENTENCES FOR CHILDREN WITH DIFFERENT EAR DOMINANCE, ANALYSED BY AGE OF THE CHILD AND BY THE NUMBER OF ERRORS A CHILD MAKES OVERALL

(a)

Age	N (*that produce errors*)	Left (%)	No dominance (%)	Right (%)
3 yr.	51	30	27	50
4 yr.	46	53	17	40

(b)

No. of errors	Left (%)	No dominance (%)	Right (%)
1	20	17	23
2	27	10	60
3 or more	54	37	63

passive sentences is always a relatively more frequent error. However, Table VI shows that, among the children who make a given number of errors on the reversible sentences overall, there is a higher tendency for right-ear and left-ear dominant subjects to make errors which reverse passive sentences than for non-dominant children.[1]

[1] The performance of subjects who show left-ear dominance is puzzling to me at the moment. First, a third of the subjects in the dichotic listening experiment who showed any dominance showed it in the left ear, which is a much larger proportion than that reported for adults. Second, left-ear dominant subjects showed almost the same tendency as right-ear dominant subjects to use the syntactic strategy on passive sentences. These facts might be true for one of three reasons: (a) some children pass through a phase of right-hemisphere dominance (associated functionally with the left ear). Evidence for this interpretation is suggested by Lenneberg's observation that about 30 per cent of young children show aphasia after injury to the right hemisphere; (b) ear dominance and the use of the linguistic strategy are associated with either right- or left-ear dominance; or (c) some of the "left-ear" dominant subjects are actually right-ear dominant, but happen to respond to the ear competition elicited in the dichotic listening tasks by focusing on the left ear input; that is, these subjects may be sensitive to the difference between the input to the two ears as a function of having a dominant ear, but the dominance may not be so strong as to preclude conscious focusing on the *non*-dominant ear.

These results support the hypothesis that the development of auditory dominance is associated with the development of the strategy of speech perception, $NVN = actor\text{-}action\text{-}object$. We have corroborated this result for the first part of the strategy, $N = actor$, with cleft-sentences that have their subject first (9a) or object first (9b). Significantly more right-dominant children reverse sentences like (9b) than do children with no dominance.

9a. It's the horse that kisses the alligator.
 b. It's the alligator that the horse kisses.

CONCLUSION

I have presented the following arguments in support of the thesis that the dominant hemisphere is the locus for the acquired strategies of speech perception. (1) It is possible to elicit qualitative behavioural differences between the right and left ear in right-handed (and presumably right-eared) subjects, without explicit auditory competition between the ears. These differences indicate a greater involvement of the right ear in the immediate processing of the speech stimulus. (2) Studies of immediate speech-processing in right-handed adults indicate the activity of an immediate processing strategy, *NVN corresponds to actor-action-object*. This strategy of speech-processing is directly available to the dominant ear and is not immediately available to the non-dominant ear. (3) This strategy emerges in the perceptual behaviour of the child at the beginning of the fourth year. Those children between 3 and 5 who show an auditory ear-preference also have a relatively large tendency to utilize this strategy in speech perception.

I mentioned above that the investigators at Haskins Laboratory (Liberman *et al.*, 1967) interpret the superiority of the right ear in consonant perception as a function of the fact that consonant perception is relatively dependent on perceptual learning.[1] This interpretation is the phonetic analogue of my interpretation of the cerebral asymmetries in the utilization of syntactic perceptual strategies. Thus, the dominant hemi-

---

[1] There are alternative explanations of this phenomenon. For example, consonants have been shown to be relatively high in "information" content (e.g., most of a written message can be decoded if only the consonants are presented and a spoken message can be understood even if all the vowels are pronounced "uh", so long as the consonants are pronounced correctly). Consequently, if the right ear is dominant for speech in general we could expect that it would be relatively more dominant for those aspects of speech which are relatively informative and relatively more attended, namely consonants. Such an explanation does not draw directly on the relative dependence of consonant perception on learned patterns.

sphere may be the locus for acquired perceptual strategies of speech at all levels of linguistic capacity.

It is important to notice that in both syntax and phonology the strategies of speech behaviour are not obviously related to basic properties of language or to sophisticated grammatical knowledge. The grammatical rules which describe the derivation of lexical and phonetic sequences from their "logical" syntactic organization, and from their "abstract" phonemic sequence, have no immediately apparent reflection in the behavioural processing system, although the processing strategies are part of a behavioural system for the deployment in actual comprehension of knowledge which is grammatically defined. I refer to the strategies as part of the speech "processing" system in order to leave open the question whether this system is immediately "perceptual" or a system of the organization of "short-term memory" (if there is a real difference between the two). The investigations reported in this paper suggest only that one component of speech behaviour is functionally and neurologically asymmetric. I must emphasize that this conclusion leaves open the possibility that the basic linguistic capacities (e.g., the capacity for reference or predication), as well as the sophisticated knowledge of linguistic structure, are neurologically reflected equally in the "dominant" and "non-dominant" hemispheres. Indeed, some recent work by Sperry and Gazzaniga (1967) on the performance of subjects with neuro-anatomically disconnected cerebral hemispheres suggests that both hemispheres have the capacity to understand the basic referential properties of some words. But it is not yet clear how general this phenomenon is, nor is it clear how to understand the implication for normal adults of research on people whose cerebral hemispheres have been physically disconnected. Notice that our results show that there are distinct *qualitative* differences between the processing habits of the two ears, as opposed to straightforward *quantitative* differences, for example, reduced attention to the non-dominant ear (suggested by Treisman and Geffon, 1968). However, the distinction between interpreting a behavioural effect as qualitative and as quantitative is inextricably muddled; an apparent qualitative difference between two behaviours can always be reinterpreted as a quantitative difference along a conceptual dimension which subsumes both behaviours. For example, one could reinterpret our apparently qualitative findings as due to the quantitative lack of attention initially paid to the non-dominant ear by the central speech-processing mechanism.

Our experiment on picture-verification time showed that, after some monaural experience, the left ear operates like the right ear with processing strategies. Such lability is puzzling if the functional auditory asymmetries are due to a structural difference (for example, the lack of relevant neurological connections to the non-dominant ear). However, a neuro-anatomically sound adult human has both higher and lower connections between the cerebral hemispheres so that experience and behavioural habits can be transmitted from one hemisphere to the other (assuming that neuro-anatomical connections are relevant in such a direct way). Thus, the functional dominance we are studying in speech is a matter of the initial localization of acquired perceptual *habits*. The ability of the non-dominant ear to mimic the performance (at least qualitatively) of the dominant ear, after experience, is not surprising whatever the neurophysiological basis for cerebral asymmetry may be. Consider your own behaviour when you use your non-dominant hand for some complicated manual skill that is usually carried out by your dominant hand (e.g., throwing a ball, eating soup with a spoon, striking a match and lighting a cigarette). At first, your manual motions are awkward and jerky; your manual improvement may appear to recapitulate the original motor learning of your dominant hand. But with enough experience some of the same integrative motor strategies used in the dominant hand appear to smooth out the activity of the non-dominant hand (although your performance may always be less good than with the dominant hand).

The ability of the non-dominant behavioural system to acquire the patterns of skill of the dominant system when given unilateral experience may explain why many behavioural ear differences depend on simultaneous stimulation of the two ears. Presumably, the non-dominant ear cannot acquire the skill of the dominant ear when they are in direct competition, but when the non-dominant ear is on its own it can quickly acquire the performance strategies of the dominant ear, thus masking many initial qualitative differences between the ears.

I should like to add a general speculation about the relative role of external experience and of internal neurophysiological maturation in the normal development of cerebral lateralization of function. It has been noted by others (e.g., Zangwill, 1960) that lack of clear cerebral dominance is often associated with learning problems in children who otherwise appear to be intelligent. This would support an hypothesis that the ability to learn from experience and cerebral lateralization are related, but does not clarify whether certain critical experiences (presumably before the age of 6) are necessary to stimulate the development of lateralization. The form of the lateralized perceptual strategies in the adults and children we have studied appears to be responsive to the actual probabilities in stimuli recognized by the child as part of his own experience. The fact that functional dominance appears to develop simultaneously with the perceptual strategies raises the possibility that cerebral lateralization is itself critically dependent on certain kinds of experience. For example, I noted that Kimura found that children from a "lower middle class" school showed less auditory dominance than children from a wealthier community. We could take this as support for the claim that cerebral lateralization is in part a function of certain kinds of intellectual experience.[1]

Of course, we can (and should) study the functional nature of cerebral dominance independent of its physiological basis and its individual onto-genesis. I have reviewed a series of scattered arguments that the dominant hemisphere and behavioural strategies of speech-processing are uniquely associated, not because the arguments *should* convince you, but because they convince me that we must pursue this possibility.

Discussion

BEVER: It seems to me, that we are all to some extent burdened with a particular notion of structure, and I want to try to modify this notion. There is a classical conflict within biological fields between analyses in terms of structures and in terms of processes. In the past 10 years of linguistics and psycholinguistics we have emphasized structure over process. This was a reaction to the preoccupation with learning pro-cesses that went on before that, when the only process that anyone could think of was free-floating association, which didn't seem to work out very well. I think now that we could try to develop an enriched concept of the kinds of psychological processes which we might find in organisms. Up till now we have taken the view that the language structure is given; that we can discover the structure by teasing out little facts here and there and then assembling them in phrase structure "trees"; and then we state the relations between trees by transformations, and only after that is done can we come to the problem of seeing how all this structure is utilized in behaviour.

Perhaps the time has come to look upon this in a different way. We

---

[1] It is intriguing to notice that the relation of localization of brain function and the variety of early experience has been demonstrated for rats (Smith, 1959). Smith found that rats reared in an undifferentiated environment follow Lashley's law of mass action and do not show functional cerebral specificity, while rats reared in an intricate environment do show cerebral localization and differentiation of functions in various learning tasks. (I am indebted to Dr. J. Church for calling my attention to this research.)

might look upon linguistic structure as the distillation, as a by-product, of active language processes. The question we should now ask is something like this: given that we know the nature of linguistic structures, what do they tell us about the linguistic processes, about the processes that result in language behaviour? One area that I have been particularly interested in lately has been concerned with the constraints that the general principles of perception might bring to bear on some of the intricate and internal linguistic structures that we find. I am arguing that these structures are the way they are because certain general perceptual constraints are present.

One example is the constraints on pronominalization in English. The general rule about pronominalization is that it *proceeds from left to right*. If you want to say:

*"Bill$_i$ talks to Bill$_i$"

and you mean the two "Bills" to be co-referential, you must say:

"Bill$_i$ talks to himself$_i$."

You can't say:

*"He$_i$ talks to Bill$_i$"

if you are talking about only one person. If you say:

"He$_i$ talks to Bill$_j$,"

you have to mean somebody else, you cannot mean *Bill was talking to himself*. However, this general left-right rule may be broken when the pronominalization is from a main clause into a subordinate clause. You can say both:

"Although Mary spoke to Bill$_i$, he$_i$ stayed late;"

and

"Although Mary spoke to him$_i$, Bill$_i$ stayed late."

"Bill stayed late" is the main clause and "although Mary spoke to him" is the subordinate clause. That is, there is a second rule of pronominalization, that it proceeds from main clause to subordinate clause. What you can't say is:

*"He$_i$ stayed late although Mary spoke to Bill$_i$."

Here the pronominalization does not satisfy the left-to-right rule and it doesn't satisfy the subordinate-clause/main-clause rule either. Several people (Postal, Ross and Langacker) discovered these two general principles about the same time. Actually, there are other difficulties about pronominalization; but let's assume for the moment that these two rules might be true and then let's look at what kind of general cognitive principle would provide the basis for them.

What seems to happen is that the pronominalization is allowed to occur whenever you know already what the pronoun refers to—as in the left-to-right rule—or when you are given a promissory note that you are about to be told what the pronominalization refers to, as in the cases with subordinate clauses. Bob Kirk, of M.I.T., argues that by the time you come to a verb in a clause, you already know whether it is a verb in a subordinate clause or the verb in a main clause of a sentence. This is because there is always some marker of subordination like *although*, *with*, *if*, and so on, or the *-ing* suffix, or the infinitive marker *to*. If Kirk is right that the subordinate clause is always marked as such when it comes first in a sentence, that means that the listener is given the promissory note that the main clause is coming. This seems to me to be the basis for a very reasonable perceptual strategy, given that what we do when we're hearing sentences is trying to sort out what the main thought is and what the qualifying thoughts are. The strategy here is that when we hear a subordinate clause we know there is more to come, and we put it aside and wait for the main clause. Since we know more is to come, a pronoun in an initial subordinate clause is acceptable. It is in this way that the structural constraints on pronominalization rules interact with perceptual strategies.

Another example has to do with the ordering of adjectives. Vendler (1967) has argued that the more noun-like an adjective is, the further away it must be from the determiner (e.g. "the") or the closer it must be to the noun. For instance, we say a *nice metal ball*, but not a *metal nice ball*. *Metal* has much more "nounness" than *nice* has, so it goes next to *ball*. Now it seems to me that a very reasonable perceptual strategy would be that, when you hear a determiner *a*, *the*, perhaps *any*, numbers and so on, there is a perceptual strategy to look for the first thing that *can* be a noun and that gives you the opportunity to establish closure at least provisionally. If we had an order which allowed *the metal nice ball*, it would incorrectly apply closure prematurely after *metal* since it can be a noun. So the constraints on the neutral, conjunctive order of adjectives can be viewed as a structural accommodation to our perceptual system.

SINCLAIR: I wonder how much this question of subordinate and main clauses has to do with topic and comment. I believe you can say in English:

"The time Bill stayed late Mary had spoken to him",

and that you can also say:

"The time he stayed late, Mary had spoken to Bill."

BEVER: Perhaps you can, but the second sentence is a surface structure in which the first clause is marked as subordinate.

KLIMA: Yes, but sentences are presumably processed via surface structure.

BEVER: O.K. it may be that the rules don't handle this, although I think they do. I did say that we hadn't yet licked all the problems of pronominalization. However, the structural constraints I mentioned handle a large number of problems.

SCHLESINGER: I would like to suggest an alternative explanation to the phenomenon of order of adjectives. Your explanation can't account for *the good old man*, for instance, or *the tough old man*, or *the stingy old man*. This seems to involve a distinction between secondary and primary qualifiers. *Old* belongs to the man, he can't help being old, but he can help being stingy.

BEVER: In certain cases that might be true, although the adjective order you give is not the neutral conjoined order in my dialect. But if we try to deal with the problem in this way, it is going to be extremely messy in any case because it allows any kind of perceptual strategies and inductive strategies which people might develop on the basis of their experience. There are going to be all kinds of intersecting types of experience which will range from such structural variables that I've been talking about here, to the richest source of induction, which is context, which we don't know how to study. There is another point here, about counter examples; what we're dealing with are perceptual *strategies*, not exceptionless rules; 20 per cent of the cases could be counter-examples and it would still be an effective perceptual mechanism to have this as a strategy.

ERVIN-TRIPP: You have been talking about a strategy for receiving other people's speech. Presumably a child develops his perceptual strategies before he learns to control his speech in the same way, and we might expect to find that some of these strategies affect speech output too. Basil Bernstein and his colleagues found that 5-year-old working-class children do not follow these rules for pronominal usage and do not use pronouns the way middle-class children do, with verbally specified antecedents. We also have some evidence that working-class children, on the input side, have learned their language more often from other children than from adults.

BEVER: Yes, clearly what we are talking about are partially induced strategies, although the perceptual system must also start with some built-in mechanisms. I'm talking about the kinds of perceptual inductions that the child develops, once his memory attains the quality or the quantity which allows him to form such inductions. He is critically dependent on getting enough cases over which to make his induction.

ROBINSON: It is quite true that, in working-class speech, they let out lots of pronouns without giving any referents, so that when they say *him*, *it*, *he*, you have no idea what they are talking about unless you are also with them; even then you might not. So, their failure to follow the rules leads to failure in communication as well.

CAZDEN: I think we need to distinguish between what is ungrammatical and what is referentially unclear. For instance:

"He kicked it and broke the window"

is not ungrammatical, but you won't understand it unless you know the context.

ROBINSON: You're right. The problem is: you get 14 pronouns in a small paragraph and three nouns for these to refer to. This is not a matter of clever violations of rules, it is just a series of pronouns.

T. INGRAM: Perhaps it's just that we don't understand it. You often find that other children from the same group understand what one of them is saying, even if what is said doesn't refer to the immediate situation.

ERVIN-TRIPP: Well, there have been a number of "back to back" communication experiments. One child is supposed to tell another child about how a number of objects are arranged, so that the second child can reproduce the arrangement. Working-class children succeed less well at this game, even with working-class hearers. These experiments normally don't pair close friends nor refer to shared experience, and these are the normal conditions under which working-class children learn the amount of specificity required for successful communication. They have not been trained to over-specify, and without feedback here may take up a style of communication that has normally worked for them, where a lot of pronouns can be used.

ROBINSON: I don't think it's a matter of familiarity with the group, as much as familiarity with the environment in which the events are occurring. I think there is a distinction here between speaking in a restricted in-group code, so that everyone knows the allusions, as against speaking egocentrically where you simply fail to provide the necessary information.

SINCLAIR: It seems to me that ability to use pronouns is something which develops with age as a cognitive function. When you first have children playing at talking on the telephone, every child, working-class or middle-class, will act as if the other child can see what he is talking about. To take your earlier example, it is as if you have an adult seeing Mary and Bill looking at each other, he can very well say to somebody else:

"Although she spoke to him he is still staying late."

You have nothing but pronouns, but it's O.K. because you can see the persons involved. When we have working-class children and middle-class children, if there is any difference in their ability, it might be that working class children don't catch on to the game that you're playing. Once you get them to understand that the game is to specify objects that are invisible to the listener, then we have never been able to find any differences between working-class children and middle-class children, except that the middle-class children catch on to this kind of game much more quickly.

ROBINSON: You may be right, it may be a perceptual problem of what the situation is about, rather than a problem of what their command of the language is. If what you're talking about turns out to be a violation of the pronominal rules, then I could argue that children that don't get the chance to learn the strategy also violate the rules.

SCHLESINGER: You could look at this in a slightly different way. It seems to me you're saying that the strategies originate in the child. Now you could say that this is a strategy which the adult adopts when he communicates with others, so that the listener is not overburdened. In other words, the child learns it from the adult, who has learnt it because he wants to help the child.

BEVER: This sounds kind of circular to me.

MEHLER: I think you could be interpreted as being circular too; because you take a structure in the language and then you say that this is due to a certain strategy, and then you say that because that structure exists that proves that your strategy is right. But the strategy of looking for the nearest nounlike word might have resulted in a language where you had determiner always followed by noun, and then all the adjectives could be piled up afterwards. Or, given that adjectives precede nouns, you could invent other strategies to account for that.

BEVER: I'm not trying to say that it is only these perceptual constraints that determine the form of the language or that all perceptual strategies are induced. As regards word order, I think it is just in those cases where the syntactic structure allows free order, that the perceptual constraints play a role in determining the preferred order.

HYMES: There's a problem here. What with the variety of conceptual

constraints and the number of different languages, how would you preserve any sort of general all-over principles? The question is very difficult, but I can think of one general constraint: language-users tolerate
only a very small amount of ambiguity. For instance, you generally need
to know where the deep structure subject, verb and object are, and
languages will have a necessary amount of case markings, or the necessary amount of ordering constraints to let you know. Of course every
language has a certain amount of ambiguity which is tolerated. In
English we have sentences like "John is quick to please", which is
ambiguous with respect to its deep-structure relations. But no language
allows itself to be totally chaotic, to allow an arbitrarily large number of
such ambiguous derivations. Terry Langendoen argues that linguistic
pressure is in the direction of resolving ambiguity. Whenever the ambiguity gets too bad, you stick in a function word to clear things up.

Learning Strategies

GENERAL DISCUSSION

MEHLER: One thing bothers me a little. There seem to be two kinds of psycholinguistics going on today. One is adult psycholinguistics, which has its own methods and procedures and the other is developmental psycholinguistics. There seems to have been very little adaptation of the methods used in adult psycholinguistics to the investigation of 6- or 7-year-old children. I don't think you can push the adult methods back to very young children, but I think there must be some attempt to use them with these slightly older children. Take the click experiment (Fodor and Bever, 1965). I think this is eminently utilizable with very young children and it hasn't been done at all. Another suggestion is the sort of experiment that Paul Kosler (1964) was doing with reading material and with certain kinds of geometrical inversions and rotations. These experiments are language independent, in the sense that he tested Hebrew and English subjects. Now I don't see any reason why this shouldn't be tried with children. Isn't it necessary now to abandon the gathering of further data, and go further into experimental techniques and more rigorous ways of studying children? Or am I too optimistic?

ERVIN-TRIPP: Well, it seems to me that with the two different approaches one finds out different things. I have just committed myself to a project for which we are collecting more data. We want to find out more about what happens naturalistically in language development; but this has different purposes from the kind of experimental hypothesis-testing you are talking about. I know of no way except observational methods by which we can discover what the actual input structure to children is, about which many very wrong statements have been made, or to discover some basic components of rules for stylistic alternations in produced speech. But in studying the structure of sentence-processing by children and adults we obviously must use experimental methods. I am for both being done.

MEHLER: I have a very modest suggestion to make. Wouldn't it be possible to start looking at how the child defines objects and concepts spontaneously? I mean, how he establishes word classes? For instance, what is the range of application of the word *dog*? This is a sort of vocabulary study; I don't know of any recent data on this. It seems to me that this could lead to some information about the way in which the child organizes his environmental experiences. An investigation into what sort of experience a child needs to establish a word class is a very important subject to study.

CHURCH: I think the problem is that everyone has his own interests and he is not likely to be shunted aside from them by someone else's interests. What you can do is find an audience of people eager to do research, and all you have to do is to publish a list of what hasn't been done and sooner or later someone is going to pick it up and do it. It is probably a matter of just spreading your ideas around and hoping that people will pick them up.

ERVIN-TRIPP: Part of the problem in naturalistic studies is access to families. The most serious problem we have had in our work is to find things that go on within the physical environment of the child. To do this you need to be there, which presents enormous practical problems. Even if you can get a tape recorder for the auditory environment, recording the visual environment is very difficult.

BEVER: Mehler seems to be arguing that we still know very little about some obvious properties. The classical studies of conservation and perceptual development create problems. They all draw on simple stimuli, with rather simple properties being manipulated, such as height and weight and volume. Regular geometric figures are normally used. But we don't really know how often it is that numerosity is correlated with apparent size in the everyday world. We can make guesses about what ought to be right, but a few facts couldn't hurt. One problem that arises, in getting developmental results, is the décalage. An example of this is that number conservation, if I remember correctly, precedes volume conservation.

Why does volume conservation develop later than number conservation? It may be that the correlation between apparent size and volume is higher in the child's experience, than the correlation between apparent size and the number of components. If this were to turn out to be the case, it would be a rather nice explanation for the different ages at which the conservations appear. Given that non-conservation behaviour is due to perceptual strategies which the child develops to be efficient for this world, when a given strategy is disconfirmed less often in the everyday experience it is going to be maintained for a longer time. To study this you must take into account everything you know about the child's visual system and perceptual analysis at the age just before these strategies develop, which we think is around $2\frac{1}{2}$. Another thing to do would be the kind of study Brunswick did, in which he followed subjects around and took photographs of everything that they looked at. Then he acquired naive judgements about the corresponding phenomenology of those objects. Now, part of our problem is to develop that methodology further so it can be used with children.

MEHLER: But what is of interest, I think, is not the *frequency* with which the child observes some correlation in nature, but rather the *way* in which the child sees some correlation. There is a completely behaviouristic view that frequency *per se* will influence behaviour one way or another; whereas I prefer to think it is the manner in which the child encodes.

BEVER: If you want to say that it is entirely due to the *manner* in which the child encodes, that would simply mean that if one correlation obtained 100 per cent of the time and the other correlation obtained 1 per cent of the time, that this difference wouldn't matter to the child. I am suggesting that, if you are trying to analyse object properties in the light of the way you understand the child's capacity to internalize them, then the variety of cases and the number of times for each case that the child sees a particular correlation becomes an important factor. I suggest that the décalage is due to the differential support which the child finds around him for the different kinds of non-conservation.

SINCLAIR: I agree that some décalages are problematic; but the particular one that you were mentioning is not. Let me take a slightly easier one, because we have done some learning experiments on it. Number conservation comes before weight and the reason for that décalage is quite clear: number conservation is not linked to the characteristic properties of the object, it doesn't matter whether you are conserving pencils or marbles or people. In weight conservation, the characteristics of the object you are dealing with obviously come into play.

BEVER: How does the child know that?

SINCLAIR: That's just the point; he doesn't, up to a certain age.

BEVER: But I don't accept that as an explanation that solves the problem; that has simply characterized or articulated a certain portion of the problem in different words.

SINCLAIR: I think the distinction between the two kinds of knowledge is important.

BEVER: I agree the distinction is important, but I don't see that there is any general basis to predict that one kind of distinction would apply to the décalage in this way.

SINCLAIR: Consider the physical situation, where the whole concept of weight has to be abstracted from the characteristics of the objects themselves; not from your handling of them as in the case of number. It has been proved to be quite possible to teach children the conservation of weight, in what one might call a logical manner. You demonstrate that you haven't added anything, you haven't taken anything away, you have just cut it up. After a few sessions, they begin to understand.

MEHLER: Where does volume come in?

SINCLAIR: Volume is a problem. Some décalages are a problem and some are not. For instance, if you teach a child deliberately—and this has been done—you get the kind of conservation of weight which is a logical one and not a physical one. It seems to us, in such cases, that you do away with the non-conservation which, in itself, is a preparation for a higher order, or at least a later physical concept; for instance pressure. The child says that little bits of clay weigh less than one big lump. It is a physical law that something which is very heavy and only rests on the floor on one little point, makes a bigger dent than a pancake that is spread out. Now, if you tease this out for the child by fixing him on the logical property of the conservation of weight simply by saying: "look, we don't take anything away, we just divide it up", you may stop the beginning of the next order of physical concept. This again comes back to the fact that there are two kinds of knowledge, one logical, one physical, one is earlier than the other, and essential for the development of the other.

BEVER: What I'm suggesting is that if we did the relevant survey and found the constant properties, then we would have a consistent explanation for décalage, rather than having to explain it differently for different sorts of problems.

MEHLER: I wonder if this is not rather closely connected with language. Isn't it a particular manifestation of the problem of the uses of the verbs *avoir* and *être*, in the sense that, wherever you make a statement about the structure of some physical embodiment of something that exists, you can define existence in more than one way? You can say *X is X* or you can say *X is Y*, or something like that. Since in our data *être* usually seemed to precede *avoir*, perhaps looking at conservation from that point of view might help to settle the question of décalage also.

SINCLAIR: This is possible.

Critical Periods in Language Learning

GENERAL DISCUSSION

BEVER: I would like us to discuss the notion of "critical period" in language. In the discussion yesterday it was said that experience, having to deal with linguistic and cognitive problems, is perhaps a critical stimulus in the development of neurological lateralization of function. We're all familiar with the phenomenon of imprinting, when a baby duck sees a large moving object before he is 48 hours old he starts following the object around, but it doesn't work after that. It is possible that certain types of linguistically deficient children may be deficient either because they didn't get enough experience with linguistic problems in time to respond by developing the basis for adult cognition, or because they did not get enough experience, before the critical time, to develop a great many of the kinds of perceptual strategies that we have been talking about. It might be interesting to look carefully at children who are having problems in acquiring their own first language, and we might also look at the problems of acquiring a second language.

T. INGRAM: If we are to talk about children who have difficulty in acquiring their own language, there are some studies, mainly French, for instance by Alajouanine, of children who have lost speech, and have had to relearn it as a result of brain injury. Alajouanine (1965) has been particularly interested in the ages at which injury is sustained in children with acquired damage, and he has been unable to demonstrate any critical period with his material. He studied 37 children very carefully, ranging from about 18 months to about 11 years of age. The only common observation across all children and across all ages was a lack of fluency and a diminished output, and even this was qualified, because he found that the children, when pressed, were able to cope with much more elaborate forms of speech than those produced in normal circumstances. Lenneberg (1967) argues very strongly for the existence of critical periods, but his material is not nearly so extensive.

MEHLER: I believe we should be very careful about relying on the conclusions that may be drawn from observations of this sort. I know that there are two big hospitals carrying out this work in Paris; they both have looked at enormous numbers of cases, and their conclusions couldn't be more different.

T. INGRAM: But it is clear that unilateral lesions in patients, aged about 15 or 20, have very damaging consequences. It does seem that there is some age where there is a rather clear shift in the sensitivity to brain damage and subsequent recovery. Luria (1966) has some very interesting findings on the pattern of different types of speech disturbance and different types of dysphasia that you get in different brain injuries at different periods of childhood. He showed that the patterns of loss became more specific as the child grew older, and that it was much easier to identify the kinds of dysphasia that you meet in adult patients, in relation to the older children than in relation to the younger children. But this seems to me to be a matter of degree, not a difference of kind. The ability to identify more specific types of loss as children grow older is a very gradual thing.

MEHLER: As I understand it, the Russian work concerns mainly the writing and the phonological aspects of speech; as far as I could see from the examples, Luria has said little about syntax or semantics.

BEVER: Let's talk about second language learning. The possibility still remains that although second language learning at an advanced stage is quite possible, even perhaps overcoming the problem of accent in some cases, nevertheless the internal capacity, the internal mechanism, which is recruited for this late second language learning may be different from the internal mechanisms which are recruited for early second language learning. I'm guessing that the critical period will be at 15 years or somewhere around that. I'm also guessing that there will be consistent differences in the underlying psycholinguistic processes and that these can be discovered experimentally. Susan Berio, George Miller and I are trying to find out just this. Mrs. Berio has collected a large body of Italian-speaking New Yorkers, who came to the United States at different times. We have some who came at a rather late age, but who speak English extremely well and claim they had no prior training, and some who came at a rather early age and speak English rather poorly. After we have got the basic socio-economic factors sorted out, we should run a series of psycholinguistic tests, and see if we can find any underlying differences.

E. INGRAM: There are some experiments on second language learning which go rather against the hypothesis of there being a critical period in language learning. Thorndike (1928) reported an experiment in which various age groups were taught Esperanto. Admittedly, the methods he used for teaching were the prevailing methods at the time, which were inductive: you gave a grammatical rule, you practised on it, you gave a variety of examples and then you tested on some new examples. The extreme groups he used were children between 9 and 18 on the one hand and adults, 35 years of age or over on the other. The children received twice the formal instruction that the adults did and yet the children learned less than half of what the adult group learned. The language was Esperanto and there was no pronunciation test. Cheydleur (1932) ran an experiment in teaching French, comparing high school pupils with adults attending evening classes, aged between 20 and 62 years, averaging the 40's. All groups had the same method, the same teachers, the same work and the same test. The comparison showed that 64 per cent of the adults in the evening classes did as well as the best 25 per cent of the children from high school. The age of the children here are perhaps a little too high to argue conclusively against the hypothesis of critical periods. But, as you know, in recent years there has been a large amount of teaching of foreign languages in primary school. It was argued that, what with starting the children early, and exposing them to language laboratories, they would learn perfectly whatever language they were being taught. But the results that are coming out show what might be expected, and that is that the children learn something, but they certainly do not learn any aspect of the foreign language perfectly, not even the pronunciation.

There might be one area where the notion of a critical period is relevant and that is in the area of pronunciation. We are all familiar with anecdotal stuff; if you are going to learn something well, like ballet dancing or ski-jumping or riding a bicycle, you are much better off if you start as a child, than if you start as a grown-up. I believe that in a matter of pronunciation, there might well turn out to be some sort of critical period, perhaps around 12 to 15, for the majority of learners.

The second point I want to make is that anything that we can demonstrate about second language learning mechanisms does not necessarily demonstrate anything in particular about first language mechanisms. Whether we discover, or do not discover, critical periods in second language learning, this does not necessarily have any implication for first language learning.

BEVER: It could be that children with different backgrounds may in fact show great internal psychological differences in the mechanisms which they bring to bear when they speak, although they speak equally well.

The Word and its Referent

BEVER: I would like us to discuss the nature of the relationship between the word and its referent and the development of this relationship in the very young child. One view on this is that, for the child, the word is inextricably a part of the object for which it stands. An example of this is from Piaget, when he asks children: "Could we call the sun the moon?", and they answer "No". He asks "Why?" and they answer "Because the moon isn't a fiery red ball". The conclusion from this is that the child argues that the sun is *necessarily* a fiery red ball. This is often referred to as *nominal realism*. I think it was Judy Brooks, at Columbia, who ran a careful experiment asking questions about changing the names of the sun and the moon. She showed that 50 per cent of 10-year-olds still have "nominal realism". They do not seem to know that names are arbitrary, and apparently they were middle-class children too. Now this seemed to me to be wrong, so I started trying to think about what sort of questions one could ask children to explore their feelings about the relationship of the word and the object for which it stands. One of the things we do is to use a giraffe, and then start playing the "part of" game:

"Is the foot part of the giraffe?" "Yes."
"Is the nose part of the giraffe?" "Yes."
"Are the eyes part of the giraffe?" "Yes."

And so on. Then we take a bracelet and put it around the giraffe's neck and then we ask the child: "Is the bracelet part of the giraffe?" Most of the children say *no*; some say *yes*; perhaps especially the younger ones, but not all of those. Then we ask:

"Is the name *giraffe* part of the giraffe?"

The children we've looked at are aged between 2 and 5 years and we find that 30 per cent say everything is part of the giraffe, everything associated with it is part of it, including its name, the other 70 per cent

271

say that the bracelet is not part of the giraffe and almost all of these say that the name is not part of the giraffe either. There is no difference in terms of age in this. The next thing we did was to ask if giraffes could change their name:

> "Could the giraffe be called a cat?"
> "Could the giraffe be called a gip?"
> "Could the giraffe be called a raffe?"

It is very difficult to establish what a child really believes about this, so there's not much point in giving figures, but you can go on asking him further questions: "If you can't call him a cat, why can't you?" One child answered: "Because he don't be small like a cat." You can ask: "Will Mummy know what you mean if you say, I saw a cat today?" and they say: "Well, Mummy will know, because she's here, but Daddy won't". (The mother usually sits in the back during the experiment.) Children that give me that answer, I think, seem to know what naming is about. When I ask: "Can we call him gip?" a much larger proportion of children accept it. Interestingly enough, two children at the age of $4\frac{1}{2}$ refused to accept either "cat" or "gip" as a name for a giraffe, but said spontaneously: "You could call it a raffe" or "You could call it a griffe".

This could be interpreted as showing nominal realism; but I think it shows they know what naming is about. In general a lot of children under 5 agree that they themselves could have a different name, and they would still be the same person, though everyone would call them a different name. They know that if I decided to call them a different name they would have to tell everyone else, or nobody would know. So a large proportion of them do not have any trouble in playing this game.

SCHLESINGER: This doesn't really refute the argument for nominal realism, because all it means is that you can play this game, and it's a kind of crazy thing, but after all a chair is a chair.

BEVER: Actually, I think the name *nominal realism* is misleading. I suspect that this is really a kind of "linguistic rigidity", and that it is something that is learnt. We may be dealing with children who haven't yet got to the stage of being very choosy about what labels they use to refer to objects in their environment. I'm arguing two things, that this so-called nominal realism might actually be a constructive higher-order association between words and things and also that it might not be the resting state of the children.

CHURCH: But I think there is quite clearly a phenomenon of linguistic realism if you like; where the child, at least initially, finds it very hard to treat a statement as a hypothetical statement, or a lie as an untruth. In fact, he is an extremely gullible creature and when you say something to him he finds it very hard to be incredulous. This is up to about 4 to 5 years.

BEVER: Children do play pretend games.

CHURCH: Yes, but characteristically the child draws a distinction between pretending and really being, but perhaps this is easier for him when he creates the game himself.

E. INGRAM: I would support the distinction between pretend play initiated by the child, and his ability to detect irony. In general, if you say something to a child, then he assumes that that is what you mean.

BEVER: All right, I think that is a clear intuition which a lot of people have, but I'm not convinced. I think a 2½-year-old is an awfully sophisticated being.

HYMES: I am reminded of the work of Luria (1961) where he found that very young children could understand the meaning of various words or commands, but that when they were engaged in an activity, a particular command to stop had no effect. He is arguing that there is a difference between understanding language and the ability to control behaviour through language.

SINCLAIR: I think one has to be very careful about what words one uses here and how one plays these games. I think, for instance, it is very dangerous to use toys; a toy lion is not a real lion at all, it is already a symbol. Secondly, I think that there are differences of reality, if you like, between some sort of words and other sorts of words; the sun and the moon are very far away, they are not touchable, you cannot inspect them. Perhaps children's reaction to something which they cannot control might be different from their reaction to toys or pictures, which they can take apart.

Also the concept of "part of" is a very tricky one. There is a kind of whole-part relationship, for instance, between cars and the wheels of the cars; and if you asked children whether they could rename either the car or the wheels, or both at the same time, you might get different sorts of results. That is, the relationship between an object and its attributes is important. For instance, I might take a red rose and suggest it was a daisy (a daisy is generally white, or at least pale pink). If I then asked "Could I call this a daisy?" or "If you called it a daisy, would it be white or red?", I might get different results. In other words, I think perhaps it is the cognitive structures that children have about things that determine their answer, rather than formal linguistic development.

E. INGRAM: Templin said to children: "This is a cow, that is a dog. Now if we call a cow a dog, and a dog a cow, what is the name of the thing we get milk from?" Below about 6 years of age, they said: "A cow of course; everybody knows you get milk from a cow." Above that age they were able to answer: "A dog". But this could be a rather difficult problem for them to sort out.

MEHLER: Yes, in the first place they have to understand the game you are playing. I also think this kind of problem is very dependent on memory storage. Jane Ellen Huttenlocher showed that memory span is dependent on the operations you do on the elements which are stored in immediate memory. For instance, if you have three cubes in the immediate memory, and then you have to record them in the inverted order, that takes up all the memory span of the child. Whereas, if you don't have to do an operation on the cubes, the child might manage to store six cubes. In this case it might very well be that the child can say "A cow is a dog" and "A dog is a cow", but when he has to do an operation on this, he cannot do it because he hasn't got enough storage space. Again, these things could be variously interpreted until we know more about the basic processes of children, such as memory storage.

CAZDEN: I'd like to ask whether you think that this ability to rename has anything to do with the complementary phenomenon of one word referring to two different things. I believe that some children have quite a bit of trouble with this. I wonder whether, if children had more experience with words, or were more aware that there were words like *run* that could refer to different things, this might help them to understand the arbitrary relationship between words and things.

CHURCH: I think most of the evidence indicates that the child doesn't seem to notice the homonym of "a run in the stocking". Asch and Nerlove (1960) showed that, when the child knows what *a sweet person* is and knows what *a sweet taste* is, he will not agree that these two *sweets* have anything to do with each other.

Clinical

Sentence Production in Normal Children, Adolescents and in Patients with Diffuse and Unilateral Cerebral Disease[1]

H. HECAEN

Centre Neurochirurgical des Hôpitaux Psychiatriques de la Seine, Paris

INTRODUCTION

ALTHOUGH SOME of the studies which I shall report have not been completed, it might be of interest to present a brief résumé of the results we have obtained on various groups of normal and pathological subjects.

Since the beginning of our multidisciplinary research on aphasia, we have been using a test of sentence production. As a result, we have a good deal of data available and our initial analyses appear to allow us to come to certain conclusions. The sentence production test was compiled with the ultimate aim of constructing a model of linguistic performance. This model includes a component representing a knowledge of linguistic rules, which constitute the component of competence; as well as such other factors as perception, memory and attention, necessary for the production of actual utterances. Ideally perhaps the establishment of such a model should be based on spontaneous speech, but, individual differences in performance being so variable, it would not be possible on such a basis to determine the role of the variables mentioned. It was in an attempt to overcome the influence of these variables to some extent that we developed a test which imposes certain syntactic and semantic constraints upon the subjects and yet allows them a certain freedom of choice in their sentence-production strategies.

[1] Travail du groupe de la R.C.P. no 41 (C.N.R.S.), effectué au Centre Neurochirurgical de l'Hôpital Sainte-Anne et avec l'aide de l'I.N.S.E.R.M.

DESCRIPTION OF THE TEST

The test consists of ten tasks: for each task, the subject is presented (orally) with a sequence of two, three or four words in a chosen order (cf. below). With these words he is requested to make a single sentence which must be as simple and short as possible. The subjects in some cases are asked to utter the sentence, and in other cases to write the sentence without erasure or corrections.

The time between two consecutive tasks is the time necessary for the subject to write or to say a sentence; it is therefore not uniform for all subjects. In this first stage of the study, the analysis of the production does not take account of the time taken to produce a sentence.

The following ten sequences of words are presented to the subjects:

   (1) fauteuil (armchair), docteur (doctor), asseoir (to sit);
   (2) bureau (desk, office), tiroir (drawer), ouvrir (to open);
   (3) maison (house, family), mère (mother);
   (4) récompense (reward, compensation), enfant (child);
   (5) lumière (light), lampe (light bulb, lamp);
   (6) maison (house), chat (cat);
   (7) enfant (child), père (father), absent (absent);
   (8) crayon (pencil), écrire (to write), feuille (sheet), bleu (blue);
   (9) détacher (detach, separate), feuille (leaf, sheet), voler (to steal);
 (10) rouge (red), voir (to see), cheval (horse).

The sequence of words has been chosen so as to constitute semi-sentences which are either (i) *agrammatical* (for instance in (1) incorrect order of the words); or (ii) *ambiguous* (for instance in (3) [mer]: mer (sea), mère (mother) or maire (mayor)); or (iii) *semantically anomalous* (for instance (10): rouge (red), voir (to see), cheval (horse)).

PERFORMANCE OF NORMAL ADULTS AND CHILDREN

The test was given (i) to 40 students at the University of Tours and the type of construction made and the ways in which ambiguities were resolved were determined; (ii) to a control group of hospitalized patients who were free from cerebral disease and who came from various social classes; the same analysis was made. In both groups, subjects with a background of 8 years schooling (obtaining the C.E.P.) produced almost completely successful performances. In contrast subjects with a lower educational level did not follow the instructions to make a single simple sentence, particularly when presented with three or four words.

Performance variations as a function of age were analysed by taking a further sample of 300 pupils (between 10 and 19 years of age) who had approximately the same social background (middle class and fairly conservative), attending a small school where the test could be given under rigorous conditions. Statistical analysis of the different schemes within each sentence gave the following results:

(1) Important differences were found between the ages of 10 and 19 years due to a change of attitude towards the task. Different strategies could be isolated: one consists in considering the words as the substance of a message to which the subject gives a content which is "meaningful" for him (recomposition); the other consists in considering the words as items capable of supporting a system of rules (reconstruction).

It is in this sense I have interpreted the development of the correspondence between the number of statements and the number of words in the task (set), that is, between the number of words added and the number of words given; thus the progressive vagueness of the response, the loss of preciseness of the message proper according to the different (possible) modalities of the utterance (possession, time, variety of words added, etc.).

(2) The change in strategy between the ages of 10 and 19 is very noticeable. In the earlier stages recomposition is the dominant strategy; later, reconstruction becomes dominant. There is a critical threshold at 14–15 years which suggests a change of strategy at about this age: as they grow older, people tend to consider language as an object and therefore their tolerance of ambiguity is increased. A study of the sentences, produced in response to the stimulus group of words *rouge, voir, cheval*, shows a decrease in the construction of complex sentences, and a rise in semantic anomaly. At the same age there is an increase in grammatically correct sentences which conform to the instructions, but which show semantic incongruities, i.e. *le cheval voit rouge*; *je vois un cheval rouge*. Such utterances are not produced by younger subjects.

Although there is this global modification in strategy, the two attitudes are constantly present in the whole of the population. Thus subjects aged 10–14 may reject their initial strategy when, after having written an anomalous sentence, they comment *"voir un cheval rouge — c'est impossible"*.

(3) On the other hand, mastery of the syntactic possibilities as opposed to the semantic ones show certain invariant results: irrespective of age, constant correlations can be found between certain sentence types.

K§

OBSERVATIONS ON PATHOLOGICAL GROUPS

Patients with Mental Disease

Fifty patients were examined at the Clinique des Maladies Mentales in Paris. Only patients whose diagnosis was established without any doubt were included. The results obtained with conversion hysterics, obsessional neurotics, and schizophrenics agreed with the results from the controls of the same educational level. This lack of effect of certain neurotic and psychotic disturbances on performance permitted us to disregard the role of personality traits in the results.

Patients with Parkinsonian Syndrome

This group of patients had not been subjected to stereotaxic therapy. Their mean sociocultural level was low average. Given the test described above, 65 per cent of the patients made one or more mistakes. The most frequent type of mistake consisted in a lack of integration of the presented words without, however, agrammatism or lack of meaning. The number of failures correlated with the number of presented words.

Patients with Lesion of Left Hemisphere

Fifty-eight subjects were given the test described above. For each patient the site of the lesion was verified either at the time of operation or after death on post-mortem examination. The analysis for each patient related the number of unsuccessfully attempted trials to the total number of trials given. This measure was termed the coefficient of failure. Another measure used was the coefficient of so-called diffusion, in which the number of test words correctly integrated was related to the total number of words contained in the utterance produced. Also the type of errors (poor combining of words, lack of grammaticality, lack of meaning) was noted.

The number of patients in this group who performed badly in the test was very high, 72·4 per cent; and the coefficient of failure per sentence was also high. These results were independent of the locus of the lesion. However, failures were decidedly less frequent (0·12) in patients whose lesions were limited to the Rolandic area (pre-central and post-central gyri). Evidently the restricted extent of the lesion was responsible for their better performance. Patients with parietal injuries showed a higher coefficient of failure (0·61); patients with temporal and frontal lesions on the other hand showed approximately the same coefficient of failures, 0·56 and 0·51 respectively.

The influence of educational level on performance was similar to that observed in normal subjects. Intellectual deterioration and confusion were associated with poor performance. In patients of good educational background, and without deterioration or confusion, failure was most frequent in those with isolated parietal or temporal lesions (44 per cent). The coefficient of failure of patients with lesions involving the temporal lobe was 0·36, while for the patients with lesions not involving the temporal lobe it was 0·31. A similar comparison gave a figure of 0·47 in patients with parietal lesions as against 0·28 in those with lesions not involving the parietal lobe.

When the findings were considered in relation to the presence or absence of neurological symptoms, it was found that the presence of motor disturbance was not related to coefficient of failure (0·52 versus 0·51). On the other hand, coefficient of failure was particularly high in patients with visual field defects (0·72) compared to those without visual field defects (0·44). The presence of sensory disturbance was also related to the coefficient of failure (0·63 versus 0·45).

Naturally the percentage of failure was considerably higher in patients with clinically evident aphasic disorders. However, this was not the case in those with purely expressive disturbances. The coefficient of failure in patients with comprehension difficulties was extremely high, 0·83. Those with constructional apraxia showed a coefficient of failure of 0·79 compared with 0·40 in those without constructional disturbances. However, 14 of the 16 apraxics also showed disturbances in verbal comprehension and it should be noted that the coefficient of failure in the apraxic, non-aphasic patients was only 0·25.

For patients who could produce sentences (either correctly or incorrectly), the length of the sentence correlated with the number of mistakes made.

Patients with Lesions of the Right Hemisphere

This group consisted of 53 right-handed patients with right hemisphere lesions (the site of the lesions having been confirmed by surgical intervention or subsequently at post-mortem examination). Twenty-five subjects (i.e. almost half the group) made one or more mistakes. Failure was particularly high in the production of sentences involving the integration of four words. The influence of educational level, mental confusion or intellectual deterioration on performance was evident. Nevertheless, the coefficient of failure in patients with an adequate educational background and without confusion or deterioration was higher than in a normal population (0·10 versus 0·02). Patients with temporal lobe lesions showed a higher frequency of defect (0·21) than those with lesion in other areas (0·08). The mistakes were primarily due to faulty integration of words, but the patients also produced a relatively high amount of agrammatical sentences (not well-formed syntactically).

Diffluency is marked in lesions of the minor hemisphere but the highest individual coefficient observed was six, while in patients with left hemisphere lesions a coefficient of 0·12 can occur. The severity of failure was more marked in patients who did not follow the instruction to produce short sentence, i.e. those who tended to be discursive. As in the preceding group, discursiveness was greatest in the patients with temporal lesions and the shortest sentences were produced by patients with Rolandic lesions.

States of Dementia

The test was given by L. Irigaray (1967a and 1967b) to 50 patients: 30 patients suffering from conditions of rather diverse etiology at the Centre Neurochirurgical Sainte-Anne, and 20 patients at the Clinique Psychiatrique Bel-Air of the University of Geneva (Prof. J. de Ajuriaguerra). Poor performance was particularly frequent when the task required the integration of three or four words. Responses conforming to the instructions were made only when extent of deterioration was relatively moderate, or when the task was not ambiguous, or when the message corresponded to the semantic experience of the subject or when the terms were semantically compatible and did not pose a problem of distribution among syntactic classes. When these subjects did succeed, the type of sentence construction reflected a strategy similar to that observed in young children.

In general, the production whether correct or incorrect showed conservation of syntactic patterns, though with disturbances in the selection of words. As a result, logical and semantic anomalies were produced.

When the patients were divided into two groups, those without signs produced by focal lesions and those with focal signs (aphasia, apraxia, agnosia), it was clear that the frequency of failure was higher in the second group, while the degree of diffusion was about the same. Moreover, it was also observed in the patients studied at Bel-Air that the frequency of failure was directly related to the degree of deterioration as judged by the operational tests of Piaget. We plan to examine this question in greater detail with specific reference to the respective roles of disabilities produced by focal lesions and degree of deterioration of performance in this test of sentence production.

These preliminary analyses of the results obtained from different types of patients given the same test seem to us to permit a fairly discriminating judgement of the verbal behaviour of the subjects and of the degree of mastery of the language which they possess. Probably a more precise analysis of the responses and the types of errors, and also the determination of the correlations with neurological signs and site of lesions will enable us to assess the operative factors determining the strategies involved in the production of utterances.

We are seeking particularly to bring to light the role of lesion localization in performance deficit on this test, but so far we have reported only the results obtained in subjects with verified unilateral lesions. The study will be extended to our total sample of patients including those for whom there is only clinical evidence for the presence of a unilateral cortical lesion. This will make possible the determination of the correlations between type of failure and various symptoms for a much larger sample (approximately 400 subjects). In this way we hope to be able to specify the role and mode of various psychological factors in verbal expression, as measured by this test of sentence production.

The Edinburgh Articulation Test

T. T. S. INGRAM

Edinburgh University

T. INGRAM: Over the past 7 years we have developed a test of articulatory development which was based on asking children to name objects and pictures (1971). It has been standardized on a representative group of Edinburgh children aged from 3 to 6 years. I hope to have it standardized for children in London, Newcastle and Leeds and I am very keen to have it standardized on American children. If there is anyone who is interested in it I would be glad to hear from them.

The test consists of a naming game in which the child is asked to name 41 objects presented as pictures. This gives a total of 68 items for analysis. These items consist of consonants and consonant clusters in word-initial, medial and final position. Vowels are excluded from consideration because they vary so much from dialect to dialect. The test is administered by a speech pathologist with perhaps a little extra training in phonetics, who studies the child's utterances at the time he makes them and also takes a tape recording which she can study later.

The test is scored according to the number of items which are considered to be pronounced in the adult form; items which are not pronounced in this way receive no score. Thus a child will receive a point for a correct *sh* sound in *fish* but will receive nothing in this scoring system for *fith* [θ]. Depending on the age of the child, the items differed somewhat in their value. For example most children aged 3 could pronounce the initial *p* in *pencil* correctly but could not articulate the medial *ns* sound. In *bridge* a great many of the younger or speech-retarded children were found to be unable to deal with the initial consonant cluster *br* and replaced it by *bw*; similarly the terminal sound in the word *bridge* [d_3] caused trouble to younger and speech-retarded children. Raw scores on the test were converted into quotients according to a conversion table.

The test was standardized on 510 Edinburgh children who were considered to be representative by sex, social class and place in family. It was

285

found that there was no significant difference between social classes I and II, II and III, III and IV or IV and V, but there were significant differences between social classes I and III, II and IV and III and V. There was no significant difference in the scores by sex. The standard deviation of the quotients was 15 points and the mean was 100.

When we examined the children who scored less than 85 on the test, they included all those with deviant speech development. All those who were considered likely to require speech therapy were included in this group; and it suggests that the articulatory test may be useful as a screening examination in picking out children who may require speech therapy, though of course not all those with quotients of less than 85 will do so.

ERVIN-TRIPP: Did they require speech therapy for other reasons than retarded speech development?

T. INGRAM: Yes, for retarded speech development and a number of other reasons. For example I was able to identify the profile of disordered articulation presented by a child with a submucous cleft palate on the results of the test.

SCHLESINGER: What kind of adult qualitative statistical analysis did you use? You have an overall score of articulatory development, but have you ever tried to analyse the patterns of development, in other words how particular groups of features are acquired?

T. INGRAM: Yes, we have looked at this but haven't got very far with the analysis as yet.

At present we are actively exploring the tape-recordings of the 510 children on whom the test was standardized to see if we can recognize different patterns in speech development, i.e. children producing different patterns of articulatory development. Already we have evidence that the majority of children with slow speech development conform to a pattern of acquisition of a speech sound, but I think it is likely that there will be deviant developers, whose pattern of sound acquisition is different from that found in the majority.

BEVER: It would be nice to verify or disprove Jakobson.

T. INGRAM: Well this is another interest I have as regards the test. I wanted to use the test on adults who suffered from dysphasia. I am also very anxious to standardize the test on other non-Scottish populations, and, since we haven't discovered in Edinburgh significant differences by sex or contiguous social classes that are at all comparable to the differences by age, I think this is a justifiable procedure. And even if representative population groups are not chosen in other centres it shouldn't matter too much for the validation of our test.

Closing Remarks

D. HYMES

University of Pennsylvania

IN MANY WAYS, I think this conference has reflected the state of current work in this field. Perhaps its strongest part has been the work in cognitive psychology. At the same time, we have had some kind of debate about different schools of thought with regard to scientific approach. I think also that some future meeting point between the sociolinguists and cognitive psychologists is beginning to emerge through the discussion of cross-cultural and comparative studies. This seems to me important from the anthropological side and from the linguistic side.

I think everybody would really agree that the problem came down to a search for the invariants, for general laws, though each of us might define the frame of reference for these somewhat differently. This has certainly been true of linguistics for some time. Jakobson has always insisted that the goal of linguistics was the search for invariants: I think if we take that particular note, then the interplay of the development of cognitive processes on the one hand, and the sociological and ethnographic analysis of the use of language on the other, do come together in very important ways. We have mentioned some of them, which are in one sense practical, ethnological problems. It is a matter of controlling the conditions under which the data are obtained, and of controlling their interpretation. It seems to me though, as it often seems to anthropologists whose research is rooted in Western society, that there must be at least a niggling concern about what it would look like if it were done with a variety of language types, in a variety of sociocultural situations. I am not saying this in order to take the view that the results will all turn out to be different and the invariant laws will disappear. I want to make sure that the invariants which appear really are the invariants for the species and not just for the cultural situation. Some work on American society, for example, which seemed to establish very interesting differences in socialization turned out to represent just a small single part of the total distribution of the phenomena in the societies in the world which were considered (Whiting, 1954). This is a very difficult problem. Dr Tripp has mentioned some work that is just beginning which compares research from a number of different societies around the world. One could count on the fingers of one's hand the number of studies of any substance of language development in children from non-western society. It does seem to me that this is one of the things which is going to be most important in the future, simply because the societies of the world are getting more and more alike. In so far as differences need to be taken into account in treating some of these things, we don't have an indefinite future in which to take advantage of these differences.

The second point I would like to repeat at the end of this conference is that, when we talk about language, we all have many different things in mind. It seemed to me that Dr Bever was leading us in this direction when he mentioned the variety of functions that language serves and the way in which the child, for example, is able to talk in a linguistic way in his own language. I am sorry myself that we didn't have the chance to pay more attention to this. One of the problems I see in our field concerns the lack of multi-lingual cases with regard to the presence of features in more than one language in the child's experience. There is also the fact that we so often find that these languages are specialized, and have a different purpose in different social groups, at different places in the child's conception of his social life. It seems to me that if we are to have a developing field of the study of language development, it is the issue of the integration of the sociological and the psychological perspective that is going to be extremely important. Pronouns would be a valuable phenomenon to study in this regard, their linguistic meaning entails reference to social roles in the speech event, and so their study would relate the development of the child's knowledge of both linguistic structure and social role.

I would also like to suggest that the biological aspects are equally important. We discussed biology from the point of view of the psychologist and social scientist, who are interested in the biological basis of human behaviour; we did not discuss it from the point of view, say, of a biologist or zoologist looking at it. We have been looking at the biological basis of behaviour in one particular direction, whereas a student of primate behaviour, or a zoologist interested in adaptation, interested in ecological points of view, might bring something important to the study of communication in the human species and of languages. This would be an essential aspect of a more general picture.

Finally, there is the innate aspect of the child's development, and the way in which it becomes integrated into the personality of the child and into its social behaviour and social life. We were thinking in that direction at one point when we were concerned with perceptual strategies and the influence of the social factors on these things. There is not much work in progress in this field, but I think it is becoming of critical importance.

We have had people at this conference who represent some of the practical and social concerns with language and our society, whose problems are of things like education and retardation. These problems can hardly be adequately approached without regard to biological concerns as well. I think the chief points of some of the goals that we *do* have in common—the study of invariants, the study of the total picture of the child in terms of language development—come down to two things, once we get past the differences between methods and ways of stating things: how are we to take this very highly developed, and very richly developing area of research in cognitive psychology, which is perhaps the most advanced aspect of the study of language development, and utilize its success to study the cross-cultural aspects, by implementing its techniques and design for studying the problems under a variety of conditions of language in a social context? And how are we to conceptualize and integrate the emergence of language itself, as part of the emergence of the child as a total communicating being in society?

Bibliography

ALAJOUANINE, T. and L'HERMITTE, F. 1965. Acquired aphasia in children. *Brain*, **88**, 633–662.

ALBERT, E. 1964. "Rhetoric", logic, and poetics in Burundi: culture patterning of speech behaviour. In J. J. Gumperz and D. Hymes (Eds.), *The ethnography of communication*. American Anthropological Association, Washington, D.C., 35–54.

ANTHONY, A., BOGLE, D., INGRAM, T. T. S. and MCISAAC, M. W. 1971. *The Edinburgh Articulation Test*. E. & S. Livingstone, Edinburgh and London.

ASCH, S. E. ad NERLOVE, H. 1960. The development of double function terms in children. In B. Kaplan and S. Wapner (Eds), *Perspectives in Psychological Theory*, 47–60. International Universities, New York.

BALTIMORE CITY PUBLIC SCHOOLS. 1964. *An early school admission project: progress report, 1963–64*. Baltimore City Public Schools, Baltimore.

BELLUGI, U. 1967. The acquisition of negation. Doctoral Dissertation, Harvard University, Cambridge, Mass.

BELLUGI, U. (in press). *The aquisition of the system of negation in children's speech*. M.I.T. Press, Cambridge, Mass.

BELLUGI, U. and BROWN, R. (Eds.) 1964. The acquisition of language. *Monographs of the Society for Research in Child Development*, **29**, 1, 1–192.

BERKO, J. 1958. The child's learning of English morphology. *Word*, **14**, 150–177.

BERNSTEIN, B. 1961a. Social structure, language and learning. *Educational Research*, **3**, 163–176.

BERNSTEIN, B. 1961b. Social class and linguistic development: a theory of social learning. In A. H. Halsey, J. Floud and E. Anderson (Eds.), *Education, economy and society*. Free Press, New York.

BERNSTEIN, B. 1971. A sociolinguistic approach to socialization: with some references to educability. In D. Hymes and J. Gumperz (Eds.), *Directions in sociolinguistics*. Holt, Rinehart and Winston, New York.

BERNSTEIN, B. and YOUNG, D. 1967. Social class differences in conceptions of the uses of toys. *Sociology*, **1**, 131–140.

BEVER, T. G. 1967. *Harvard Center for Cognitive Studies Report*. Cambridge, Mass.

BEVER, T. G. 1970. The cognitive basis for linguistic structures. In J. R. Hayes, *Cognition and the development of language*. Wiley, New York. 279–362.

BEVER, T. G., FODOR, J. and WEKSEL, W. 1965. The acquisition of syntax: a critique of contextual generalization. *Psychological Revue*, **72**, 467–82.

BEVER, T. G., KIRK, R. and LACKNER, J. 1968. An automatic reflection of syntactic structure. *Neuropsych.* **7**, 23–28.

BEVER, T. G., LACKNER, J. and KIRK, R. 1969a. The underlying structure sentence is the primary unit of speech perception. *Perception and Psychophysics*, **5**, 225–234.

BEVER, T. G., LACKNER, J. and STOLZ, W. 1969b. Transitional probability is not a general mechanism for the segmentation of speech. *Journal of Experimental Psychology*, **79**, no. 3.

BEVER, T. G., MEHLER, J. and EPSTEIN, J. 1968. What children do in spite of what they know. *Science*, **162**, 921–924.

BEVER, T. G., MEHLER, J. and VALIAN, V. (in press). Linguistic capacity in very young children. In T. G. Bever and W. Weksel (Eds.), *Structure and psychology of language*. Holt, Rinehart and Winston, New York.

BEVER, T. G. and STEIN, N. (in preparation) *Auditory asymmetries in the location of tones during speech.*

BIRDWHISTELL, R. L. 1971. A kinesic-linguistic exercise. In J. J. Gumperz and D. Hymes (Eds.), *Directions in sociolinguistics: the ethnography of communication*. Holt, Rinehart and Winston, New York.

BLOOM, L. M. 1970. Language development: form and function in emerging grammars. The M.I.T. Press, Cambridge, Mass.

BLOOMFIELD, L. 1927. Literate and illiterate speech. *American Speech*, **2**, 432–439. Reprinted in D. Hymes (Ed.) *Language and culture in society: a reader in linguistics and anthropology*, 1964, 391–396. Harper and Row, New York.

BLOOMFIELD, L. 1933. *Language*. Holt, Rinehart and Winston, New York.

BLUMENTHAL, A. 1967. Observations with self-embedded sentences. *Psychon. Sci.* June.

BOWER, T. G. R. 1966. Slant perception and shape constancy in infants. *Science*, **151**, 832–834.

BOWER, T. G. R. 1966. The visual world of infants. *Scientific American*, **215**, 80–92.

BOWER, T. G. R. 1967. Phenomenal identity and form perception in an infant. *Perception and Psychophysics*, **2**, 74–76.

BRAINE, M. D. S. 1963. The ontogeny of English phrase structure: the first phrase. *Language*, **39**, 1–13.

BRANDIS, W. and HENDERSON, D. 1970. *Social class, language and communication*. Routledge and Kegan Paul, London.

BRIGHT, W. 1966. *Sociolinguistics*. Mouton, The Hague.

BRIMER, M. A. and DUNN, L. M. 1962. *The English picture vocabulary tests*. National Foundation for Educational Research, London.

BROWN, R. 1968. The development of wh- questions in child speech. *Journal of Verbal Learning and Verbal Behavior*, **7**, No. 2, 279–290.

BROWN, R., CAZDEN, C. B. and BELLUGI, U. 1969. The child's grammar from I to III. In J. P. Hill (Ed.), 1967, *Minnesota symposium on child psychology*, 28–73. University of Minnesota Press, Minneapolis.

BROWN, R. and HANLON, C. 1970. Derivational complexity and order of acquisition in child speech. In J. R. Hayes (Ed.), *Cognition and language learning*, 11–53. Wiley and Sons, New York.

BRUNER, J. S. 1966. *Studies in cognitive growth*. Wiley and Sons, New York.

BRUNSWICK, E. 1956. *Perception and the representative design of psychological experiments*. University of California, Berkeley.

BRYDEN, M. P. 1965. Tachistoscopic recognition, handedness, and cerebral dominance. *Neuropsych.* **3**, 1–8.

BULLOWA, M., BEVER, T. G. and JONES, L. G. 1964. The development from vocal to verbal behaviour in children. *Monographs of the Society for Research in Child Development*, **29**, 1.

BURKE, K. 1945. *A grammar of motives*. Prentice-Hall, New York.

CALDWELL, B. M. 1964. *Directions for setting up child-environment interactions and a check-list for observed reactions and early language assessment scale*. Mimeographed.

CAREY, P., MEHLER, J. and BEVER, T. G. 1970. When do we compute all the interpretations of an ambiguous sentence? In G. D'Arcais and W. Levelt (Eds.), *Advances in Psycholinguistics: Proceedings of the Bressonone Conference*. North Holland Publishing Company, Amsterdam.

CARROLL, J. B. and CASAGRANDE, J. B. 1958. The function of language classifications in behaviour. In E. L. Hartley, E. E. Maccoby and T. M. Newcomb (Eds.), *Readings in social psychology*. Holt, Rinehart and Winston, New York.

CATTELL, P. 1940. *Infant intelligence scale record form*. Psychological Corporation, New York.

CAUDILL, W. and WEINSTEIN, H. 1966. Maternal care and infant behaviour in Japanese and American urban middle class families. In R. Konig and R. Hill (Eds.), *Yearbook of the International Sociological Association*.

CAZDEN, C. B. 1966. Subcultural differences in child language: an interdisciplinary review. *Merrill-Palmer Quarterly*, **12**, 185–219.

CAZDEN, C. B. 1967. On individual differences in language competence and performance. *Journal of Special Education*, **1**, 135–150.

CAZDEN, C. B. 1968. The acquisition of noun and verb inflections. *Child Development*, **39**, 433–448.

CAZDEN, C. B. 1970. The neglected situation in child language research and education. In F. Williams (Ed.), *Language and poverty: perspectives on a theme*. Markham Publishing Co., Chicago. 81–101.

CHARLESWORTH, W. R. 1968. Cognition in infancy; where do we stand in the midsixties? *Merrill-Palmer Quarterly*, **14**, 25–26.

CHEYDLEUR, F. D. 1932. An experiment in adult learning of French. *Journal of Educational Research*, **26**, 259–275.

CHOMSKY, N. 1957. Syntactic structures. Mouton, The Hague.

CHOMSKY, N. 1965. *Aspects of the theory of syntax*. M.I.T. Press, Cambridge, Mass.

CHOMSKY, N. 1968. *Language and mind*. Harcourt, Brace and World, Inc., Chicago.

CHURCH, J. 1966. *Language and the discovery of reality*. Vintage, New York.

CHURCH, J. 1969. Cognitive consequences of social disadvantage. Paper read at Symposium on New Ways of Viewing the Disadvantaged Child, New York State Psychological Association.

CHURCH, J. 1970. Techniques for the differential study of cognition in early childhood. In J. Hellmuth (Ed.), *Cognitive studies*, Vol. I. Brunner-Mazel, New York. 1–23.

COLLER, A. R. and VICTOR, J. 1967. *Early childhood inventories project*. New York University, School of Education, Institute for Developmental Studies, New York.

COULTHARD, M. and ROBINSON, W. P. 1968. The structure of the nominal group and elaborateness of code. *Language and Speech*, **11**, 234–250.

CROTHERS, E. and SUPPES, P. 1967. *Experiments in second language learning*. Academic Press, New York.

DE BARDIES, B. 1969. Memorization of negation: syntax and semantics. In J. Mehler (Ed.), *Psycholinguistique et grammaire générative*. Paris. 111–118.

DE CAMP, D. 1971. A generative analysis of a post creole speech continuum. In D. Hymes (Ed.), *Pidginization and creolization of languages*. Cambridge University Press, Cambridge.

DIEBOLD, A. R. 1963. Code switching in Greek–English bilingual speech. *Report of the Thirteenth Round Table Meeting in Linguistics and Language Study*. Georgetown University Monograph, No. 15. Washington, D.C.

DIXON, J. D. 1957. Development of self recognition. *Journal of Genetic Psychology*, **91**, 251–256.

DRILLIEN, C. M. and HUTTENLOCHER, J. 1957. The social and economic factors affecting the incidence of premature birth. Part I. *Journal of Obstetrics and Gynaecology of the British Empire*, **64**, 161–184.

DUBOIS, J. and IRIGARAY, L. 1966. Approche expérimentale de la constitution de la phrase minimale en Français. *Language*, **3**, 90–125.

DUBOIS, J., ASSAL, G. and RAMIER, A. M. 1968. Production de phrases dans une population d âge scolaire. *Journal de Psychologie*, **2**, 183–208.

EPSTEIN, J. 1969. Recall of word lists following learning of sentences and random strings. *Journal of Verbal Learning and Verbal Behavior*, **8**, 20–25.

ERVIN-TRIPP, S. 1966. Language development. In L. W. Hoffman and M. L. Hoffman (Eds.), *Review of child development research*, 2. Russell Sage Foundation, New York. 55–105.

ERVIN-TRIPP, S. 1969. Sociolinguistics. In L. Berkowitz (Ed.), *Advances in experimental social psychology*. Vol. 4. Academic Press, New York and London.

FERGUSON, C. A. 1966. On sociolinguistically oriented surveys. *Linguistic Reporter*, **8** (4), 1–3.

FILLMORE, C. J. 1968. The case for case. In E. Bach and R. J. Harmes (Eds.), *Universals in linguistic theory*. Holt, Rinehart and Winston, New York.

FISCHER, J. L. 1958. Social influences on the choice of a linguistic variant. *Word*, **14**, 47–56.

FLAVELL, J. H. 1963. *The developmental psychology of Jean Piaget*. Van Nostrand, New York.

FODOR, J. 1966. How to learn to talk: some simple ways. In F. Smith and G. Miller (Eds.), *The genesis of language*. M.I.T. Press, Cambridge, Mass. 105–122.

FODOR, J. and BEVER, T. G. 1965. The psychological reality of linguistic segments. *Journal of Verbal Learning and Verbal Behavior*, **4**, 414–420.

FODOR, J. and GARRETT, M. 1966. Some reflections on competence and performance. In J. Lyons and R. Wales (Eds.), Psycholinguistic papers. Edinburgh University Press, Edinburgh. 135–154.

GAHAGAN, G. A. and GAHAGAN, D. M. 1968. Paired associate learning as partial validation of a language development program. *Child Development*, **39**, 1119–1132.

GARDENER, P. 1966. Symmetric respect and memorate knowledge: the structure and ecology of individualistic culture. *Southwestern Journal of Anthropology*, 22.

GARFINKEL, H. 1971. Remarks on ethno-methodology. In J. J. Gumperz and D. Hymes (Eds.), *Directions in sociolinguistics: the ethnography of communication*. Holt, Rinehart and Winston, New York.

GARRETT, M. and FODOR, J. 1968. Psychological theories and linguistic constructs. In T. Dixon and D. Horton (Eds.), *Verbal behaviour and general behaviour theory*. Prentice-Hall, Englewood Cliffs, New Jersey. 451–477.

GEBER, M. 1958. The psycho-motor development of African children in the first year and the influence of maternal behaviour. *Journal of Social Psychology*, **47**, 185–195.

GESCHWIND, N. 1965. Disconnection syndromes in animals and man, Part I. *Brain*, **88**, 237–294.

GIBSON, J. J. 1966. *The senses considered as perceptual systems.* Houghton Mifflin, Boston.

GOFFMAN, E. 1963. *Behavior in public places.* Collier Macmillan, Free Press of Glencoe, New York.

GOLDSTEIN, K. and SCHEERER, M. 1941. Abstract and concrete behavior. *Psychological Monographs*, vol. 53, no. 2.

GOODENOUGH, W. H. 1962. *Co-operation in change.* Russell Sage Foundation, New York.

GOODMAN, N. 1967. The epistemological argument. *Synthèse*, **17**, 23–28.

GOUGH, P. B. 1966. The verification of sentences: the effects of delay of evidence and sentence length. *Journal of Verbal Learning and Verbal Behavior*, **5**, 492–496.

GRÉGOIRE, A. 1937, 1947. *L'apprentissage du langage* (2 volumes). Droz, Liège and Paris.

GRUBER, J. 1967. Topicalisation in child language. *Foundations of language*, **3**, 37–65.

GUNTER, R. 1966. On the placement of accent in dialogue: a feature of context grammar. *Journal of Linguistics*, **2**, 159–179.

HALL, E. T. 1961. *The silent language.* Fawcett Publications Inc., Greenwich, Conn.

HALLIDAY, M. A. K. 1964. Syntax and the consumer. In C. I. J. M. Stuart (Ed.), *Report of the Seventeenth Annual Round Table Meeting on Language and Linguistics.* Georgetown University Press, Washington. 11–24.

HALLIDAY, M. A. K., MCINTOSH, A. and STREVENS, P. 1964. *The linguistic sciences and language teaching.* Longmans, London.

HAYES, C. 1951. *The ape in our house.* Harper, New York.

HEBB, D. O. 1949. *The organisation of behaviour.* John Wiley and Sons, New York.

HECAEN, H. and DE AJURIAGUERRA, J. 1964. *Left-handedness.* Grune and Stratton, New York.

HELD, R. 1965. Plasticity in sensory motor systems. *Scientific American*, **213**, 84–94.

HEMMENDINGER, L. 1951. A genetic study of structural aspects of perception as reflected in Rorschach test performance. Ph.D. Dissertation, Clerk University, Worcester, Mass.

HESS, R. D. and SHIPMAN, V. C. 1965. Early experience and the socialization of cognitive modes in children. *Child Development*, **36**, 869–886.

HOCKETT, C. F. 1965. Sound change. *Language*, 41.

HUBEL, D. H. and WIESEL, T. N. 1963. Receptive fields of calls in the striate cortex of very young, visually inexperienced kittens. *Journal of Neurophysiol.* 26.

HYMES, D. 1964. Introduction: toward ethnographies of communication. In J. J. Gumperz and D. Hymes (Eds.), *The ethnography of communication.* American Anthropological Association, Washington. 1–34.

HYMES, D. 1967. The anthropology of communication. In F. Darce (Ed.), *Human communication theory: original essays.* Holt, Rinehart and Winston, New York. 1–35.

HYMES, D. 1968. Linguistic problems in defining the concept of the tribe. In J. Helm (Ed.), *Proceedings, 1967 Spring Meeting of the American Anthropologist.* 23–78.

HYMES, D. 1971. Sociolinguistics and the ethnography of speaking. In E. Ardener (Ed.), *Linguistics and social anthropology* (ASA Monograph). Tavistock Publications, London.

IRIGARAY, L. 1967a. Approche psycholinguistique du langage chez les dements. *Neuropsychologia*, **5**, 25–52.

IRIGARAY, L. 1967b. La production de phrases chez les dements. *Language*, **5**, 49–66.

JAKOBSON, R. *Selected writings*, Vol. 1. *Phonology*. Mouton, The Hague.

JOHN, V. P. and MOSKOVITZ, S. 1968. *A study of language change in integrated and homogeneous classrooms*. Project Report No. 2. Yeshiva University, New York.

JONES, J. 1966. Social class and the under-fives. *New Society*, **221**, 935–936.

KAGAN, J. 1968. On cultural deprivation. In D. C. Glass (Ed.), *Environmental influences*. Rockefeller University Press and Russell Sage Foundation, New York. 211–250.

KATZ, J. J. 1966. The philosophy of language. Harper and Row, New York.

KATZ, J. J. and POSTAL, P. 1964. An integrated theory of linguistic descriptions. M.I.T. Press, Cambridge, Mass.

KESSEN, W. and SALAPATEK, P. 1966. Visual scanning of triangles by the human newborn. *Journal of Experimental Child Psychology*, **3**, 155–167.

KIMURA, D. 1963. Speech lateralisation in young children as determined by an auditory test. *J. Comp. Physiol. Psychol.* **56**, 889–902.

KIMURA, D. 1967. Functional asymmetry of the brain in dichotic listening. *Cortex*, **111**, 163–178.

KLIMA, E. 1964. Negation in English. In J. Fodor and J. Katz (Eds.), *The structure of language*. Prentice-Hall, Englewood Cliffs, New Jersey. 246–323.

KLIMA, E. and BELLUGI, U. 1966. Syntactic regularities in children's speech. In J. Lyons and R. Wales (Eds.), *Psycholinguistic papers*. Edinburgh University Press, Edinburgh. 183–213.

KOLERS, P. A., EDEN, M. and BOYER, A. 1964. Reading as a perceptual skill. *M.I.T. Res. Lab. of Electronics*, *Quart. Prog. Rep.* **74**, 214–217.

KUČERA, H. 1955. Phonemic variation of spoken Czech. *Word*, **11**, 575–602.

KUHN, T. S. 1962. *The structure of scientific revolutions*. University of Chicago Press, Chicago.

LABOV, W. 1965. Stages in the acquisition of standard English. In R. Shuy (Ed.), *Social dialects and language learning*. National Council of Teachers of English, Champaign, Illinois. 77–103.

LABOV, W. 1966. *The social stratification of English in New York City*. Center for Applied Linguistics, Washington, D.C.

LABOV, W. 1967. Some sources of reading problems for negro speakers of non-standard English. *New directions in elementary English*. National Council of Teachers of English, Champaign, Illinois. 140–167.

LABOV, W. 1969. Contraction, deletion and inherent variation of the English copula. *Language*, **45**, 715–762.

LABOV, W. 1970. The study of language in its social context. *Studium Generale*, **23**, 30–87.

LABOV, W. and COHEN, P. 1967. *Systematic relations of standard and non-standard rules in the grammar of negro speakers*. Paper for 7th Project Literacy Conference, Cambridge, Mass.

LABOV, W., COHEN, P. and ROBINS, C. 1965. *A preliminary study of the structure of English used by negro and Puerto Rican speakers in New York City*. Columbia University, Co-operative Research Project No. 3091, New York.

LAKOFF, G. P. 1965. *On the nature of syntactic irregularity in mathematical linguistics and automatic translation*. Report No. NSF-16. Computational Laboratory of Harvard University, Cambridge, Mass.

LANGACKER, R. W. 1969. On pronominalisation and the chain of command. In Reibal and Shane (Eds.), *Modern studies in English: readings in transformational grammar*. Prentice-Hall, Englewood Cliffs, New Jersey.

LAWTON, D. 1968. *Social class, language and education*. Schocken Books Inc., New York.

LENNEBERG, E. 1967. *The biological foundation of language*. John Wiley and Sons, New York.

LESSER, G. S., FIFER, G. and Clark, D. H. 1965. Mental abilities of children in different social and cultural groups. *Monogr. Soc. Res. Child Development*, **30**, No. 4 (Serial No. 102).

LEVY, D. M. 1960. The infant's earliest memory of inoculation: a contribution to public health procedures. *Journal of Genetic Psychology*, **96**, 3–46.

LEWIN, K. 1935. *A dynamic theory of personality*. McGraw-Hill, New York.

LIBERMAN, A. M., COOPER, F. S., SHANKWEILER, D. P. and STUDDERT-KENNEDY, M. 1967. Perception of the speech code. *Psychological Review*, **74** (6), 431–461.

LITTLE, A. N. D. (n.d.) *Object relationships, differentiation of space, causality sequence, temporal (memory) sequence, and imitation sequence*. Department of Psychology, University of Western Australia. Mimeographed.

LOBAN, W. D. 1966. *Language ability: grades seven, eight and nine*. Co-operative Research Monograph 18, U.S. Dept. of Health, Education and Welfare, Office of Education. Washington, D.C.

LURIA, A. R. 1961. *The role of speech in the regulation of normal and abnormal behaviour*, ed. by J. Tizard. Pergamon Press, Oxford.

LURIA, A. R. 1966. *Higher cortical function in man*. Tavistock Publications, London.

LYONS, J. 1968. *Introduction to theoretical linguistics*. Cambridge University Press, Cambridge.

LYONS, J. and WALES, R. (Eds.) 1966. *Psycho-linguistic papers*. Edinburgh University Press, Edinburgh.

MACMAHON, L. E. 1963. Grammatical analysis as part of understanding a sentence. Harvard University doctoral dissertation. Cambridge, Mass.

MCNEILL, D. 1966a. Developmental psycholinguistics. In F. Smith and G. Miller (Eds.), *The genesis of language*. M.I.T. Press, Cambridge, Mass. 15–84.

MCNEILL, D. 1966b. The creation of language by children. In J. Lyons and R. Wales (Eds.), *Psycholinguistic papers*. Edinburgh University Press, Edinburgh. Pp. 115–125.

MEAD, M. and MACGREGOR, F. C. 1951. *Growth and culture: a photographic study of Balinese childhood*. Putnam, New York.

MEHLER, J. 1964. How some sentences are remembered. Unpublished Doctoral Dissertation, Harvard University, Cambridge, Mass.

MEHLER, J. 1969. La mémoire de la couleur chez les très jeunes enfants. In *Travaux du Centre d'Etude des Processus Cognitifs et du Langage*. C.N.R.S., Paris.

MEHLER, J. and BEVER, T. G. 1967. A cognitive capacity of very young children. *Science*, **158**, 141–142.

MEHLER, J. and BEVER, T. G. 1968a. Quantification, conservation and nativism: a reply to J. Piaget. *Science*, **162**, 979–981.

MEHLER, J. and BEVER, T. G. 1968b. The study of competence in cognitive psychology. *International Journal of Psychology*, **3**, 273–280.

MEHLER, J. and CAREY, P. 1968. The interaction of veracity and syntax in the processing of sentences. *Perception and Psychophysics*, **3**, 109–111.

MEHLER, J. and SAVIN, H. B. (in press). Memory processes in the language user. In
T. G. Bever and W. Weksel (Eds.), *Structure and psychology of language*. Holt,
Rinehart and Winston, New York.

MEYER, V. and YATES, A. J. 1955. Intellectual changes following temporal lobectomy
for psycho-motor epilepsy. *J. Neurol. Psychiat.* **18**, 44–52.

MILLER, G. A. 1962. Some psychological studies of grammar. *American Psychologist*,
17, 748–762.

MILLER, G. A. (in press). Linguistic aspects of cognition: predication and meaning.
In J. Mehler (Ed.), *Cognitive psychology handbook*. Prentice Hall, Englewood
Cliffs, New Jersey.

MILNER, B. 1962. Laterality effects in addition. In M. B. Mountcastle (Ed.), *Interhemispheric relations and cerebral dominance.* Johns Hopkins, Baltimore. 177–196.

MOUNTCASTLE, M. B. (Ed.) 1962. *Interhemispheric relations and cerebral dominance*.
Johns Hopkins, Baltimore.

NAKAZIMA, S. 1962. A comparative study of the speech developments of Japanese
and American English in childhood. *Studia Phonologica*, **2**, 27–46.

NEWMAN, S. S. 1940. Linguistic aspects of Yokuts style. In A. H. Gayton and S. S.
Newman (Eds.), *Yokuts and western mono myths*, 4–9. (University of California
Publications, Anthropological Records, **4** (1).) University of California Press,
Berkeley. Cited from D. Hymes (Ed.), *Language in culture and society* (New
York, 1964).

OLIM, E. G., HESS, R. D. and SHIPMAN, V. C. 1967. Role of mothers' language styles
in mediating their pre-school children's cognitive development. *The School
Review*, **75**, 414–424.

PIAGET, J. 1946. *La formation du symbole chez l'enfant*. Delachaux et Niestle, Neu-
châtel et Paris.

PIAGET, J. (English translation, 1950) *The psychology of intelligence*. Harcourt, Brace
and World, New York.

PIAGET, J. (English translation, 1952) *The child's conception of number*. Routledge
and Kegan Paul, London.

PIAGET, J. 1956. *La psychologie de l'intelligence*. Arnaud Colin, Paris.

PIAGET, J., GRIZE, J.-B., SZEMINSKA, A., VINH-BANG. 1968. *Épistémologie et psychologie de la fonction*. Volume 23, Etudes d'Epistémologie Génétique, Presses
Universitaires de France, Paris.

PIAGET, J. and INHELDER, B. 1968. *Mémoire et intelligence*. Presses Universitaires
de France, Paris.

PIERCE, C. S. 1957. The logic of abduction. In V. Thomas (Ed.), *Pierce's Essays in the
philosophy of science*. Liberal Arts Press, New York.

POLGAR, STEVEN 1960. Biculturism in Mesquaki education. *American Anthropologist*,
62, 217–35.

POSTAL, P. 1966. On so-called pronouns in English. In F. P. Dineen (Ed.), *Linguistics
and language study*. 17th Round Table Annual Report. Georgetown University
Press, Washington, D.C.

QUIRK, R. 1968. *Essays on the English language, medieval and modern*. Longmans
Green, London.

RACKSTRAW, S. J. and ROBINSON, W. P. 1967. Social and psychological factors related
to variability of answering behaviour in five-year-old children. *Language and
Speech*, **10**, 88–106.

RAVEN, J. C. 1951. *The Crichton vocabulary scale*. Lewis, London.

RAVEN, J. C. 1963. *The coloured progressive matrices.* Lewis, London.

ROBINSON, W. P. and CREED, C. D. 1968. Perceptual and verbal discriminations of "elaborated" and "restricted" code users. *Language and Speech,* **11,** 182–193.

ROBINSON, W. P. and RACKSTRAW, S. J. 1967. Variations in mothers' answers to children's questions as a function of social class, verbal intelligence test scores, and sex. *Sociology,* **1,** 259–276.

ROSS, H. 1967. *On the cyclic nature of English pronominalisation. To honor Roman Jakobson.* Mouton, The Hague.

SAPIR, E. 1938. Why cultural anthropology needs the psychiatrist. *Psychiatry,* **1,** 7–12.

SAPIR, E. 1949. *Selected writings of Edward Sapir.* D. Mandelbaum (Ed.). University of California Press, Berkeley and Los Angeles.

SAUSSURE, F. DE. 1959. *Cours de linguistique générale.* (First ed. 1916.) English translation of 5th edition by Wade Baskin, *Course in general linguistics.* New York Philosophical Library.

SAVIN, H. B. and PERCHONOK, E. 1965. Grammatical structure and the immediate recall of English sentences. *Journal of Verbal Learning and Verbal Behavior,* **4,** 348–353.

SCHEGLOFF, E. 1968. Sequencing rules in conversational openings. *American Anthropologist,* **70,** 1075–1095.

SCHIFF, W. 1965. Perception of impending collision. *Psychol. Monogr.,* **79,** No. 11.

SCHLESINGER, I. M. 1967. A note on the relationship between psychological and linguistic theories. *Foundations of language,* **3,** 397–402.

SCHLESINGER, I. M. (in press). Production of utterances and language acquisition. In D. I. Slobin (Ed.), *The ontogenesis of grammar.* Academic Press, New York.

SHANKWEILER, D. P. and STUDDERT-KENNEDY, M. 1967. Identification of consonants and vowels presented to left and right ears. *Quart. Jour. Exper. Psychol.* **19,** 59–63.

SHRINER, T. H. and MINER, L. 1968. Morphological structure in the language of disadvantaged and advantaged children. *Journal of Speech and Hearing Research,* **11,** 605–610.

SHUY, R., WOLFRAM, W. A. and RILEY, W. K. 1967. Linguistic correlation of social stratification in Detroit speech. *Final Report, Co-operative Research Project,* No. 6, 1347. United States Office of Education.

SLOBIN, D. I. 1966. Grammatical transformations and sentence comprehension in childhood and adulthood. *Journal of Verbal Learning and Verbal Behavior,* **5,** 219–227.

SLOBIN, D. I. (Ed.) 1967. *A field manual for cross-cultural study of the acquisition of communicative competence.* Associated Students' Bookstore, Berkeley, California.

SLOBIN, D. I. 1968. Recall of full and truncated passive sentences in connected discourse. *Journal of Verbal Learning and Verbal Behavior,* **7,** 876–881.

SMITH, C. J. 1959. Mass action and early environment in the rat. *Journal of Comparative and Physiological Psychology,* **51,** 154–162.

SMITH, F. and MILLER, G. A. (Eds.) 1966. *The genesis of language.* M.I.T. Press, Cambridge, Mass.

SPERRY, R. and GAZZANIGA, M. 1967. Language after section of the cerebral commissures. *Brain,* **90,** 131–148.

STEWART, W. 1965. Urban negro speech: socio-linguistic factors affecting English teaching. In R. Shuy (Ed.), *Social dialects and language learning.* National Council of Teachers of English, Champaign, Illinois.

STODOLSKY, S. C. and LESSER, G. 1967. Learning patterns in the disadvantaged. *Harvard Educ. Rev.*, **37,** 546–593.

TEMPLIN, C. M. 1957. *Certain language skills in children.* University of Minnesota Press, Minneapolis.

TESNIÈRE, L. 1959. *Éléments de syntaxe structurale.* Klincksieck, Paris.

TEUBER, H. L., BATTERSBY, W. and BENDER, M. B. 1960. *Visual field defects after penetrating missile wounds of the brain.* Harvard Univ. Press, Cambridge, Mass.

THORNDIKE, E. L. 1928. *Adult learning.* MacMillan, New York.

THORNE, J. P., BRATLEY, P. and DEWAR, H. 1968. The syntactic analysis of English by machine. In D. Michie (Ed.), *Machine intelligence,* 3. Edinburgh University Press, Edinburgh.

TINBERGEN, N. 1951. *The study of instinct.* Clarendon Press, Oxford.

TREISMAN, A. and GEFFON, G. 1968. Selective attention and cerebral dominance in perceiving and responding to speech messages. *Quarterly Journal of Exper. Psychol.* **20,** 139–150.

TYLER, S. 1966. Context and variation in Koya kinship terminology. *American Anthropologist,* **68,** 693–707.

UZGIRIS, I. C. and HUNT, J. McV. 1966. *An instrument for assessing infant psychological development.* Psychological Development Laboratory, University of Illinois. Mimeograph.

VENDLER, Z. 1967. Singular terms. In *Linguistics in philosophy.* Cornell University Press, Ithaca.

WALLACE, A. F. C. 1961a. *Culture and personality.* Random House, New York.

WALLACE, A. F. C. 1961b. On being just complicated enough. *Proceedings of the National Academy of Sciences,* **47,** 438–464.

WATERHOUSE, V. 1963. Independent and dependent sentences. *International Journal of American Linguistics,* **27,** 45–54.

WECHSLER, D. 1965. *The Wechsler intelligence scale for children: manual for Scottish standardisation.* Scottish Council for Research in Education, Edinburgh.

WEINREICH, U. 1953. *Language in contact.* Linguistic circle of New York, New York.

WERNER, H. 1948. *Comparative psychology of mental development.* Follet, Chicago.

WERTHEIMER, M. 1961. Psychomotor coordination of auditory and visual space at birth. *Science,* **134,** 1962.

WHITE, B. L., CASTLE, P. and HELD, R. 1964. Observations on the development of visually directed reaching. *Child Development,* **35,** 349–364.

WHITING, J. 1954. Cross cultural method. In G. Lindzey (Ed.), *Handbook of social psychology.* Addison Wesley, Cambridge, Mass.

WILLIAMS, F. and NAROME, R. C. 1969. On the functional analysis of social class differences in modes of speech. *Speech Monographs,* 36.

WRIGHT, P. 1968. Sentence retention and transformation theory. *Quart. Jour. Exper. Psychol.* **20,** 265–272.

ZANGWILL, O. L. 1960. *Cerebral dominance and its relation to psychological function.* Oliver and Boyd, London.

ZAZZO, R. 1957. Le problème de l'imitation chez le nouveau-né. *Enfance,* **2,** 135–142.

Author Index

Numbers in italics refer to pages where References are listed in full

Subject Index

A

Abduction, 223
Acceptability, 8, 26, 222
Accommodation, 121, 131
Actor–action–object relation, 131f
  and NVN strategy, 240ff
Actor–action relation, 91, 169f
Actor–non-actor distinction, 170
Actor–object distinction, 170
Adjective order in English, 257f
Agents as pivots, 85ff
Agnosia, 282
Alor, 28
Alternation rules, 32f
Ambiguity, 261
  completion of ambiguous sentences, 142
Animate–inanimate distinction, 89, 141, 142
Aphasia, 233, 251n, 277ff
Appropriateness, 10, 13ff
  judgements of, 14
Apraxia, 282
Arabic, 7
Articulation in early utterances, 163f
Articulatory development, 285f.
  and social class, 286
Ashanti, 27
Assimilation, 121, 131
Auditory asymmetry, 232ff.
  and NVN strategy, 242ff.
Aurecanians, 27
Auxiliary inversion
  in non-standard Negro English, 30
  in children's questions, 96ff., 116
Axiomatic systems, 220f.
  vocabulary of, 220f.

B

Base structure (cf. deep structure), 209, 221, 226f.
Basic capacities in cognition, 232
Behavioural strategies in speech perception (cf. perceptual strategies, learning strategies), 231f., 240ff.
  and hemispheric dominance, 234
Berber, 7
Blessing Way Ceremony, 34
Book of Common Prayer, 34
Burundi, 9

C

Case marking
  in children's pronouns, 96, 107ff., 116
Causative verbs, 171
Cause and effect
  as a cognitive relation, 132, 179
Centrality of syntax, 150f.
Centre-embedded sentences, 153f.
  immediate recall of, 241
Cerebral dominance, 231ff.
Chaga, 28
Cleft sentences, comprehension of, 252
Closed-type role systems, 70
Code, 19, 49f., 67
  contextual features of, 50
  elaborated, 21, 49f., 58, 59, 61, 68ff.
  restricted, 21, 49f., 58, 68ff., 259
Code relationships, 20
Code switching, 20
Cognitive universals, 177
Colour names, 189
Communicative acts, 177
Communicative competence, 7, 12, 15, 18, 22, 24

305